JUVENILE JUSTICE

JUVENILE JUSTICE
IMPACT AND IMPLEMENTATION IN INDIA

G.S. Bajpai

BLOOMSBURY
NEW DELHI • LONDON • OXFORD • NEW YORK • SYDNEY

BLOOMSBURY INDIA
Bloomsbury Publishing India Pvt. Ltd
Second Floor, LSC Building No. 4, DDA Complex, Pocket C – 6 & 7,
Vasant Kunj, New Delhi 110070

BLOOMSBURY, BLOOMSBURY INDIA and the Diana logo are trademarks of
Bloomsbury Publishing Plc

First published in India 2019
This export edition published in 2020

ISBN: HB: 978-93-88414-64-7; eBook: 978-93-88414-65-4

Typeset in Manipal Digital

Contents

List of Tables vii

Acknowledgements ix

Chapter I Introduction 1

Chapter II Literature Review 14

Chapter III Analysis of Legislative Framework 34

Chapter IV Analysis of Judicial Trends 71

Chapter V Juvenile: Pre-Institutionalisation 101

Chapter VI Juvenile: In Conflict with Law 117

Chapter VII Juvenile: Inside the Home 134

Chapter VIII Juvenile: Post-Release Prospects 145

Chapter IX Major Findings 156

Chapter X Juvenile Justice (Care and Protection of Children) Act, 2015: Opening Pandora's Box 187

Chapter XI Conclusion 206

Annexure I *Sample of Interview Schedule* 227

Annexure II *List of Heinous Offences* 235

Annexure III *Cross-Tabulation Tables* 239

Glossary 285

Bibliography 287

Index 303

About the Author 307

List of Tables

3.1 Quantity of Bedding 45
3.2 Quantity of Clothing (Boys) 45
3.3 Quantity of Clothing (Girls) 46
3.4 Nutritional and Diet Scale 47
3.5 Suggested Staffing Pattern 64
3.6 Quantity of Bedding 65
3.7 Quantity of Clothing (Boys) 66
3.8 Quantity of Clothing (Girls) 66
3.9 Diet and Nutrition Scale 67

5.1 Demographic Information of the Respondents 101
5.2 Frequency Table for Information about Family/Significant Others 108
5.3 Frequency Table for Psycho-Social Factors 111

6.1 Information about Delinquent Behaviour 117
6.2 Interaction with the Justice System 125

7.1 Information about Homes and the Quality of Services 134

8.1 Information Regarding Post-Release Plan 145

10.1 Cases Registered against Juveniles in Conflict with Law and Crime Rate in 2015 196

Acknowledgements

Juvenile justice in India has witnessed significant challenges in the past four decades. The transformation in juvenile justice has brought forth problems and challenges to policies, and the Juvenile Justice Act 2015 is a major development in this area. This Act envisages a very progressive approach to juvenile offending and its treatment. While the potential of this instrument is laudable, Indian states inevitably suffer ineffective implementation.

The present study is an empirical attempt to explore the experiences of implementing the Juvenile Justice Act 2015. In the process, the researchers visited all the major stakeholders in the selected states to understand the ground realities of implementing this Act. Conducting fieldwork was not an easy task. This project was greatly assisted by Virendra Kumar, Field Researcher, who carried out extensive fieldwork in the selected states of India, and brought tremendous insight for us to present a critique on the existing problem. I'm indeed thankful and grateful for his efforts. Ankit Kaushik, Research Consultant, has been a great support to this study in terms of analysing the data and preparing the initial draft. His dedication was remarkable and augmented this study significantly. I also thank Kavisha Mann, who contributed significantly in improving the draft report.

I am greatly indebted to Professor (Dr) Ranbir Singh, Vice-Chancellor, National Law University, Delhi, whose guidance and patronage provided an enabling environment to accomplish this project. I express my gratitude to the University Grants Commission for sponsoring this project. I am sure this research would go a long way in providing useful insight for significant policy development to improve the implementation of juvenile justice in India.

Professor G.S. Bajpai

Chapter I
Introduction

There can be no keener revelation of a society's soul than the way in which it treats its children.

—Nelson Mandela

Oscar Wilde once said, 'Every saint has a past and every sinner has a future.' A corollary to this statement is Mahatma Gandhi's remark that one should hate the crime and not the criminal. This is especially true in the case of juvenile justice, where the principle of reformation as the dominant mode of punishment when dealing with children in conflict with the law has been accepted by the international community as a cornerstone.

The concept of juvenile justice has been derived from a belief that the problems of juvenile delinquency in abnormal situations are not amenable to resolution within the framework of traditional process of criminal law.[1] The main reason for this is that a young person is believed to be less blameworthy than an adult, as he is prone to act in haste due to lack of judgement, easily influenced by others. John Pitts said, 'From their inception, youth justice system has preceded from the assumption that the children and young people, by dint of their relative immaturity, are

[1] Ved Kumari, *The Juvenile Justice in India: From Welfare to Rights* (New Delhi: Oxford University Press), 1.

less able to control their impulses, less able to understand the seriousness of the offences and less able to foresee the consequences of their actions.'[2]

Juveniles have to be treated differently as they are less culpable and less capable of looking after themselves.[3] As far back as 1860, the Indian Penal Code, which works on the theory of deterrence and retribution, recognised that a child who is less than seven years old cannot commit a crime. A child who is over seven but below 12 years cannot commit a crime if they are immature and cannot understand the act they have done, the consequences of their actions or what they have done is wrong. The Reformatory School Act (enacted in 1876 and modified in 1897) was the next landmark legislation in the treatment of juvenile delinquents. It empowered local governments to establish reformatory schools, and the sentencing court could detain boys in such institutions for a period of two to seven years. The Code of Criminal Procedure of 1898 outlined specialised treatment for juvenile offenders, including the commitment of juvenile offenders up to 15 years of age to reformatory schools and probation for good conduct to offenders up to the age of 21.[4] Later, as per the Report of Indian Jail Committee 1919–20, reformatory schools were established, and it advocated reformation and decriminalisation of the juvenile justice system as well.

Consequently,[5] by 1960, various states in India had passed their respective Children's Act,[6] which included provisions for homes, certified schools and release on probation. Children were to be dealt by juvenile courts. The Children's Act of 1960 was also the first piece of central legislation prohibiting the imprisonment of juvenile offenders in union territories and laying down separate mechanisms to deal with them and juveniles in need of care. The Supreme Court, in *Sheela Barse* v. *Union of India*,[7] observed: 'We would suggest that instead of each state having

---

[2] John Pitts, 'Youth Justice in England and Wales,' in *The New Politics of Crime and Punishment*, ed. Roger Matthews and Jock Young (Willan Publishing, 2003), 71.

[3] Ved Kumari, *Relevant Date for Applying the Juvenile Justice Act*, (2000) 6 SCC (Jour) 9.

[4] Code of Criminal Procedure, 1898, Sections 29B, 399 and 562.

[5] Satadru Sen, 'A Separate Punishment: Juvenile Offenders in Colonial India,' *The Journal of Asian Studies*, Vol. 63, no. 1 (February 2004): 81–104.

[6] Namely: Madras Children Act, 1920, Bengal Children Act, 1922, Bombay Children Act, 1924.

[7] (1986) 3 SCC 632.

its own Children's Act in other States (sic) it would be desirable if the Central Government initiates Parliamentary Legislation on the subject, so that there is complete uniformity in regard to the various provisions relating to children in the entire territory of the country.' Though the act of 1960 called for absolute restraint on imprisonment, there were still a few state acts that allowed imprisonment in exceptional circumstances.

Since its enactment, there has been concentrated effort on the part of everyone involved to ensure that the sole concern of society dealing with juveniles in conflict with the law should be the protection of their rights and liberties. This includes a multi-pronged approach with measures ranging from inculcation of social values to prevent further legal conflicts to the rehabilitation and reintegration of offenders and everything in-between.

In this context, two acts, namely the Central Children Act (1960) and the Juvenile Justice Act of 1986, deserve special mention; the former because it enunciates the basic philosophy of care, protection, maintenance, welfare, training, education and rehabilitation of neglected and delinquent children, and the latter for bringing about a uniform juvenile justice system in the country by consolidating all related legislations in the country. The Juvenile Justice Act could be proclaimed as the first pan-India child welfare enactment, seeking to promote 'the best interests of the juveniles' by incorporating into its fold not only some of the major provisions and clauses of the Indian constitution and national policy resolution for children but also universally agreed principles and standards for the protection of juveniles. These include the United Nations Standard Minimum Rules for the Administration of Juvenile Justice of 1985, commonly known as the Beijing Rules.

Among international frameworks and provisions that promote reformation, most prominently Article 40 of the UN Convention on the Rights of the Child, which has been signed by India, declares that the 'state parties recognise the right of every child alleged as, accused of, or recognised as having infringed the penal law to be treated in a manner… which takes into account the child's age and the desirability of promoting the child's reintegration and the child's assuming a constructive role in society'.

Role of the State

The Juvenile Justice (Care and Protection of Children) Act, 2000 was enacted with the aim to 'consolidate and amend the law relating to juveniles in conflict with law and children in need of care and protection, by providing for proper care, protection and treatment by catering to their development needs, and by adopting a child-friendly approach in the adjudication and disposition of matters in the best interest of children and for their ultimate rehabilitation through various institutions established under the enactment'.

While the provisions of this act have been analysed in detail in subsequent chapters, it is important to understand why there is a need for differential treatment of juveniles under a distinct justice system, and the role to be played by the state in lieu of such a need.

As of 2001, India had over 422 million children,[8] constituting around 41 per cent of its population, the largest for any country in the world, placing an enormous responsibility on the state and the nation to rear them as responsible and law-abiding citizens. The life experience of each child is unique and incomparable to that of children born before or after him. The experiences of the underprivileged are shaped largely by poverty, barriers to education, hunger, multiple and intersecting forms of discrimination, violence and limited opportunities of growth and employment.[9] On the other hand, the experiences of those born in privileged homes are honed to a certain extent not by economic considerations mixed with lack of opportunity, but psychological, familial, legal and societal considerations. In this context, the state assumes responsibility in all cases where the child is found to be in need of care and protection or in conflict with the law.

In early 2000, through the landmark Juvenile Justice (Care and Protection) Act, India recognised its obligation to its children. The law

---

[8] 'Age Structure and Marital Status,' Office of the Registrar General & Census Commissioner, Ministry of Home Affairs, accessed 15 March 2019, http://censusindia.gov.in/Census_And_You/age_structure_and_marital_status.aspx.

[9] 'UNDP Youth Strategy 2014–17: Empowered Youth, Sustainable Future,' UNDP, accessed 15 March 2019, http://www.undp.org/content/dam/undp/library/Democratic%20Governance/Youth/UNDP_Youth-Strategy-2014-17_Web.pdf.

governed the experience of children in conflict with law,[10] referring to individuals alleged or found to have committed an offence who have not completed 18 years on the date of commission of such offence. These children are torn in a society, which is—in economic, sociological, political and legal contexts—backward for one segment of the population and forward for another. They desire to participate in the process of upward mobility witnessed in some parts of the country but lack the opportunities to do so. Above all, they strive to become part of a society that continually fails to nourish them with enriching lives. Such aspirations and strife in young and adolescent minds, largely ill-equipped to handle them, produce conflict. The role of the state is then to push for their inclusion in society, give them opportunities to become contributory members and ensure direct proportion between the growth of the country and society, and the growth of these children.

Their development has received minimal attention in budgetary allocations. Against the demand for a grant of ₹ 20,755 crore[11] for the flagship Integrated Child Development Services programme, the Ministry of Women and Child Development was allocated ₹ 22,095 crore[12] for its entire gamut of operations, including the Integrated Child Protection Scheme (ICPS). A compelling query arises with respect to the government's perspective of inclusive growth, when one of the most marginalised and vulnerable sections of society do not get requisite attention. Though children received more share from the total allocation, there have been major reductions in some of the key programmes related to children belonging to minorities—pre-matric scholarship for minorities reduced by 10.48 per cent, post-matric scholarship for minorities reduced by 5.19 per cent, scheme for providing education to madrasas/minorities reduced by 68.04 per cent, and incentives to children of vulnerable groups among scheduled castes reduced by 90 per cent.

---

[10] Section 2 (13) of the Juvenile Justice Act, 2015.

[11] Ministry of Finance, *Statement 3b, Demand for Grants, Budget 2017-18,* http://indiabudget.nic.in/ub2017-18/eb/stat3a.pdf, accessed on 12/09/2017.

[12] Ministry of Finance, *Statement 3a, Annual Financial Statement, Budget 2017-18,* http://indiabudget.nic.in/ub2017-18/eb/stat3b.pdf, accessed on 12/09/2017.

As per a 2015–16 economic survey, there is a decline in government school enrolments in rural areas—from 72.9 per cent in 2007 the number dropped to 63.1 per cent in 2014. It emphasised the need to increase these numbers substantially to achieve universalisation of education.[13] But in light of such suggestions, funds allotted to the Sarva Shiksha Abhiyan were raised by a mere 2 per cent. There exists only one welfare scheme related to child labour—scheme for the welfare of working children in need of care and protection—and that too observed a 70 per cent decrease in funding.

It is pertinent to note that children in need of care and protection as well as children in conflict with the law barely find any place in budget allocation. The child protection sector remains the most under-resourced—the 2016–17 budget allocated ₹ 397 crore to ICPS, down 1.3 per cent from ₹ 402 crore in 2015–16. An increase in crimes against children and by children makes them even more vulnerable, hence the lack of attention to child protection is disconcerting. Reducing funding for necessary schemes is bound to have a negative impact on the reformative and rehabilitative approach adopted by the acts of 2000 and 2015.

Institutional Contact with Children in Conflict with Law

The first point of contact for a child in conflict with the law is the police. It is well established that a considerable amount of police discretion is exercised in handling juveniles. Although this is necessary and part of police work, the potential of abuse exists because there is no way to routinely review this practice. In their study, Irving Piliavin and Scott Briar[14] observed that the police exercised wide discretion while responding to juvenile offenders, but it was affected by the demeanour of the apprehended individual, prior offence record, race, etc. The social judgement of the officer influenced the description of an individual as a delinquent. This often depended on how the juvenile presented himself to the officer rather than the actual

---

[13] Department of Economic Affairs, Ministry of Finance, Economic Survey of India 2015-16.

[14] Irving Piliavin and Scott Briar, 'Police Encounters with Juveniles,' *American Journal of Sociology*, Vol. 70, no. 2 (September 1964): 206–14.

offence. According to Piliavin and Briar, the decisions made by the police are crucial.

Police behaviour in this context is also critical to shaping the child's experience. In their study of Finnish adolescents, A. Dirikx and Jan Van den Bulck[15] observed that treating people fairly during personal encounters was crucial for the police; these encounters also impacted adolescents' belief and trust in the police. Physical abuse, arrest and detention are common a child's interaction with law enforcement. It is the nature of police work, which, in most cases, allows individual police officers to decide how they will handle the incident as well as those discovered independently in the course of their work on the ground. In their study, Robert Brown et al.[16] found that juveniles were more likely to be arrested than adults, and officers' behaviour varied considerably during their interaction with juveniles and adults. According to Bonnie et al., adolescents are different from adults and require a different response from the justice system.[17]

Thus, the police are an important point of contact who influence juveniles' perceptions about the justice system, so it is necessary to train officers to sensitise them to the needs of children and respond to juvenile offenders. This training should not only inform them about existing laws related to children but also teach officers to handle children with care and sensitivity. One should bear in mind that the involvement of a youth with the justice system may impact his future and how he is perceived. The juvenile may be left with the daunting task of handling stigma from his family members, in the neighbourhood and society at large. Thus, the work to be done does not merely include reforming the juvenile and preventing recidivism, but also the community and society, to give offenders a second chance to build their lives constructively.

---

[15] Astrid Dirikx and Jan Van den Bulck, 'Media Use and the Process-Based Model for Police Cooperation: An Integrative Approach Towards Explaining Adolescents' Intentions to Cooperate with the Police,' *The British Journal of Criminology*, Vol. 54, no. 2 (March 2014): 344–65.

[16] Robert A. Brown et al., 'Identifying variation in police officer behaviour between juveniles and adults,' *Journal of Criminal Justice*, Vol. 37 (2009): 200–8.

[17] R.J. Bonnie et al., 'Reforming Juvenile Justice: A Developmental Approach,' *National Research Council*, National Academic Press, Washington DC (2013): 91.

The police can prevent the stigma a juvenile may face by restraining from harassment and scapegoating the child as a 'criminal' post his release. They are instrumental in ensuring the smooth entry of the juvenile in the justice system. Rough handling by the police can scar the child and cause him to see himself as a bad character that can impact his self-esteem and self-confidence, which are crucial for his future growth. Needless to say, it may also impact the child negatively towards the justice system.

Institutional authorities such as probation officers and counsellors constitute the second stage of interaction for juveniles, and they are the lynchpins of a successful juvenile justice system. They serve an integral role at every stage of the juvenile's contact with the system, from their intake to the follow-up after the juvenile formally exits the system. An ideal juvenile justice structure would serve the goals of accountability towards the people, rehabilitation of juveniles and individualised case management. Such officers make the achievement of these goals possible by recognising that a brief presence in court or juvenile justice board is not enough.

One of the most prominent and revolutionary features of the Act of 2000 was the establishment of juvenile justice boards.[18] Each board is required to determine the age, question of bail, and the question of commission of offence, and pass appropriate orders. The composition of the board includes a principle magistrate and two social workers, thereby ensuring that not only are legal intricacies covered but the socioeconomic, psycho-social and familial circumstances are considered as well. The social workers involved in the juvenile justice system are also known as forensic social workers or correctional social workers internationally. Their presence is to enforce the belief that with the right counselling and opportunities an individual can change into a law-abiding citizen.[19] However, inordinate delays in proceedings, resulting in a backlog of cases, as well as inadequate infrastructure to handle them leads to deferred justice.

---

[18] Ved Kumari, 'Juvenile Justice: Securing the Rights of Children during 1998–2008,' *NUJS Law Review*, Vol. 2, no. 4 (2009): 557.

[19] Patricia Brownell and Albert R. Roberts, 'A Century of Social Work in Criminal Justice and Correctional Settings,' *Journal of Offender Rehabilitation*, Vol. 35, no. 2 (2002): 1–17.

Social workers can work towards the reintegration of the juvenile within society. The involvement with the justice system may cause stigma and isolation, and impact the minor's future education and employment prospects. Social workers may work with the family, neighbourhood and schools, enabling them to accept the child and support him in rebuilding his life. Officers can encourage schools to readmit juveniles and maintain continuity of schooling, preventing drop-out rates. Admission to open schools may also be supported where the juvenile can continue his education via home schooling and work simultaneously to support himself and his family. Social workers should help juveniles find jobs and work with employers to induct them. Working with the family can prevent them from labelling the child 'useless' and encourage him to reshape his future by being a productive member of society.

Lastly, correctional institutions under the enactment emphasise understanding human behaviour and psychology through personal contact to assist young offenders to correct deviant behaviour, with the cooperation of their family and support of the society.[20] However, a review of the literature upon the same enlightens us with respect to the gap between the theoretical principles and the implementation of those principles.

Punitive measures alone overlook the challenges posed in a familial environment such as child abuse and neglect,[21] which can be a risk factor for delinquency.[22] Thus, it is also important to address the factors that make the individual susceptible to delinquency. One may take the family as the unit to work with and deal with issues such as poor socioeconomic status, poor parenting, etc. It could prevent the involvement of other siblings in delinquent activities.

It appears that children entering the juvenile justice system frequently face grave threats to their individual rights, yet their plight

---

[20] Rupam Jagota, 'Juvenile Justice System in India: An Attempt at Reformation,' *RMLNLUJ*, Vol. 2 (2010): 84.

[21] Cathy S. Widom and Michael G. Maxfield, 'An Update on the "Cycle of Violence",' *National Institute of Justice Research in Brief*, US Department of Justice, Office of Justice Programs (February 2001).

[22] Peters, 'Social Work,' 355–65.

is often ignored.[23] Police abuse is commonplace in some jurisdictions. Children languish in the system for years, either as residents of our decrepit detention facilities without access to meaningful education and employment, or as the subject of endless proceedings that draw them away from education or employment, resulting in an economic crisis for the child's family.[24]

If this is the case, not only do we fail the children as a state, but also when they come in conflict with law. Wizner and Keller discussed the juvenile criminal justice system, stating, 'It has neither provided adequate protection for society from juvenile crime nor succeeded in rehabilitating young offenders.'[25]

This book is an attempt to examine the provisions of contemporary juvenile justice laws, and the jurisprudence that guides them within the context of the impact and implementation of such provisions. In the interest of preserving the momentum behind the recent changes in our juvenile justice system, this book conducts a study of the reformative and rehabilitative services provided in special and observation homes in Delhi, Haryana and Punjab, and attempts to identify issues relating to the implementation of the system's principles.

Research Methodology

It has been hypothesised that the institutional set-up required under the Juvenile Justice Act (JJA) has not been established fully and district-level institutions are generally deficient of infrastructure and staff to effectively implement it. This hinders the rehabilitative and reformative aspects of the system, leading to a failure in achieving stated aims of rehabilitation and reintegration. There has been little or no focus on structured rehabilitative schemes. Moreover, the performance of staff is sub-par given that training requirements have not been met. The attitude and aptitude required to enforce the act are missing in the concerned

---

[23] Erika Rickard and Jason M. Szanyi, 'Bringing Justice to India's Children: Three Reforms to Bridge Practises with Promises in India's Juvenile Justice System,' *UC Davis Journal of Juvenile Law & Policy*, Vol. 14, no. 1 (Winter 2010): 109.

[24] Rickard and Szanyi, 'Bringing Justice,' 109.

[25] Stephen Wizner and Mary F. Keller, 'The Penal Model of Juvenile Justice: Is Juvenile Court Delinquency Jurisdiction Obsolete?' Faculty Scholarship Series. Paper 1857.

personnel and there is no proper coordination between different levels and functionaries.

The principle objectives of this book are to study the preparedness of Delhi, Haryana and Punjab in terms of availability of resources and infrastructure to enforce the act; the adequacy and availability of trained manpower at observation and special homes; the identification of performance indicators for officials and institutions; and an objective assessment of the performance of the state vis-à-vis budget allocations and infrastructure provisions. Issues and problems have been identified and examined, and suitable suggestions or workable recommendations have been drawn up as well.

This book has incorporated doctrinal and empirical research. The former makes for in-depth analysis of existent laws on juvenile justice in terms of delinquency and the march of law thereafter, as seen in their application and interpretation by a higher judiciary.

To fulfil empirical objectives, primary and secondary data collection was carried out. To examine various hypotheses, an interview schedule incorporating a set of structured questions was created to guide researchers. Their conversations with various interest and pressure groups such as advocates, employees and staff of homes, members of boards, counsellors and non-profit organisations were enlightening with regard to prevailing grass-root conditions.

Three observation homes and special homes in Delhi, Haryana and Punjab each were selected for in-depth study. Pre-structured questions were used during interviews with juvenile inmates and staff of observation and special homes. Permissions were obtained to visit juvenile detention centres from appropriate authorities and visits were made to the Delhi Gate, Kingsway Camp and Special Home Majnu Ka Tila observation homes in Delhi. In Haryana, observation homes for boys in Faridabad and Hisar as well as a special home at Ambala were visited. Juvenile detention facilities in Ludhiana and Faridkot as well as a special home in Hoshiarpur were visited in Punjab. In total, the staff and detainees of nine facilities in three states were used as samples.

The questions covered socioeconomic variables, quality of service provided by the institution and performance indicators for officials. Data was collected from around 30 officers and 300 juveniles who are either under trial and kept in observation homes or those serving detention periods in special homes. Personal interviews were conducted and data compiled to gather information and identify issues in the implementation of the act. The schedule for officials and inmates uses a Likert scale procedure to calculate the index of performance.

The data collected in this study was processed with the help of Statistical Package for Social Sciences. Overall, 55 variables for data analysis were identified during our interactions with the children. Forty-five frequency tables and 89 Cross-Tabulations were generated during analysis. The latter were analysed to pinpoint trends and explain the situation of institutions where data was collected. The findings of this study can be used to enhance the service and environment of these homes, improve the rehabilitation processes of juveniles and elevate the in-house training and vocational facilities of institutions. The data also offers insight into the backgrounds of delinquents and their families.

Brief Overview of the Book

The first chapter of the book is the introduction itself; the second chapter reviews, examines and summarises the existing literature on the subject; the third chapter analyses the Act of 2000 and the rules thereunder as well as Act of 2015 and the rules thereunder; the fourth chapter analyses the patterns and trends in application and interpretation of laws by the higher judiciary; the fifth chapter documents the frequencies and Cross-Tabulations with respect to the child prior to institutionalisation; the sixth chapter examines the frequencies and Cross-Tabulations of variables when the child comes in conflict with the law and at the first point of contact; the seventh chapter analyses the frequencies and Cross-Tabulations of variables when the child in lodged inside the home; the eight chapter documents the frequencies and Cross-Tabulations of post-release prospects of the children; the ninth chapter lists the major empirical findings of the book and, finally, the tenth chapter concludes the book and notes down observations after correlation of the empirical and doctrinal parts of the book while giving effective and practicable solutions and suggestions.

Operational Definitions

The operational definitions of terms used in the hypothesis have been deduced from the existing normative framework of juvenile justice laws.

Reformation and rehabilitative service means service that fulfils the objective of ensuring the physical, emotional, intellectual, social and moral development of a juvenile in conflict with law, and his successful reintegration and re-socialisation post-release.

The term proper infrastructure alludes to the physical infrastructure of the institution to ensure individualised and holistic treatment of the juvenile as envisaged under the normative framework of JJA.

The term resources includes funds; material resources such as books and vocational training equipment; adequate number of well-qualified and well-trained staff; and links to governmental and non-governmental voluntary organisations that ensure the implementation of reformative and rehabilitative initiatives.

The term structured rehabilitative scheme includes targeted and goal-oriented therapeutic treatment, which ensures individualised attention and targets risk factors; life skills and personality development sessions; gainful vocational training; proper pre-release and post-release plans; proper mental health assessment; and periodic inspections to ensure implementation of institutional programmes.

Proper coordination at various levels and between various functionaries includes timely response and effective communication by decision-making authorities on any proposal by the institution. It also includes sharing of information related to the juvenile, such as social investigation report, psychological assessment, behavioural reports, etc. when he is transferred from one institution to another.

Chapter II
Literature Review

Literature review is one of the most vital parts of any research project, helping the researcher focus on grey areas that earlier studies have not covered. Hence, it is important to review existing literature and study material relating to the impact and implementation of juvenile justice in general and the Act of 2000 in particular.

Theories of Cause and Effect

There are different theories that explain delinquency and varied factors—such as peer influence, poor parenting, disrupted families, lack of academic achievement, etc.—that influence juvenile delinquency.

General strain theory, as propounded by Robert Agnew, explains the reason for people to engage in crime as a result of stress or strain. Indulging in crime may help them reduce stress, such as stealing to reduce financial problems or seeking revenge against someone who has harmed them. There are two categories that can contribute to crime: (a) being prevented by others to achieve the goal you have; (b) things that are valuable to you are taken away by others or being presented by negative stimuli. Crime may be caused by failure to achieve goals related to money, status and independence from adults, in case of adolescents.[1]

---

[1] 'Crime Causation: Sociological Theories—Strain Theory,' Law Library—American Law and Legal Information, accessed 16 March 2019, http://law.jrank.org/pages/814/Crime-Causation-Sociological-Theories-Strain-theory.html,' Crime Causation: Sociological Theories—Strain Theory.

The theory of social disorganisation developed by Clifford Shaw and Henry McKay suggests that crime is unequally distributed in the city. Economically deprived areas are socially disorganised and there's low social control over institutions like family, school, etc. Shaw and McKay also theorised that criminal behaviour is passed down from one generation to another.[2]

Child abuse and neglect also provoke delinquent behaviour. Cathy Widom and Michael Maxfield found that these factors increased the risk of future delinquency by 29 per cent, and the likelihood of arrest as an juvenile by 59 per cent. They suggested more attention be given to families where children are malnourished and abandoned.[3]

Research has also found that children with strong social bonds commit less crime than those who don't.[4] If a child develops anger and mistrust, then he loses his conscience and exhibits anti-social behaviour. Hirschi observed, 'If the bond to the parent is weakened, the probability of delinquent behaviour increases; if this bond is strengthened, the probability of delinquent behaviour declines.'[5] In their study with 506 boys, David Farrington et al. found that poor parental supervision is significantly correlated to delinquency.[6] They also found that poor housing—where the boys were living in bad neighbourhood—can be linked to delinquency. Then, Machteld Hoeve et al., in the meta-analysis of 161 studies, observed that parenting is linked to delinquency. Their findings were in line with previous research that emphasised that poor supervision and parental rejection, as well as neglect and hostility,[7]

---

[2] 'Review of the Roots of Youth Violence: Literature Reviews,' Vol. 5, Chapter 4, Ontario Ministry of Children, Community and Social Services, accessed March 16, 2019, http://www.children.gov.on.ca/htdocs/English/professionals/oyap/roots/volume5/chapter04_social_disorganization.aspx.

[3] Cathy S. Widom and Michael G. Maxfield, 'An Update on the "Cycle of Violence",' *National Institute of Justice Research in Brief*, US Department of Justice, Office of Justice Programs (February 2001).

[4] Travis Hirschi, *Causes of Delinquency* (New Jersey: Transaction Publishers, 2002).

[5] Hirschi, *Causes of Delinquency*, 88.

[6] David P. Farrington et al., 'Are Within-Individual Causes of Delinquency the Same as Between-Individual Causes?' *Criminal Behaviour and Mental Health,* Vol. 12, no. 1 (2002): 53–68.

[7] Machteld Hoeve et al., 'The Relationship between Parenting and Delinquency: A Meta-analysis,' *Journal of Abnormal Child Psychology*, Vol. 37, no. 6 (August 2009): 749.

link to delinquency. Roland Chilton and Gerald Markle point to studies that strongly correlate living in disruptive families to delinquency, with few exceptions. They also found that delinquents with more serious offences were from incomplete families, and that income was important in understanding delinquent behaviour.[8] Lastly, Terence Thornberry et al. studied 4,000 youth to figure out the relationship between delinquency and drug use, and the influence of multiple changes in family structures. They observed that more family transitions link to delinquency and drug use.[9]

From these studies, one can observe the impact parenting and family have on delinquents. Proper parenting is important to prevent felonious behaviour, and parents must give love and warmth to children while disciplining them at the same time. They require close supervision as well. Family conditions also have a bearing on delinquency; family stability is important for the child and multiple transitions due to divorce, separation and changing partners can have a negative impact. However, this phenomenon needs to be explored further.

J.B. Kupersmidt and K.A. Dodge[10] maintain there are two extreme hypotheses, which specify the different roles of peers in developing aggressive and antisocial behaviour in a child, and focus on individual characteristics that may cause delinquency among children. Dana Haynie and D. Wayne Osgood found that 'adolescents engage in more delinquency if they have delinquent friends or if they spend a great deal of time in unstructured socialising with friends. Yet these influences from the peer domain are no more or less important than social control processes in the realms of family and school.'[11]

---

[8] Roland J. Chilton and Gerald E. Markle, 'Family Disruption, Delinquent Conduct and the Effect of Subclassification,' *American Sociological Review*, Vol. 37, no. 1 (February 1972): 93–99.

[9] Terence P. Thornberry et al., 'Family Disruption and Delinquency,' *Juvenile Justice Bulletin*, US Department of Justice, Office of Juvenile Justice and Delinquency Prevention (September 1999).

[10] J.B. Kupersmidt and M.E. DeRosier, 'How Peer Problems Lead to Negative Outcomes: An Integrative Mediational Model,' in *Children's Peer Relations: From Development to Intervention*, eds. J.B. Kupersmidt and K.A. Dodge (Washington DC: American Psychological Association, 2004), 119–38.

[11] Dana L. Haynie and D. Wayne Osgood, 'Reconsidering Peers and Delinquency: How Do Peers Matter?', *Social Forces*, Vol. 84, no. 2 (December 2005): 1125.

Mark Warr studied the influence of family and friends on delinquency and found that spending more time with parents could negate peer influences.[12] Adolescents who are attached to their parents may not choose to be with delinquent friends. Following previous research, Joseph Murray et al.[13] concluded that 'having delinquent peers was most likely to be correlated rather than a cause of boy's offending'.[14] Thus, spending time with delinquent peers may negatively influence the juvenile. Additionally, Haynie and Osgood found supporting evidence for two perspectives—the socialisation perspective, where associating with delinquents has a casual influence, and the opportunity perspective that focuses on 'time spent with peers as a potential source of opportunities that promote delinquency'.[15]

Don Weatherburn and Bronwyn Lind observed that the reasons for delinquency in urban and rural areas were the same—social and economic stress, child neglect and child abuse.[16] Social and economic disadvantages are the root causes, which lead to an increasing rate of offences such as theft and robbery. In their study, Robert Sampson and John Laub[17] found that poverty had an indirect influence on delinquency, hindering the family's ability to have informal social control, resulting in delinquent behaviour among adolescents. They state, 'Cohesive families characterised by consistent, loving and reintegrative punishment, effective supervision and close emotional ties appear to have overcome these disadvantaged conditions in producing a low risk of adolescent delinquency.'[18] Rashmita Mistry et al. observed that economic difficulties negatively influence parenting, which,

---

[12] Mark Warr, 'Parents/Peers, and Delinquency,' *Social Forces*, Vol. 72, no. 1 (September 1993): 247–64.

[13] Joseph Murray and David P. Farrington, 'Risk Factors for Conduct Disorder and Delinquency: Key Findings from Longitudinal Studies,' *The Canadian Journal of Psychiatry*, Vol. 55, no. 10 (October 2010): 633–42.

[14] Murray and Farrington, 'Risk Factors,' 638.

[15] Haynie and Osgood, 'Reconsidering Peers,' 1124.

[16] Don Weatherman and Browyn Lind, 'Poverty, Parenting, Peers and Crime Prone Neighbourhoods,' *Trends and Issues in Crime and Criminal Justice*, Australian Institute of Criminology, No. 85 (April 1998): 1–6.

[17] Robert J. Sampson and John H. Laub, 'Urban Poverty and the Family Context of Delinquency: A New Look at Structure and Process in a Classic Study,' *Child Development*, Vol. 65, no. 2 (April 1994): 523–40.

[18] Sampson and Laub, 'Urban Poverty,' 538.

in turn, impacts the child's well-being. Parents under financial stress tend to show less affection towards their children than those who are not.[19] The link between socioeconomic status and delinquency has been widely studied, and poverty does have a relationship with the delinquency. But this relationship extends to parenting as well. Thus, proper parenting can prevent delinquent behaviour despite low socioeconomic status.

Furthermore, there is substantial evidence linking children's social and academic functioning. However, Melissa DeRosier and Stacey Lloyd[20] point out that 'most studies to date have been cross-sectional or correlational indicating that problems in one area tend to co-occur with problems in the other area'.[21] A great deal of research on children's peer relations has focused on social acceptance or the degree to which a child is liked by their same-grade peers at school as opposed to disliked or rejected by them.[22] Children with high social acceptance tend to experience positive academic, social and behavioural adjustment both concurrently and in the future. Conversely, children with low social acceptance (for example, peer rejection) tend to experience concurrent problems across these domains and are at substantial risk of myriad negative outcomes, including suicide, drug abuse, educational underachievement, delinquency, antisocial behaviour and depression. R.E. Tremblay et al.,[23] while exploring the links between early disruptive behaviour, poor school achievement and antisocial behaviour, did not conclude that poor school achievement was a

---

[19] Rashmita S. Mistry et al., 'Economic Well-being and Children's Social Adjustment: The Role of Family Process in an Ethnically Diverse Low-Income Sample,' *Child Development*, Vol. 73, no. 3 (May/June 2002): 935–51.

[20] Melissa E. DeRosier and Stacey W. Lloyd, 'The Impact of Children's Social Adjustment on Academic Outcomes,' *Reading & Writing Quarterly*, Vol. 27, no. 1–2 (2010): 25–47.

[21] DeRosier and Lloyd, 'The Impact of Children's Social Adjustment,' 25–47.

[22] J.G. Parker et al., 'Peer Relationships, Child Development, and Adjustment: A Developmental Psychopathology Perspective,' in *Developmental Psychopathology: Vol 2. Risk, disorder, and adaptation*, eds. D. Cicchetti and D. Cohen (Oxford: Wiley, 1995), 96–161.

[23] R.E. Tremblay et al., 'Early Disruptive Behaviour, Poor School Achievement, Delinquent Behaviour and Delinquent Personality: Longitudinal Analyses,' *Journal of Consulting and Clinical Psychology*, Vol. 60, no. 1 (February 1992): 64–72.

causal factor of delinquency for boys. Antonis Katisyannis et al.[24] reviewed previous literature and concluded that 'a clear relation exists between poor academic achievement and juvenile delinquency and repeat offending'.[25] In their meta-analysis Eugene Maguin and Rolf Loeber found that poor academic performance was not only linked to delinquency but also to its onset and level of seriousness. This association, in their observation, was stronger for males than females. Based on existing intervention studies, Maguin and Loeber also found that better academic performance was linked to a reduction in delinquent acts, and that intelligence and a poor attention span also correlated to poor academic performance and delinquency.[26] Thus, poor academic performance links to delinquent behaviour while the opposite better academic performance ties to lower delinquency rates. Additionally, poor performance may either cause delinquency or become a by-product of delinquent behaviour. This can be explored further.

Dr Mahendra Tiwari et al.[27] attribute the rise of delinquency in India to socioeconomic and psychological reasons. 'Poverty, broken homes, family tensions, emotional abuse, rural-urban migration, breakdown of social values and joint family system, atrocities and abuses by parents or guardians, faulty educational system, the influence of media besides the unhealthy living conditions of slums and such other conditions explain the phenomena of juvenile delinquency. The neglect of children by their parents, family, society and the nation create a detrimental effect on their physical and mental growth and overall development.'[28]

In India, migration often occurs from rural to urban areas, larger cities and metros, and migrants tend to be left with poor housing, bad

---

[24] Antonis Katsiyannis et al., 'Juvenile Delinquency and Recidivism: The Impact of Academic Achievement,' *Reading & Writing Quarterly*, Vol. 24, no. 2 (2008): 177–96.

[25] Katsiyannis et al., 'Juvenile Delinquency and Recidivism,' 190.

[26] Eugene Maguin and Rolf Loeber, 'Academic Performance and Delinquency,' *Crime and Justice*, Vol. 20 (1996): 145–264.

[27] Mahendra Tiwari and Mohan Shakti, 'Analytical View on the Concept of Juvenile Delinquency,' *International Journal of Research in Economic and Social Sciences*, Vol. 5, no. 9 (September 2015).

[28] D.A. Kumar, 'Juvenile Delinquency and its Justice System in India: A Critical Study with Special Reference to Juvenile Justice (Care And Protection of Children) Act, 2000,' accessed 12 December 2018, http://shodhganga.inflibnet.ac.in/bitstream/10603/188816/2/01%20summary.pdf.

neighbourhoods, low incomes and incomplete families. These may disrupt a child's development and his education, and expose him to negative peer influence. He may also be subjected to child labour in factories or early employment, hindering schooling. A labouring child is exposed to long working hours in unhealthy conditions with minimal pay, which has a negative impact on his emotional, psychological and physical health. The child may desire a better lifestyle, which could lead to delinquent behaviour. Unsupervised media exposure can also affect the child—violence or content that promotes wrong beliefs could hack away at the child's social values.

Different theoretical models have been formulated to help us understand the link between academic and social difficulties. The incidental model suggests that problems in early childhood peer relations are an artefact of other underlying disorders or deviancies, such that peer problems are merely incidental to other causal processes (Jeffrey G. Parker and Steven R. Asher).[29] Social and academic problems may occur together in a correlational fashion, but the former do not independently predict the latter.

Conversely, the causal model suggests that academic problems are causally related to earlier disruption in socialisation processes, such that peer problems contribute independently to the prediction of later academic difficulties.

According to Jean Piaget, 'The ability to understand and interpret his or her world proceeds in a series of stages, beginning with sensorimotor period, which lasts roughly from birth until two years of age and ends with the formal operations period, which lasts from roughly age 11 through adulthood. During this period, the child is able to understand and interpret the world differently because of his or her ability to engage in more abstract thought. In addition, the development of the child's cognitive abilities is, to some extent, influenced by the child's environment.'[30]

This, however, doesn't demarcate the thought process of adults, who take measured and informed decisions, and the thought process of adolescents, who are significantly more likely to indulge in thoughtless risk-taking behaviours. In his feature for the American Bar Association magazine,

---

[29] Jeffrey G. Parker and Steven R. Asher, 'Peer Relations and Later Personal Adjustment: Are Low Accepted Children at Risk?' *Psychological Bulletin*, Vol. 102, no. 3 (1987): 357–89.

[30] Preston Elrod and R. Scott Ryder, *Juvenile Justice: A Social, Historical, and Legal Perspective, Third Edition* (Boston: Jones and Bartlett, 2011), 9.

Mark Hansen[31] mentions three experiments that differentiate between the minds of adolescents and adults. In the first experiment, a group of people aged ten to 30 is given a puzzle involving the rearrangement of a stack of coloured balls in placeholders in as few moves as possible. While the adolescents almost always started to move the balls around immediately, the adults took more time to consider their first move. In the second experiment, the group was asked to choose between smaller but immediate rewards or long-term high-paying rewards. The adolescents took the smaller reward for its shorter time period, while the adults were more willing to wait for the higher reward. In the third experiment, the group was given a computer simulation of a situation, wherein they were driving and had to choose between running a series of traffic lights, which were about to turn red—alone and in the company of friends. Invariably, the younger subjects took greater risks when their friends were present, while older subjects did not alter their driving in either case.

A study published in *The Lancet Child & Adolescent Health*[32] found that while adolescence sets in at 10 years now, the understanding of the child with respect to continued growth has lifted the end point age well into the 20s. What this and other studies with respect to the age of adolescence tells us is that the age of maturity is rather subjective. Unfortunately, policies and legislations rarely prioritise subjectivity over objectivity. Even so, the extent to which the subjectivity of the age of maturity is factored into objective tests laid down by the law requires an in-depth analysis, of both the provisions and the factors surrounding their implementation.

Steven Levitt[33] examines the rate of crimes from an economic point of view. The divergence of adult and juvenile crimes, he argues, may not be the result of teenagers who differ categorically from earlier generations, but rather a rational response to a change in relative incentives for juveniles and adults to engage in criminal activities. If criminal activity involves learning by doing or investment in crime related human capital, then changes in the expected punishment of juveniles may affect not only their current crime

[31] Mark Hansen, 'What's the Matter with Kids Today?' *ABA Journal*, July 2010, 50.

[32] Susan M. Sawyer et al., 'The Age of Adolescence,' *The Lancet Child & Adolescent Health*, Vol. 2, no. 3 (March 2018): 223–28.

[33] Steven D. Levitt, 'Juvenile Crime and Punishment,' *Journal of Political Economy*, Vol. 106, no. 6 (December 1998): 1156–85.

involvement but also future involvement. Levitt[34] suggested that punishment may bring about long-run changes in the individual's engagement with crime. To exemplify this, if juvenile detention centres facilitate the acquisition of criminal human capital or stigmatise those in custody, then harsh punishment of juveniles may reduce crime in the short run but increase its probability over a longer time. He said, 'Juvenile offenders are at least as responsive to criminal sanctions as adults. Sharp drops in crime at the age of majority suggest that deterrence (and not merely incapacitation) plays an important role. There does not, however, appear to be a strong relationship between the punitiveness of the juvenile justice system that a cohort faces and the extent of criminal involvement for that cohort later in life.'[35]

The *Coalition for Juvenile Justice 2000 Annual Report*[36] concludes that unchecked mental health problems play a large role in criminal behaviour among juvenile offenders. Youth with untreated mental health problems are filling up courts, detention centres and correctional facilities, and society needs to recognise, acknowledge and publicise the prevalence of mental health problems among the youth. For those juveniles who must be placed in detention, the time so spent must be humane and safe, and every youth must be properly diagnosed, assessed and monitored for their mental health needs. Patricia Kerig et al.[37] support the theory that trauma interferes with adolescent development especially in girls, correlating trauma exposure and mental health problems.

Thomas Grisso[38] noted that three mental health studies on youth in juvenile justice systems found that 60 per cent to 70 per cent of the youth had mental disorders, and that their prevalence is higher among girls

---

[34] Levitt, 'Juvenile Crime,' 1156–85.

[35] Levitt, 'Juvenile Crime,' 1156.

[36] 'Handle with Care: Serving the Mental Health Needs of Young Offenders,' *Coalition for Juvenile Justice 2000 Annual Report*, accessed 17 March 2019, https://files.eric.ed.gov/fulltext/ED453465.pdf.

[37] Patricia K. Kerig et al., 'Posttraumatic Stress as a Mediator of the Relationship between Trauma and Mental Health Problems among Juvenile Delinquents,' *Journal of Youth and Adolescence*, Vol. 38, no. 9 (October 2009): 1214.

[38] Thomas Grisso, Gina Vincent and Daniel Seagrave, eds., *Mental Health Screening and Assessment in Juvenile Justice* (New York: The Guilford Press, 2005).

than boys. In another article,[39] he pointed out that previous studies indicate mental health problems as a cause of delinquent behaviour. Gail Wasserman et al.[40] found that more than half of their sample in a juvenile justice setting indicated mental disorders. Around 14 per cent reported lifetime suicide attempts, prompting the researchers to state, 'the importance of justice setting in defining mental health needs'.[41]

The area of mental health and delinquency requires more work by the authorities. A large percentage of delinquent children are found with mental disorders, and poor home conditions can worsen their condition. Untreated mental disorders can impair normal functioning of the youth, affecting their work performance and hence impacting their professional sustainability. This could lead to worse economic conditions and a lot of free time post-release. Young delinquents may also suffer from depression and suicidal tendencies, which need to be addressed to make them productive and do better psychologically. Involving families can be important in the treatment process. Name calling and stigmatisation, as well as disruptive and unhealthy relationships involving the juvenile can be detrimental to his well-being, so the family needs to play a supportive role and provide a cordial environment for speedy recovery. Efforts must especially be made for substance addicts so they don't fall back into addiction after release or have company who could trigger abuse.

However, despite significant amounts of research around the causes and risk factors contributing to delinquency, their application remains minimal.

Arvind Narrain[42] criticises the Act of 2000 for the lack of application of various studies and ensuing recommendations in the field of juvenile justice. 'What is shocking [is] that in an age when our knowledge about wrongdoing has increased exponentially wherein the traditional

---

[39] Thomas Grisso, 'Adolescent Offenders with Mental Disorders,' *The Future of Children*, Vol. 18, no. 2 (Fall 2008): 143–64.

[40] Gail A. Wasserman et al., 'Psychiatric Disorder, Comorbidity, and Suicidal Behaviour in Juvenile Justice Youth,' *Criminal Justice and Behavior*, Vol. 37, no. 12 (December 2010): 1361–76.

[41] Wasserman et al., 'Psychiatric Disorder,' 1369.

[42] Arvind Narrain, 'A Critique of Juvenile Justice Act 2002,' accessed 17 March 2019, http://altlawforum.org/publications/a-critique-of-the-juvenile-justice-act-2002/.

criminological approaches of classical/positivist have long been contested by other explanatory frameworks, which locate the reason for wrongdoing in societal structures, the Act bears no trace of any new thinking… the Act reflects no such theoretical shift in thinking. If social control theories were even considered, then juvenile justice would have focused more strongly on ensuring that one concentrated on building the social bonding between the juvenile and society, rather than subjecting the juvenile to a prison regime of limited contact with the outside world, which, in effect, alienates him/her even further from society.'[43]

Thus, the Act and its implementing agencies need to take into account the social well-being of the juvenile, his relationship with his family, and social reintegration for better functioning.

Theories and Practices of Prevention, Rehabilitation and Reformation

Professor B.B. Pandey[44] eloquently sums up the vision behind the enactment of the Act of 2000: 'The Juvenile Justice Act, 2000, amendment, 2006 and Juvenile Justice Model Rules 2007 envisage to usher in a child-friendly justice delivery system that provides for dealing with "juveniles in conflict with law" and "children in need of care and protection" in terms of distinct and exclusive rules for apprehension, bail release, pre-adjudication custody, adjudication, disposition and post disposition custodial care. The Juvenile Justice Act, 2000 has been in operation for the past 13 years, but still we need to go a long way before the Act is fully operational.'

There is, however, debate with respect to the theory that should guide the juvenile justice system—should it be reforming and rehabilitative, or should it be deterrent and punitive? Stevens Clarke[45] distinguishes the proponents of the two sides of the debate as 'treaters' and 'punishers'. He states that treaters argue the prisons are cruel, expensive and non-rehabilitative, while punishers contend that while prisons may be

---

43 Narrain, 'A Critique.'

44 B.B. Pandey, 'Child Rights Law,' *Annual Survey of Indian Law*, Vol. XLIX (2013): 93.

45 Stevens H. Clarke, 'Getting Em' Out of Circulation: Does Incarceration of Juvenile Offenders Reduce Crime?' *The Journal of Criminal Law and Criminology*, Vol. 65, no. 4 (1974): 538.

non-rehabilitative, incarceration prevents those crimes the offender may commit if not imprisoned. He explores the question of whether and to what extent incarceration prevents criminal acts that may have occurred but for the imprisonment. After rigorous data analysis in the context of the US, Clarke concludes that even if the number of juvenile offenders incarcerated was to be doubled, the overall decrease in the nationwide index of offences would only be 1 to 4 per cent. Considering the problems, the benefit was not worth the cost.

Richard Lundman[46] observed that the reasons for juvenile institutionalisation have changed, and the state wants to send a message to society that it intends to deal with juveniles strictly. This reinforces the idea that doing time in juvenile correctional facilities is painful rather than a treatment all institutions provide. This, according to Lundman, makes a lasting impression.

In the Indian context, Kailash Jeenger[47] argues that the age of 18 years set by the Act of 2000 is an abomination and provides blanket cover to all juvenile delinquents, blindly ignoring the rise in juvenile delinquency as well as the paradigm shift in a child reaching an age of discretion, discernment and maturity. Jeenger points out that the Beijing Rules allow discretion to the state to decide the age of criminal responsibility, so, to avoid the child from mingling with adult prisoners, he should be housed in a separate cell. Also, such punitive measures make space for reformation in children in that they teach them a lesson at a tender age.

In her review of the role of institutions, Maharukh Adenwalla[48] states that whatever be the noble reasons for institutionalising a child, he perceives the loss of freedom as punishment in itself. This protection advanced by the Juvenile Justice Act is not welcomed by inmates and looked upon as an intrusion, as most of them are already independent.

---

[46] Richard J. Lundman, *Prevention and Control of Juvenile Delinquency, Third Edition* (Oxford University Press, 2001), 29.

[47] Kailash Jeenger, *Excessive Protection to Juveniles and Minors: A Plea for Legislative Amendments to the Law*, Supreme Court Cases 3 (2), 2015.

[48] Maharukh Adenwalla, *Child Protection and Juvenile Justice System for Juvenile in Conflict with Law*, Childline India Foundation (December 2006).

Donna Bishop[49] recognises that there has been a spurt in legislations that allow the prosecution of adolescents under the adult criminal justice system. The proponents assert that the juvenile court sanctions and services constitute neither just nor effective responses to juveniles and offenders, and propose proportionate punishment under the criminal justice system. This provides better and effective deterrence as well as incapacitation. Bishop asserts that empirical evidence, though limited, proves the assertions of the proponents to be false. She argues that such prosecution will send many non-threatening juveniles into the adult system and move adolescents with special needs to correctional systems ill-prepared to handle them.

Shiladitya Rakshit[50] observes that the government's argument for harsher punishment seems to be a reaction of moral panic rather than of well-thought, empirically supported propositions. Research indicates that restorative justice is effective and should be adopted. This is also the case for more serious offences because such children are thought to be most in need of closure and assistance. Referring to the Act of 2015, Rakshit regrets that the fate of youth offenders in India has been sealed by a public vote in favour of revenge, rather than constitutionally and internationally sound principles of youth crime regulation. The need of the hour is to return to the view that juvenile delinquency is essentially a behavioural problem and not a criminal problem. Mark Umbreit et al.[51] point out that early efforts of Victim Offender Mediation (VOM) focused on helping the victim and reforming the offender, involving direct interaction between the victim and offender in front of a trained mediator. This provided an opportunity to victims to get answers to questions they may have, and to the offender to take responsibility for their behaviour. Umbreit et al. reviewed seven studies to see if victims participating in juvenile VOM were satisfied at all. The findings indicated that around 80 per cent to 97 per cent of victims were satisfied except in one

---

[49] Donna M. Bishop, 'Juvenile Offenders in the Adult Criminal Justice System,' *Crime and Justice*, Vol. 27 (2000): 81.

[50] Shiladitya Rakshit, 'Missing the "Justice" in the Juvenile Justice (Care and Protection of Children) Bill, 2014,' *Law and Policy Brief*, Vol. 1, no. 8 (August 2015).

[51] Mark S. Umbreit et al., 'Victim Impact of Meeting with Young Offenders: Two Decades of Victim Offender Mediation Practice and Research,' in *Restorative Justice for Juveniles: Conferencing, Mediation and Circles*, eds. Allison Morris and Gabrielle Maxwell (Oxford—Portland Oregon: Hart Publishing, 2001), 121–43.

study where 56 per cent of the victims were satisfied. Then, in her study, Nancy Rodriguez[52] found that 'juveniles in the restorative justice program were less likely to recidivate than juveniles in the comparison group when controlling for legal and extra-legal factors'.[53] It can be assumed, therefore, that the impact of restorative justice has been effective in victim satisfaction and reducing recidivism. In fact, restorative justice can more successfully reintegrate the juvenile in the society, and rehabilitate him.

Karen Kolivoski et al.[54] observed that the youth who experienced out-of-home placement in child welfare systems are more likely to have justice system involvement. They identified five groups on the basis of their age in conflict with law—no/low involvement, early age involvement, late/adult age involvement, short-term/highly involved, and chronically involved. They found that placement factors affect each group differently. The study demonstrates the need to better understand the heterogeneity of child-level characteristics within the child welfare population as a necessary step towards disentangling the complex relationship between child welfare populations and the juvenile justice system.

Robert Zabel and Frank Nigro[55] observe that juvenile offenders, particularly those with disabilities, were at a higher risk of school failure and diminished educational employment and social opportunities, leading to social maladjustment as adults. To understand the occupational preferences and aptitudes of offenders, a sample group was asked to complete an inventory of occupational interests and aptitude. On the basis of the results, Zabel and Nigro recommended multifaceted intervention programmes, beginning in middle school, which keep students in school, remediate academic and social

---

[52] Nancy Rodriguez, 'Restorative Justice at Work: Examining the Impact of Restorative Justice Resolutions on Juvenile Recidivism,' *Crime & Delinquency*, Vol. 53, no. 3 (July 2007): 355–79.

[53] Rodriguez, 'Restorative Justice,' 336.

[54] Karen M. Kolivoski et al., 'Developmental Trajectories and Predictors of Juvenile Detention, Placement, and Jail among Youth with Out-of-Home Child Welfare Placement,' *Journal of the Society for Social Work and Research*, Vol. 5, no. 2 (Summer 2014): 137.

[55] Robert Zabel and Frank Nigro, 'Occupational Interests and Aptitudes of Juvenile Offenders: Influence of Special Education Experience and Gender,' *Journal of Correctional Education*, Vol. 58, no. 4 (December 2007): 337.

problems, engage students in prevocational and vocational programmes with transition specialists, and teach self-determination skills.

Dr T.H. Khan[56] fervently speaks out in favour of reformation. 'Juvenile delinquency is the culmination of several maladjusting experiences that a child had to pass through … that a child treated through community-based correction is certainly at a much greater stake for social conformity than the one subjected to penal detention and labelled as a delinquent and that no formal system can undo the aberration of a larger social system.'

According to Amol Kanth, in *Juvenile Justice System*[57] the involvement of social workers and non-governmental organisations at different stages of apprehension, treatment and rehabilitation of juveniles is an essential element of correctional strategy under this law. The concepts of 'place of safety' and 'fit person/institution', and the recognition of voluntary institutions as observation homes, juvenile homes, special homes and after-care homes have yet to materialise in most of the states. Social workers can be an important link between juveniles and their families, schools and local communities. They can help juveniles with admission in schools and employment, recommend new career opportunities, and link them with important agencies, such as employment agencies. They can also keep a check on the child's involvement in any further delinquent acts and motivate him to improve his academic or work performance. Social workers can undertake work with dysfunctional families as well and link them with important funding sources where possible, or inform them about government schemes and programmes and assist them in accessing them.

Information from previous studies reveals that Bombay had taken the lead in establishing the Juvenile Aid Police Unit (JAPU) in 1952. Subsequently, JAPUs were established in Calcutta (1956), Hyderabad (1958), Madras (1960), Patna and Ranchi (1961), Poona, Sholapur and Nagpur (1967), Calicut (1970), and Bhilai, Indore and Jabalpur (1974). However, progress on the subject is unknown at a national level, though there are sporadic reports on juvenile clubs being run by the police in certain places, such as Prayas in Delhi.

---

[56] T.H. Khan, 'Juvenile Justice System in India: An Appraisal,' *Central India Law Quarterly*, Vol. VIII, no. 1 (1994): 61.

[57] Vijay Hansaria and P.I. Jose, *Juvenile Justice System* (New Delhi: Universal Law Publishing, 2010).

Ved Kumari,[58] after conducting an empirical study, concluded that vocational training provided in an institution setting under the juvenile justice system is not helpful towards earning a stable livelihood, and most juveniles spend their time sitting idle in observation or special homes. Even if gainful vocational training is provided, reformation and rehabilitation remain a distant dream due to lack of opportunity after release and restoration in the environment of deprivation. Another challenge is the variable length of stay of a juvenile in a home. Additionally, there is lack of information that could reflect the record of reformation and rehabilitation by the institution. Kumari's study also pointed out the need for proper infrastructure to provide a therapeutic environment and properly trained staff to handle juveniles with appropriate sensitivity. The behaviour of the police and the environment in the police station, for howsoever a brief period, are the first encounters of these children with the state machinery; these determine their attitude towards the *parens patriae* regime of juvenile justice system to a large extent.

A study by Thomas Ollendick and Michel Hersen[59] demonstrated that an experimental group that was exposed to social skills training, as compared to a control group, showed significant improvement in their social skills. They learnt interpersonal skills and had reduced anxiety. Edward Ameen and D.L. Lee[60] suggested creating career opportunities for the youth in detention through vocational training, while Mark Lipsey,[61] in his meta-analysis of the impact of rehabilitative programmes on serious offenders in the juvenile justice setting, found that they were effective in reducing recidivism. However, it requires focused effort to implement effective programmes. The time spent at the detention centres can be proper utilised by providing the juvenile with educational opportunities and vocational training. They can be taught English and basic computer

---

[58] Ved Kumari, *The Juvenile Justice System in India: From Welfare to Rights* (Oxford University Press, 2004).

[59] Thomas H. Ollendick and Michel Hersen, 'Social Skills Training for Juvenile Delinquents,' *Behaviour Research and Therapy*, Vol. 17, no. 6 (1979): 547–54.

[60] Edward J. Ameen and D.L. Lee, 'Vocational Training in Juvenile Detention: A Call for Action,' *The Career Development Quarterly*, Vol. 60, no. 2 (June 2012): 98.

[61] Mark W. Lipsey, 'Can Intervention Rehabilitate Serious Delinquents?' *The ANNALS of the American Academy of Political and Social Science*, Vol. 564, no. 1 (July 1999): 142–66.

courses that can help them get a job after release. Other skills such as cooking, stitching, etc. can also be taught so that juveniles can use them for self-employment, especially in cases where they are unable to find suitable jobs. Vocational training centres can link up with agencies who can use the services of juveniles and provide them with income. Thus, offenders may not only learn skills but also use them to earn a livelihood.

Rupam Jagota[62] attributes economic factors, deprivation, cut-throat competition, technological changes, cultural variations, disintegration of the joint family system and increased industrialisation leading to mass migration as contributory to juvenile delinquency. While appreciating the provisions of the Act of 2000, the author concedes that there is lack of proper implementation of provisions due to structural imbalances. Jagota outlines the need for coordination between agencies at state and district levels, and the development of a new value system among educators, which will foster positive work attitude, self-esteem and job skills in children. He implores the community to step up to provide a sense of belonging to juveniles.

Based on her review of existing literature, Anne Rankin Mahoney found that the community can react negatively to delinquents, and that chances of them getting employed are affected. Juvenile delinquents may experience ostracisation from family members or relatives or be removed from the family to stem negative influences on other siblings.[63]

Erika Rickard and Jason Szanyi[64] hail the Act of 2000 as a commitment to India's international obligations to its children, and its change in philosophy, guiding the treatment of the country's most marginalised youth. They found evidence, however, that even after a decade of enactment, the reforms were yet to trickle down to the local level, where they can have a deep positive impact. Rickard and Szanyi

---

[62] Rupam Jagota, 'Juvenile Justice System in India: An Attempt at Reformation,' *RMLNLUJ*, Vol. 2 (2010): 84.

[63] Anne Rankin Mahoney, 'The Effect of Labelling Upon Youths in the Juvenile Justice System: A Review of the Evidence,' *Law & Society Review*, Vol. 8, no. 4 (1974): 583–614.

[64] Erika Rickard and Jason M. Szanyi, 'Bringing Justice to India's Children: Three Reforms to Bridge Practises with Promises in India's Juvenile Justice System,' *UC Davis Journal of Juvenile Law & Policy*, Vol. 14, no. 1 (Winter 2010): 109.

surmise that for many children, the promise of a just and equitable system remains elusive, and suggest that universal training should be mandated for all who come in contact with the children. Other recommendations include issue-based guidance; employment of alternative policing models; diversion as an explicit goal; limited use of secure detention; professional probation officers with well-defined roles, and a system of accountability. Probation officers responsible for investigating facilities for juveniles are often overworked and lack adequate training.

According to Robin Walker Sterling,[65] the Supreme Court of the US has recognised that 'children are different from adults', concluding that these differences must inform how we treat children accused of serious offences. She argues that if children are treated differently in homicide cases and sentenced to life without parole, then, by extension, they should be treated differently when they're accused of sexual offences and face mandatory lifetime sexual offender registration, in line with the principle of a fresh start.

The 2013 Justice Verma Committee emphasised that children who have been deprived of parental guidance and education have very little chance of mainstreaming and rehabilitation, with the provisions of Juvenile Justice Act being reduced to mere words on paper. A report submitted by the Centre for the Child and the Law, National Law School of India University, notes that there is no substantial data on whether juveniles committing serious offences are indeed receiving the treatment and reformatory services necessary for their rehabilitation and reintegration into the mainstream.

After conducting detailed research at observation homes in Delhi, Ruzbeh N. Bharucha[66] concluded that despite the Act of 2000 providing for the establishment of Special Juvenile Police Units and Child Welfare Officers (CWOs) in every police station to deal with children in conflict with law, the situation remains grim. In many states, no such units have been established or there's lack of awareness within the department. The CWOs also handle other cases, resulting in a heavy workload and running from one court to another. Bharucha also criticised the lack of political

---

[65] Robin Walker Sterling, 'Juvenile Sex Offender Registration: An Impermissible Life Sentence,' *The University of Chicago Law Review*, Vol. 82, no. 1 (2015): 295.

[66] Ruzbeh N. Bharucha, *My God is a Juvenile Delinquent* (New Delhi: Sainathann Communication, 2008).

will to change, and a restrictive attitude of the government with regard to apathy about the continued usage of terms like detention and release.

Justice Anjana Prakash[67] observes the irony that it is not the juvenile offenders, the victims of social evils fostering at the behest of adults, that the society needs protection from; it is rather on account of the failure of civilised society and its various organs that juveniles turn into offenders. The author surmises that the need of the hour is not just the introduction of a new 'well researched and more comprehensive' Act or an Amendment, but rather an imperative for the legislature to take steps to ensure that the authorities act in an honest and diligent manner and further, the outlook of the masses needs to be changed.

Professor Pandey[68] states that traditionally understood juvenile justice relates to an all-embracing concept that aims at providing, first, an alternative system of justice, and second, justice and fairness for the child, not only at the trial stage, but also at the investigation, pre-trial custody, bail and remand-proceeding stages. However, he reasons that conceiving juvenile justice too widely is the main reason for many implementation-level flaws and crises within the system today. He mentions three reasons: it leads to the merger of two, almost opposed, welfare and justice jurisdictions; it generates problems of coordination between the functions of diverse agencies like the police, adjudicators and the welfare administration; and it inhibits specialised approach to the issue.

In as far back as 1968, the Sinha Committee Report pointed out that there should be at least one juvenile court and juvenile welfare board in each district to deal with cases of neglected and delinquent juveniles. 'For this purpose it is necessary to have 244 more juvenile courts and 327 welfare boards in the country in the fourth plan. According to the statistical surveys published by the National Institute of Social Defence, the number of juveniles courts in 1976 stood at ninety-five (statistical survey—Children Courts and Child Welfare Boards, Social Defence, 1981).'

---

[67] Justice Anjana Prakash, 'Juvenile Justice Act, 1986: An Outline,' *CNLU Law Journal*, Vol. 1 (2010): 107

[68] B.B. Pandey, *Rethinking Juvenile Justice: Amit Das Style*, (2000) 6 SCC (Jour) 1.

In 1984–85, the official figure of districts without a juvenile court stood at 230, those and without a board at 419.[69]

The Parliamentary Standing Committee, in its 264th report, noted that while there has been notable research as far as the condition of juvenile homes are concerned, none of these studies have addressed the need to trace the level of reform and rehabilitation of children in conflict with law after they are released. More importantly, there is no data or record with regard to juveniles who committed crimes after attaining majority or leaving the homes. Training and treatment of juvenile offenders is likely to go waste if their difficult transition from institution to outside world is not helped and guided by humane and efficient after-care programmes.

Gauri Pillai and Shrikrishna Upadhyay[70] state that although the proposed policy under the Act of 2015 was contrary to the established principles of juvenile justice, the solution wasn't reversion to the position under the Act of 2000 with focus on its implementation. They hold that the Act of 2000 didn't take into account that heinous offences should carry with them a higher punishment than just three years, which falls short of guaranteeing effective rehabilitation. After an analysis of the Acts, they conclude that the Act of 2000 was more offender-centric and didn't acknowledge the plight of victims. They suggest that while retaining the emphasis on rehabilitation, principles of restorative justice ought to be annexed as the mandatory second limb for the formulation of a comprehensive juvenile justice policy in India.

Overall, the literature points towards poor parental supervision, poor family conditions and neighbourhoods, peer influence and poor academic performance as some of the linking factors to delinquency. It also points towards the need to address mental health issues and to provide better vocational and educational facilities to inmates, thus improving the response of juveniles to the justice system. It also suggests that the justice system include the overall context of the juvenile, his family and socioeconomic conditions.

---

[69] Kumar, 'Juvenile Delinquency.'

[70] Gauri Pillai and Shrikrishna Upadhyay, 'Juvenile Maturity and Heinous Crimes: A Relook at Juvenile Justice Policy in India,' *NUJS Law Review*, Vol. 10, no. 1 (2017).

Chapter III

Analysis of Legislative Framework

As seen in the introduction and literature review, a distinct set of principles focused on reformation and rehabilitation has dominated academic and political discourse with respect to the drafting of laws relating to juvenile justice and children in conflict with law. The Juvenile Justice Act of 1986 and its subsequent amendments can be considered in many ways a landmark in signifying changes in the thought process of lawmakers.

At the turn of the twenty-first century, a need was felt to update the laws bearing in mind prescribed standards set by the UN Convention on the Rights of the Child, 1989; the UN Standard Minimum Rules for Administration of Juvenile Justice, 1985,[1] as well as the UN Rules for Protection of Juveniles Deprived of their Liberty, 1990. The legislative exercise subsequently culminated into the Juvenile Justice (Care and Protection of Children) Act, 2000,[2] along with the Juvenile Justice (Care and Protection of Children) Model Rules of 2000, as replaced by the Juvenile Justice (Care and Protection of Children) Model Rules of 2007.[3]

In the wake of the 2012 Delhi gangrape and murder case, one of the accused, who was a juvenile, was sentenced to three years in a reformation home as per the provisions of the Juvenile Justice Act, 2000.

---

[1] Hereafter referred to as the Beijing Rules.

[2] Hereafter referred to as the Act of 2000.

[3] Hereafter referred to as the Model Rules of 2000.

In light of the Supreme Court[4] judgement upholding the constitutional validity of the Act, in December 2015, the Delhi High Court[5] held itself to be bound by the provisions, and refused to extend the sentence of the accused. This led to a widespread feeling of miscarriage of justice, with the masses protesting in solidarity with the victim's family. Drawing much flak from various sections to correct the supposed lacunae in the previous act, the government introduced the Juvenile Justice (Care and Protection of Children) Bill, 2014, which was passed by the parliament in its present form on 22 December 2015. It received the President's assent on 31 December 2015, and came into effect on 15 January 2016, as the Juvenile Justice (Care and Protection of Children) Act, 2015.[6]

The march of law and the circumstances surrounding it have had profound implications on the principles governing juvenile justice in India. In this chapter, the researchers have attempted to mark such changes by doctrinally analysing the various acts and rules, which were legislated in this century.

Juvenile Justice (Care and Protection of Children) Act of 2000

The preamble to the Act of 2000 bares the intention of lawmakers, in that they sought to consolidate and amend the law relating to 'children alleged and found in conflict with law and children in need of care and protection, by catering to their basic needs through proper care, protection, development, treatment, social reintegration, by adopting a child-friendly approach in the adjudication and disposal of matters in the best interest of children and for their rehabilitation through processes provided, and institutions and bodies established.'

Section 2 (k) of the Act of 2000 defines the term juvenile as any person who has not completed the 18th year of age, while Section 2 (l) defines juvenile in conflict with the law as any juvenile who is alleged to have committed an offence. Section 2 (p) defines offence as any offence punishable by any law in force at the time.

---

4 *Dr. Subramanian Swamy & Ors.* v. *Raju Thr.*, (2014) 8 SCC 390.

5 *R.K. Tarun* v. *Union of India*, (2015) SCC Online Del 13461.

6 Hereafter referred to as the Act of 2015.

Procedure with Regard to Children in Conflict with Law

Section 4 of the Act of 2000 instructs the setting up of a Juvenile Justice Board[7] consisting of a metropolitan magistrate and two social workers. Section 6 empowers the board with exclusive jurisdiction to deal with all proceedings under the Act with relation to children in conflict with law. In order to avoid the prosecution of juveniles in other courts, Section 7 lays down the procedure for other magistrates not empowered by the Act, wherein the magistrate is required to note his opinion that a person brought before him is a juvenile and forward the juvenile to the board.

It is important to distinguish between a special home and an observation home as institutions created under the Act of 2000. Under Section 8, state governments have been empowered to establish observation homes as required for a 'temporary reception' of juveniles in conflict with law during the pendency of any inquiry. In contrast, special homes are to be established under Section 9 for the reception and rehabilitation of juveniles. They receive those juveniles for whom alleged charges have been confirmed by the board in its final order.

Section 10 of the Act of 2000 details the procedure to be followed after the apprehension of the juvenile. As soon as the juvenile is apprehended by the police, he must be placed under the charge of the Special Juvenile Police Unit[8] or a designated police officer who must report the matter to the board within 24 hours.[9] Irrespective of whether the offence alleged is bailable or non-bailable, the juvenile must be released on bail with or without surety, unless there are 'reasonable grounds for believing that the release would bring him association with known criminals, or expose him to moral, physical or psychological danger or that his release would defeat the ends of justice'.[10]

In the event the juvenile is not released, he must be sent to an observation home until he can be brought before the board.[11] The board cannot commit the juvenile to prison, but order for him to be sent to an observation home or a 'place of safety' pending the duration of enquiry.[12]

---

[7] Hereafter referred to as the board.

[8] Hereafter referred to as the SJPU.

[9] As amended via the Amendment Act of 2006.

[10] Section 12 (1), Act of 2000.

[11] Section 12 (2), Act of 2000.

[12] Section 12 (3), Act of 2000.

Under no condition can the juvenile be placed in a police lockup/judicial custody.[13]

Section 13 makes it a duty of the officer-in-charge of the station or SJPU to inform the parents/guardians of the child as soon as the arrest is made and direct them to be present before the board. Such officer is also duty-bound to inform the probation officer of such arrest to enable him to collect the antecedents and family background of the juvenile, in order to assist the board in its enquiries.

Officers who frequently or exclusively deal with juveniles are to be specially trained and instructed in order to enable them to perform their duties effectively.[14] One officer in every police station is to be designated a juvenile or Child Welfare Officer (CWO), to handle juveniles in coordination with the police.[15]

After the enquiry, to be conducted within a stipulated period of four months,[16] the board, if satisfied that the juvenile has committed the alleged offence, may pass the following orders:[17]

1) Allow the juvenile to go home after admonition following counselling of the parents.
2) Direct the juvenile to participate in group counselling.
3) Direct the juvenile to perform community service.
4) Order the parents of the juvenile, or the juvenile himself (if above 14 years of age) to pay a fine.
5) Direct the juvenile to be released on probation and placed under the care of any parent, guardian or fit person, for a period not exceeding three years.
6) Direct the juvenile to be released on probation and placed under the care of any fit institution for a period not exceeding three years.
7) Make an order directing the juvenile to be sent to a special home:
    i. In case of a juvenile over 17 but less than 18, for not less than two years.
    ii. In case of any other juvenile, for a period till he ceases to be a juvenile.

---

[13] Section 9, Amendment Act of 2006.

[14] Section 63 (1), Act of 2000.

[15] Section 63 (2), Act of 2000.

[16] Section 14, Act of 2000.

[17] Section 15, Act of 2000.

These orders must keep in mind the social investigation report by the probation officer.[18] In furtherance of orders passed under Sections 15 (d), 15 (e) and 15 (f), the board may appoint a probation officer for a period not exceeding three years to supervise the conduct of the juvenile thereafter. In case of misconduct during probation, the court may send the juvenile to a special home.

Ordinarily, convictions under certain sections of the Indian Penal Code (IPC) or other enactments carry some disqualifications, such as in government appointments or under the Representation of People Act 1951.[19] However, Section 19 of the Act of 2000 removes the disqualification in case of juveniles who have committed an offence, and the records of such commission shall be removed after the passing of the period of appeal or any other reasonable period of time.

If the authority finds that the presence of a parent or guardian of the child is sine qua non at the proceedings, it is empowered under Section 45 of the Act of 2000 to give such directions.[20] Under Section 46, competent authorities have been empowered to dispense with the presence of the juvenile during proceedings if found to be inessential to the conduct of such proceedings.

If it appears to the board that the person brought before it is a juvenile, the board is required to conduct an enquiry to determine the age of the person, take evidence as necessary and record the findings.[21] Further, the report of the probation officer or social worker has to be treated as confidential, providing access to its substance only to the juvenile, parent or guardian, to provide them with the opportunity of producing such evidence as may be necessary to the matter.[22]

An appeal against the order of the board can be made only to a Court of Sessions, while no appeal can be made against an order of acquittal by the board.[23] No second appeals may be made against the order of the Court of Sessions passed in appeal; however, the High Court may, on

---

[18] Section 15 (2), Act of 2000.

[19] Sections 8, 8A, 9, 9A, 10 and 10A, Representation of People Act, 1951.

[20] Section 45, Act of 2000.

[21] Section 49, Act of 2000.

[22] Section 51, Act of 2000.

[23] Section 52, Act of 2000.

its own motion or an application, call for the record of any proceedings in the Court of Sessions or before the board to satisfy itself with respect to the legality of such an order.

The board may, if it deems fit, transfer any child addicted to narcotics or psychotropic substances to a treatment centre not exceeding the period for which he is required to be kept there, or as maybe certified by the medical officer, necessary for the proper treatment of the juvenile.[24]

Penal Provisions

The publication of names, addresses, schools or any other particulars, which may lead to the identification of the juvenile, in any newspaper, magazine, news sheet or visual media is strictly prohibited under Section 21 of the Act of 2000. Any contravention of such provisions carries a fine of ₹ 25,000.[25]

The act penalises cruelty to a juvenile, with a six-month sentence with or without fine. For the purpose, it defines cruelty as assault, abandonment, exposure or neglect in a manner likely to cause such juvenile or child unnecessary mental or physical suffering, or procurement of the child for any of the above reasons.[26]

The act sets out a sentence of three years' imprisonment with or without fine for the employment or use of any juvenile or child for begging.[27] Section 2 (b) defines begging as:

1) Soliciting or receiving alms in a public place or entering into private premises for the purpose of soliciting or receiving alms, whether under any pretence.
2) Exposing or exhibiting with the object of obtaining or extorting alms, any sore, wound, injury, disability or deformity, whether of himself or any person or animal.

Section 25 of the Act of 2000 makes the giving of alcohol in a public place, or any narcotic or psychotropic substance to a juvenile punishable with a three-year sentence with or without fine. Further, the procurement of

---

[24] Section 58, Act of 2000.

[25] Section 15, Amendment Act of 2006.

[26] Section 23, Act of 2000

[27] Section 24, Act of 2000.

a child for the purpose of employment in a hazardous industry, keeping him in bondage, withholding the child's earnings and using the same for his own purposes has been made punishable with a sentence of three years with or without fine.[28]

Procedure with Regard to Children in Need of Care and Protection

The Act of 2000 calls for the establishment of a Child Welfare Committee[29] consisting of one chairperson and four other members, which shall function as a bench of magistrates and have power as conferred by the Code of Criminal Procedure, 1973 on a metropolitan magistrate or a judicial magistrate first class.[30] The committee is empowered to dispose cases for the protection, care, treatment, development and rehabilitation of children as well as to provide for their basic needs and secure human rights.[31] Any child in need of care or protection may be produced before the committee by:[32]

1) Any police officer, SJPU, or a designated police officer.
2) Any public servant.
3) Any social worker or public-spirited citizen authorised by the state government.
4) By the child himself.
5) Childline, a registered voluntary organisation, or by any other voluntary organisation as recognised by state governments.

Upon the receipt of the report under Section 32, an enquiry is initiated by the committee and for the purpose, may send the child to a children's home for a speedy investigation by a social worker.[33] If, after the completion of the enquiry, the committee is satisfied that the child has no

---

[28] Section 26, Act of 2000.

[29] Hereafter referred to as the committee.

[30] Section 29, Act of 2000.

[31] Section 31, Act of 2000.

[32] Section 32, Act of 2000.

[33] Section 33 (1), Act of 2000.

parents or ostensible support, it may allow the child to continue staying in the children's home or shelter home till he attains the age of 18 years.[34]

Juvenile Justice (Care and Protection of Children) Rules, 2007

The Juvenile Justice (Care and Protection of Children) Rules, 2007[35] were notified by the Ministry of Women and Child Development on 26 October 2007, in pursuance of the power to make rules granted under Section 68 (1) of the Act of 2000. The rules were made with a view to better implement the Act of 2000 in its true spirit and substance.

The Rules define an individual care plan as a comprehensive development plan for a juvenile based on age- and gender-specific considerations as well as the history of the juvenile.[36] The plan is to be made in consultation with the juvenile in order to restore his self-esteem and sense of self-worth, and nurture him to become a responsible citizen. The following factors must be kept in mind:

1) Health needs
2) Emotional and psychological needs
3) Educational and training needs
4) Leisure, creativity and play
5) Attachments and relationships
6) Protection from abuse, neglect and maltreatment
7) Social mainstreaming
8) Follow-up post-release and restoration

The rules also recognise and elaborately enumerate 14 principles to be followed by state governments, boards, committees and other competent authorities in their implementation, thereby forming a set of guidelines for the interpretation of the provisions of the Act of 2000 as well as the Rules of 2007.

1) **Principle of Presumption of Innocence:** The rules cite the Beijing Rules and state clearly that around the world, persons in

[34] Section 33 (3), Act of 2000.

[35] Hereafter referred to as the rules.

[36] Section 2 (h), Rules of 2007.

conflict with law below the age of 18 are considered intellectually and mentally immature. The principle states that all juveniles and children are to be presumed to be innocent of any mala fide or criminal intent up to the age of 18. Such presumption is then mandated to be respected throughout the process of justice and protection; from initial contact to alternative care, including aftercare. A corollary to this presumption is the rule mandate upon the state to provide legal aid to the juvenile and other assistance through legal services at the expense of the state.

2) **Principle of Dignity and Worth:** The rules imbibe Article 1 of the Universal Declaration of Human Rights, that all humans are born free and equal in dignity and rights. It defines dignity as not being humiliated, respect for one's personal boundaries and space, not being stigmatised and discriminated, being offered choices and information, and not being blamed for their acts. This principle imposes that the dignity and worth of the child should be respected through the process.
3) **Principle of the Right to be Heard:** One of the foremost principles of natural justice—*audi alteram partem*—has been incorporated as the principle of the right to be heard. It lays down ways to develop appropriate tools and processes of interacting with the child, promote the child's role in decision-making with respect to his own life, and provide opportunities for discussions and debates.
4) **Principle of Best Interest:** The primary consideration of all processes should be the best interest of the child. By ensuring his emotional, physical, intellectual and moral development, it seeks to ensure that the child reaches their full potential. It is further clarified in the rules that this principle means the traditional objectives of criminal justice—retribution and repression—must give way to rehabilitation and restoration.
5) **Principle of Family Responsibility:** With the primary responsibility of raising children being with the biological parents, or foster or adoptive parents in extraordinary circumstances, this principle seeks to ensure that all decision-making for the child involves the family or parents.

6) **Principle of Safety:** This seeks to ensure that right from the point of his conflict with law to restoration and rehabilitation, the child shall not be abused, neglected, mistreated, punished corporally or confined to jail. Extreme care and precautions are needed to protect the sensitivity of the child.
7) **Principle of Positive Measures:** The state shall take all possible measures to promote the well-being of the juvenile through individual care plans formulated after interactions with the child, the family, volunteers and other organisations including schools and communities. The rules list certain positive measures that are illustrative, such as creating avenues for health, education, relationships, livelihood, leisure, creativity and play.
8) **Principle of Non-Stigmatising Semantics, Decisions and Actions:** This principle prohibits the use of stigmatising semantics and adversarial as well as accusatory terms such as remand, warrant arrest, accused, trial, charge sheet, prosecution, summons, conviction, inmate, delinquent, custody or jail in juvenile justice processes.
9) **Principle of Non-Waiver of Rights:** No waiver of rights, whether by the juvenile, any acting authority or claimant to such authority, or competent authority, can be done.
10) **Principle of Equality or Non-Discrimination:** There can be no discrimination on the basis of sex, race, caste, age, place of birth, disability, health, status, ethnicity, religion, cultural practices, work, activity or behaviour of the juvenile, his parents or guardians.
11) **Principle of Right to Privacy and Confidentiality:** The right to privacy and confidentiality of the juvenile needs to be respected throughout the proceedings.
12) **Principle of Last Resort:** The institutionalisation of a child should be a measure of last resort after due enquiry, and for as short a period as necessary.
13) **Principle of Repatriation and Restoration:** This principle confers the right upon the juvenile to be reunited with his family and restored to the same socioeconomic and cultural conditions he enjoyed before coming under the purview of the Act.
14) **Principle of Fresh Start:** This ensures that the juvenile gets a new beginning and all records with relation to his conflict with the law

are erased. Furthermore, the state shall endeavour to promote ways for dealing with juveniles who break penal law without resorting to judicial proceedings.

Section 12 lays down the procedure with respect to the determination of age, which the board or court has to make on the basis of the physical appearance or documents such as matriculation certificates, birth certificate or certificate given by municipal authority or panchayat as the case may be. In case of absence of documents, the opinion of a medical board should be sought.

Upon production of the juvenile before the board, it shall review the report indicating the juvenile's background, circumstances of apprehension and offences alleged. The board may dispose of the case if the charges appear to be unfounded or the offence is trivial, release the juvenile in supervision of fit persons or institutions, detain him in an observation home, or transfer the case to a committee pertaining to children in need of care and protection.[37]

In order to ensure a fair and speedy trial, the board is expected to satisfy itself that the juvenile has not been ill-treated by the police or any other person, keep a child-friendly atmosphere during proceedings, give the juvenile the opportunity to be heard, and dispose petty cases while following the due process of enquiry in detail in case of heinous offences. A period of four months is prescribed for disposal of cases, and in case of offences other than serious, the proceedings shall stand terminated following delay beyond a period of four to six months.

Section 14 guarantees legal aid to the juvenile and the legal officer of the District Child Protection Unit (DCPU), and State Legal Aid Services are obliged to extend free legal aid to the juvenile. Section 16 states that the observation and special homes need to have segregated setups on the basis of age and gender. Every such institution is required to keep a copy of the Act and the rules, and make available simple and child-friendly versions in regional languages as well.

In chapter VI of the Rules of 2007, standards of care at institutions have been meticulously set. Section 40 reiterates the requirement for segregation of juveniles on the basis of age, gender and nature of offences.

[37] Section 13, Rules of 2007.

It further sets the minimum area requirement for the homes at 8,495 square feet, with norms regarding the division of spaces. It calls for smooth flooring to prevent accidents, adequate lighting, heating and cooling arrangements, safe drinking water, clean toilets; first-aid kits, fire extinguishers, regular review of electric installations, proper storage and inspection of food articles, and a stand-by arrangement for water and lighting.

Section 41 calls for the provision of clothing and bedding as per the climactic conditions. The minimum standards are provided in Schedule 1 (see Tables 3.1–3.3).

Table 3.1: Quantity of Bedding

No.	*Article*	*Quantity to be provided per child*
1.	Towels	Four per year
2.	Cotton bedsheets	Two for two years
3.	Pillow (cotton-stuffed)	One for two years
4.	Pillow covers	Two for two years
5.	Woollen blankets	Two for two years
6.	Cotton *durry*	Two for two years
7.	Cotton-filled quilt	One for two years (in cold regions)
8.	Mattress	One for two years
9.	Mosquito net	One for two years

Table 3.2: Quantity of Clothing (Boys)

No.	*Clothing*	*Quantity to be provided per child*
1.	Shirts	Five sets per year
2.	Shorts	Five sets per year for younger boys
3.	Pants	Five sets per year for older boys
4.	Vests	Four sets per year
5.	Underwear	Four sets per year
6.	Woollen jerseys	Two for two years (for cold regions)
7.	Scarves	Two for two years (for cold regions)

Table 3.3: Quantity of Clothing (Girls)

No.	*Clothing*	*Quantity to be provided per child*
1.	Skirt and blouse, or salwar kameez, or half sari with blouses and petticoats	Five sets per year for girls depending on their age and regional preferences
2.	*Banyans* (one metre each)	Six per year for younger girls
3.	Brassieres	Six per year for older girls
4.	Panties (one metre cloth each)	Six per year
5.	Sanitary towels	Twelve packs per year for older girls
6.	Woollen sweaters	Two for two years (in cold regions)
7.	Woollen shawls	One for two years (in cold regions)

With respect to sanitation, Section 42 necessitates the installation of water filters for safe drinking water; sufficient water for bathing and washing clothes, the maintenance and cleaning of premises; proper drainage system; arrangement for disposal of garage; protection from mosquitoes; annual pest control; airy and well-lit toilets in proportion of one toilet to seven children; airy and well-lit bathrooms in proportion of one bathrooms to seven children; sufficient space for washing; clean and fly-proof kitchen and separate area for washing utensils; and sunning of bedding and clothing, and maintenance of cleanliness in the medical centre.

Section 43 requires a daily routine to be set in consultation with the children's committee for a regulated, disciplined life. These include personal hygiene and cleanliness, physical exercise, yoga, educational classes, vocational training, organised recreational games, moral education, group activities, prayer and community singing and special activities for Sundays and holidays.

Per Section 44, children are required to be given minimum of four meals daily, including breakfast. The food must be provided as per the nutritional standards prescribed in Schedule II (see Table 3.4).

Table 3.4: Nutritional and Diet Scale

Name of food product	*Scale per head per day*
Rice/Wheat/Ragi/Jowar	600 g (700 g for 16–18-year-olds), of which at least 100 g to be wheat, ragi or jowar.
Dal/Rajma/Chana	120 g
Edible oil	25 g
Onion	25 g
Salt	25 g
Turmeric	5 g
Coriander powder	5 g
Ginger	5 g
Garlic	5 g
Tamarind/Mango powder	5 g
Milk (at breakfast)	150 mL
Dry chillies	5 g
Vegetables: leafy/non-leafy	100 g/130g
Curd or buttermilk	100 g/mL
Chicken (once a week) or eggs (four days a week)	115 g
Jaggery and groundnut seeds or paneer (vegetarians only)	60 g each (100 g paneer), once a week.
Sugar	40 g
For 50 children per day Pepper	 25 g
Cumin seeds	25 g
Black gram *dal*	50 g
Mustard seeds	50 g
Ajwain seeds	50 g
For 10 kg of chicken Garam masala	 10 g
Copra	150 g
Khus-khus	150 g
Groundnut oil	500 g

Name of food product	*Scale per head per day*
For sick children	
Bread	500 g
Milk	500 mL
Other items	
LPG for cooking only	

Section 45 prescribes the minimum standards of medical care to be followed by the institutions. This includes maintenance of a medical record based on monthly medical check-ups; medical facilities including a doctor on call; sufficient medical equipment to handle minor health problems; training all staff in first-aid; immunisation coverage; preventive measures against outbreak of contagious diseases; surgical treatments, only with the consent of parents or guardians, or in emergencies, the officer-in-charge; regular counselling for every juvenile; and referring children addicted to drugs to abuse prevention and rehabilitation programmes, at specialised centres administered by qualified personnel.

Section 46 seeks to ensure the all-round well-being of juveniles by focusing on mental health. It requires every institution to maintain a mental health record of every juvenile, and calls for environment-based interventions and individual therapy. It imposes the obligation to have trained counsellors on board, or collaborations with external agencies such as childcare institutions, psychological and psychiatric departments, and other governmental and non-governmental organisations.

In accordance with Section 47, every juvenile is required to be educated keeping in mind their age and ability, inside the institution as well as outside. Institutions are required to provide a range of educational opportunities, including at inclusive mainstream schools, bridge schools, and open schools, as well as non-formal education and the guidance of special educators. The provision of vocational training is mandatory under Section 48, while Section 49 mandates recreational activities such as indoor and outdoor games, music, television, picnics and outings, cultural programmes and library access.

Section 55 establishes a management committee within every institution, including a member of the children's committee. Every institution is to maintain complaint and redressal mechanisms and set up a children's suggestion box. The officers-in-charge of the institution must set up children's committees in every institution. This committee should participate in improving the institution; review the standards of care; prepare daily routines and diet scales; develop educational, recreational and vocational plans; report abuse and exploitation by peers; encourage the creative expression of views; and manage the institution via a management committee.

According to Section 57, positive reinforcement by way of rewards and earnings should be granted by officers-in-charge to encourage steady work and good behaviour. The juvenile's family is allowed to visit once a month under the Rules of 2007, or more frequently at the discretion of the officer-in-charge.

Duties of Various Agencies and Institutions

Section 10 lays down the functions of the board to achieve the objectives of Act, that is, to adjudicate and dispose of cases pertaining to children in conflict with law. Other functions include the cognisance of crimes under Sections 23–28 of the Act of 2000; monitoring the institutions; dealing with non-compliance on the part of government functionaries and voluntary organisations; directing district authorities or police to create infrastructure facilities; and taking suitable action for dealing with unforeseen circumstances.

Under Section 80, the State Child Protection Unit is tasked with the implementation of the Act of 2000, and the supervision of agencies and institutions under the Act. It is also responsible for setting up, supporting and monitoring DCPUs; making necessary funds available to DCPUs; coordinating with all government departments to build intersectoral links, including the departments of health, education, social welfare, urban basic services, backward classes and minorities, youth services, police, judiciary, labour, and State AIDS Control Society; training all personnel under the Act; and establishing minimum standards of care for all institutions and supervising their implementation.

As per Section 81, the DCPU is required to ensure the effective implementation of the Act at a district level; identify families at risk and children in need of care and protection; implement family-based non-institutional services such as sponsorship, foster care, adoption and aftercare; set up district-, block- and village-level child protection committees; develop tools for the supervision of institutions and agencies; and train and build the capacity of all personnel.

The duties of institutional officers-in-charge are laid down in Section 86 and broadly include ensuring compliance with the provisions of the Act and Rules, as well as orders of the board and committee; providing a homely environment with love, affection, care, development and welfare for juveniles or children; maintaining minimum standards of care and protection in the institution; maintaining buildings and premises, security measures and periodic inspections; supervising and monitoring juveniles; taking action to meet emergencies; ensuring accident and fire-safety measures are met; organising national and regional festivals in the institution; organisation field excursions and picnics; preparing budgets and controlling financial matters; and coordinating with legal officers in the DCPU to ensure every juvenile has free legal aid.

Section 88 points to the duties of the house father or house mother regarding handling the juvenile, giving him love and affection, ensuring the welfare of the juvenile or child, maintaining discipline, as well as sanitation and hygiene, implementing daily routines, looking after the inmate's safety and security within the premises as well as whenever they are sent out of the home.

Juvenile Justice (Care and Protection of Children) Act, 2015

Section 1 of the Act of 2015 makes its provisions applicable to all matters pertaining to children in conflict with law and children in need of care and protection, irrespective of any other laws in force for the time-being. These include apprehensions, detention, prosecution, penalty, imprisonment, rehabilitation and social reintegration. The inclusion of the term 'imprisonment' in the very first section serves as a prelude to what follows.

Definitions and Principles

Section 2 (12) defines a child as a person not having completed 18 years, while Section 2 (13) defines 'child in conflict with the law' as alleged or found to have committed an offence and has not completed 18 years on the date of commission of such offence. Section 2 (24) defines corporal punishment as subjecting a child to physical punishment by any person, involving the deliberate infliction of pain as retribution for an offence or to discipline or reform.

A children's court has been defined under Section 2 (20) as one established under the Commissions for Protection of Child Rights Act, 2005, or a special court instituted under the Protection of Children from Sexual Offenses Act, 2012. In case of their absence, a Court of Sessions with the jurisdiction to the try the offences under the Act is to function as a children's court. Section 2 (33) defines 'heinous offences' as offences for which the minimum punishment under the IPC or any other law for the time-being in force is imprisonment for seven years or more. Section 2 (54) defines 'serious offences' as offences for which the maximum punishment under the IPC or any other law for the time-being in force is imprisonment between three and seven years. Petty offences as defined under Section 2 (45) as offences for which the maximum punishment under the IPC or any other law for the time-being in force is imprisonment up to three years.

Unlike the Act of 2000 wherein the principles regarding juvenile justice were laid down in the Rules of 2007, the Act of 2015 provides 16 principles in Section 3 of the Act. The principles are largely in pari materia with the principles in the Rules:

1) Principle of presumption of innocence
2) Principle of dignity and worth
3) Principle of participation
4) Principle of best interest
5) Principle of family responsibility
6) Principle of safety
7) Principle of positive measures
8) Principle of non-stigmatising semantics
9) Principle of non-waiver of rights
10) Principle of equality and non-discrimination
11) Principle of right to privacy and confidentiality
12) Principle of institutionalisation as a measure of last resort
13) Principle of repatriation and restoration
14) Principle of fresh start
15) Principle of diversion
16) Principle of natural justice

The last two principles are additions to those already illustrated in the Rules of 2007. The principle of diversion states that measures dealing with the juvenile without resorting to judicial provisions shall be promoted. However, in the same breath, lawmakers have clarified that the principle is not set in stone and can be overlooked in the event of proceedings being in the best interests of the juvenile or society as a whole. Both terms—'best interests of the juvenile' and 'best interests of society'—are subject to a broad interpretations, which have not been clarified. The principle of natural justice applies to all bodies and persons acting in a judicial capacity under the Act. It states the right to fair hearing, rule against bias and the right to review, but the list is illustrative, not exhaustive.

Procedure with Regard to Children in Conflict with Law

Section 4 of the Act of 2015 mandates a Juvenile Justice Board on the same lines as in the Act of 2000. Section 8 (1) empowers the board to deal with all cases of children in conflict with the law. The key procedural difference between the two acts is that while under Section 6 of the Act of 2000, the board was granted exclusive jurisdiction to the try all pertinent cases, the provision in such absolute terms is absent in the Act of 2015. Section 8 (1), in this context, expressly excludes those provisions of the Act that may infringe upon such jurisdiction.

Section 8 (3) lays out the functions and responsibilities of the board—ensuring informed participation of the child, parent or guardian; ensuring the child's rights are protected throughout the process; ensuring the availability of legal aid; providing an interpreter or translator; directing the probation officer to undertake social investigations and submit his report; adjudicating and disposing cases; passing a final order including an individual care plan for the child's rehabilitation; conducting at least one inspection visit per month of residential facilities; ordering the registration of an FIR in case of offences committed against children in need of care and protection; and conducting regular inspections of adult jails to check if children, if any, are lodged therein.

Section 5 clarifies that if the child turns 18 during the pendency of enquiry, the enquiry should proceed as though he is a child. Under Section 6, if a person above the age of 18 is apprehended for committing an offence when he had not attained majority, such person shall be treated as a child during the enquiry.

Section 9 is analogous to Section 7 of the Act of 2000 and lays down the procedure for magistrates not empowered by the Act, wherein they're required to note that a person brought before them is a juvenile and forward him to the board. The difference between the two provisions is that while the Act of 2000 called for enquiry into the age of the child through a competent authority defined by the board or committee, the Act of 2015 empowers the court before which the claim for minority is made to conduct said enquiry and take evidence. Such claim can be raised at any stage of the trial, even after the final disposal.

After the juvenile is apprehended, he must be placed under the charge of the SJPU or a designated Child Welfare Police Officer (CWPO), who shall produce the child before the board within the stipulated 24 hours.[38] A person who appears to be a child, whether apprehended for bailable or non-bailable offences, must be released on bail by the officer-in-charge or the board unless there are reasonable grounds for believing that release is likely to bring the child into association with known criminals, expose him to moral, physical or psychological danger, or would defeat the ends of justice. The board shall record the reasons for denying bail and the circumstances that led to the decision.[39] If bail is not granted by the officer-in-charge, the juvenile must be kept in an observation home until brought before the board.[40] In case bail is not granted by the board, it must order the juvenile to an observation home during pendency of the enquiry.[41]

Observation homes have been established under Section 47 of the Act of 2015 with the objective of temporary reception, care and rehabilitation of any child alleged to be in conflict with law, pending enquiry. Special homes under Section 48 rehabilitate children found

---

[38] Section 10, Act of 2015.

[39] Section 12 (1), Act of 2015.

[40] Section 12 (2), Act of 2015.

[41] Section 12 (3), Act of 2015.

to have committed an offence and so placed by an order of the board under Section 18. Sections 47 and 48 mandate that every child sent to the institution must be segregated on the basis of age and gender, the child's mental and physical state, and the degree of offence.

Where a child alleged to be in conflict with law is apprehended, the SJPU or CWPO shall inform the parents or guardians, and second, the probation officer or CWO for the social investigation report to be submitted to the board within two weeks of apprehension.[42] When the child is brought before the board, it shall hold enquiries and pass orders as it deems fit.[43] If the board is satisfied that the child has not committed an offence, it shall pass an order to such effect.[44] However, if it finds that the child has committed the alleged offence, it may pass any of the following orders.[45]

1) Allow the juvenile to go home after admonition, following the counselling of parents.
2) Instruct the juvenile to undertake group counselling.
3) Direct the juvenile to perform community service.
4) Order the parents of the juvenile, or the juvenile himself (if over 14 years old) to pay a fine.
5) Direct the juvenile to be released on probation and placed under the care of any parent, guardian or fit person, for a period not exceeding three years.
6) Direct the juvenile to be released on probation and placed under the care of any fit institution for a period not exceeding three years.
7) Direct the child to be sent to a special home for not more than three years for reformative services, including education, skill development, counselling, behaviour modification therapy and psychiatric support during the stay.

The Act of 2015 differs from the Act of 2000 in that it creates a separate mechanism for the disposal of cases pertaining to heinous offences. As per Section 14 (f), the enquiry would be conducted by the board in case the

[42] Section 13, Act of 2015.

[43] Section 14, Act of 2015.

[44] Section 17, Act of 2015.

[45] Section 18, Act of 2015.

juvenile is under 16 years on the date of commission of offence. However, if the heinous offence was committed by the juvenile after he turned 16, procedures under Section 15 need to be followed. It requires a preliminary assessment of the mental and physical capacity of the child to commit the offence, his ability to understand the consequences of the offence, and the circumstances in which he allegedly committed it. This assessment must be completed within three months of the juvenile's first appearance before the board.[46] The board may take the assistance of a psychologist, a psycho-social worker or other experts for this purpose. If the board is satisfied that the child must be tried as an adult, it may order the case transferred to the Children's Court with jurisdiction to try such offences.[47] But if the board is satisfied that it should dispose of the matter, it shall follow the procedure for summons cases under the Code of Criminal Procedure, 1973.[48] An appeal against the board's order can be filed under Section 16, which shall be determined by the Court of Sessions. The court will consider the opinions of experienced psychologists and medical specialists, excluding those who assisted the board in said matter.[49] The High Court, which has the power of revision, may on its own motion or through an application call for records of proceedings where a board or children's court has passed an order, and adjudicate as it deems fit.[50]

After receiving the board's preliminary assessment, the Children's Court shall decide if there is need to try the child as an adult, and pass appropriate orders subject to the provisions of the Act considering the special needs of the child, tenets of fair trial and maintaining a child-friendly atmosphere.[51] If the Children's Court decides there no need to try the child as an adult, it may conduct an enquiry and pass orders as per Section 18 of the Act.[52]

The final order of the Children's Court must include an individual care plan for the child's rehabilitation.[53] He must be sent to a place

[46] Section 14(3), Act of 2015

[47] Section 18 (3), Act of 2015.

[48] Section 15 (2), Act of 2015.

[49] Section 101 (2), Act of 2015.

[50] Section 102, Act of 2015.

[51] Section 19 (1)(i), Act of 2015.

[52] Section 19 (1)(ii), Act of 2015.

[53] Section 19 (2), Act of 2015.

of safety until he turns 21, and thereafter transferred to jail.[54] Periodic follow-ups by the probation officer of the DCPU should be mandated by the Children's Court to check on the child's progress and ensure there's no ill-treatment in any form.[55]

As per Section 20, if the child has completed 21 years but is yet to complete the term of stay, the Children's Court instruct an evaluation to understand if the child has undergone reformation and if he can be a contributing member of society.[56] On the basis of the report, the court shall either release the child on conditions it deems fit, or direct the child to complete the remainder of his term in jail.[57] In no case, however, can the child be sentenced to life imprisonment with no possibility of release, or death.[58]

The child shall suffer no disqualification attached to any conviction of an offence.[59] However, the same does not apply to a child over 16 years who is tried as an adult. Further, whereas Section 24 (2) calls for destruction of all records after the period of appeal or any other reasonable period, the same is not applicable to juveniles tried as adults.

If a child in a special home or an observation home is of unsound mind or addicted to narcotics or psychotropic substances, the board may order his transfer to a psychiatric hospital or nursing home in accordance with the Mental Health Act, 1987.[60]

Procedure with Regard to Children in Need of Care and Protection

A Child Welfare Committee comprised of one chairperson and four other members is set up under Section 27 of the Act of 2015. Section 29 empowers the committee to dispose of cases for the care, protection, treatment, development and rehabilitation of children, provide for their basic needs and protect human rights.

---

[54] Section 19 (3), Act of 2015.

[55] Section 19 (4), Act of 2015.

[56] Section 20 (1), Act of 2015.

[57] Section 20 (2), Act of 2015.

[58] Section 21, Act of 2015.

[59] Section 24(1), Act of 2015.

[60] Section 93, Act of 2015.

The functions of the committee include[61] taking cognisance of and receiving children produced before it; conducting enquiries on all issues relating to the safety and well-being of the children; directing CWOs or probation officers to conduct social investigations and submit reports; conducting enquiries into fit persons for the care of the children; directing the placement of a child in foster care; ensuring care, protection and appropriate rehabilitation of children based on individual care plans; selecting registered institutions for placement of a child in need of institutional care; inspecting the residential facilities for children; certifying the execution of the surrender deed by parents; ensuring that all efforts are made for the restoration of abandoned or lost children to their respective families; declaring orphans, and abandoned and surrendered children as legally free for adoption; taking *suo motu* cognisance of cases and reaching out to children; and accessing appropriate legal services for children.

Any child in need of care and protection can be produced before the committee by:[62]

1) Any police officer, SJPU, or a designated police officer.
2) Any public servant.
3) Childline, a registered voluntary organisation.
4) Any social worker or public-spirited person authorised by the state government.
5) By the child himself.
6) Any nurse, doctor or the management of a nursing home, hospital or maternity home.

Any of these parties who take charge of a child in need of care and protection must inform Childline services, the nearest police station or committee, or DCPU within 24 hours, or hand over the child to an institution registered under the Act.[63] Under Section 32 (1), failure to inform is an offence[64] punishable by imprisonment of up to six months, a fine of ₹ 10,000 or both.[65]

[61] Section 30, Act of 2015.

[62] Section 31, Act of 2015.

[63] Section 32, Act of 2015.

[64] Section 33, Act of 2015.

[65] Section 34, Act of 2015.

Upon receiving a report under Section 31, the committee may pass an order to send the child to a children's home for speedy enquiry by a social worker or CWO.[66] The social investigation must be completed within 15 days so the enquiry can be completed within four months of receiving the order.[67] After completion of the enquiry, if the committee opines that the child has no family or ostensible support, it may send him to a specialised adoption agency if he's under six years or allow the child to remain in the children's home or special home until suitable rehabilitation is found or he turns 18.

If committee believes the child needs care and protection, it shall consider the social investigation report and the child's wishes (in case of maturity) and pass one or more of the following orders.[68]

1) A declaration that the child is in need of care and protection.
2) Restoration of the child to parents or guardians, with or without the supervision of a CWO or designated social worker.
3) Placement of the child in a children's home, shelter home or specialised adoption agency.
4) Placement of the child with a fit person for temporary or long-term care.
5) Foster care orders under Section 44.
6) Sponsorship orders under Section 45.
7) Directions to persons, institutions or facilities in whose care the child is placed regarding care, protection and rehabilitation of the child.
8) Declaration that the child is legally free for adoption under Section 38.

Children's homes have been established under Section 50 of the Act for their care, treatment, education, training, development and rehabilitation.

Rehabilitation and Reintegration Services in Institutions

Section 53 of the Act of 2015 expressly delineates the services all institutions under it must provide with respect to the rehabilitation and reintegration of children.

---

[66] Section 36 (1), Act of 2015.

[67] Section 36 (2), Act of 2015.

[68] Section 37, Act of 2015.

1) Basic requirements such as food, shelter, clothing and medical attention.
2) Equipment such as wheelchairs, prosthetic devices, hearing aids, Braille kits, and other aids and appliances as required by children with special needs.
3) Appropriate education, including supplementary education, special education and education for children with special needs.
4) Skill development
5) Occupational therapy and life skills education.
6) Mental health intervention, including counselling specific to the needs of the child.
7) Recreational activities including sports and cultural activities.
8) Legal aid where required.
9) Referral services for education, vocational training, deaddiction and treatment of diseases where required.
10) Case management, including preparation and follow-up of individual care plan.
11) Birth registration
12) Assistance in obtaining proof of identity.
13) Any other service to ensure the well-being of the child.

Penal Provisions

Section 74 of the act penalises the disclosure of name, address, school or other particulars that may lead to the identification of a child in conflict with law, a child in need of care and protection, a child victim, or a child witness in any newspaper, magazine, news sheet, audio-visual media or other forms of communication, with a sentence of six months, a fine of ₹ 200,000 or both.

Under Section 75, whoever having actual charge of or control over a child assaults, abandons, abuses, exposes or wilfully neglects him, or causes or procures a child to be assaulted, abandoned, abused, exposed or neglected in a manner likely to cause such child unnecessary mental or physical suffering, shall be punishable with imprisonment up to three years, a fine of ₹ 100,000 or with both.

The employment of any child for begging, or causing a child to beg is punishable with imprisonment up to five years and a fine of ₹ 100,000.[69]

---

[69] Section 76, Act of 2015.

Giving liquor, narcotics or psychotropic substances, and tobacco products (except on the order of a qualified medical practitioner) shall be punished with imprisonment up to seven years or a fine of ₹ 100,000.[70] Similar punishment is reserved for using children to peddle, vend, carry, supply or smuggle liquor, narcotics or psychotropic substances.[71] Additionally, 'Whoever ostensibly engages a child and keeps him in bondage for the purpose of employment or withholds his earnings or uses such earning for his own purposes shall be punishable with rigorous imprisonment for a term, which may extend to five years and shall also be liable to fine of one lakh rupees.'[72]

Section 81 of the Act of 2015 states: 'Any person who sells or buys a child for any purpose shall be punishable with rigorous imprisonment for a term, which may extend to five years and shall also be liable to fine of one lakh rupees.'[73]

Section 82 prohibits the use of corporal punishment to discipline a child by any person in charge or employed in a childcare institution. A fine of ₹ 10,000 may be imposed on the first conviction followed by imprisonment of up to three months, a fine or both every subsequent conviction. Section 83 deems the use or recruitment of any child for any purpose by a self-styled, non-state militant group punishable with imprisonment of up to seven years, a fine ₹ 500,000, or both.

Procedure with Regard to Determination of Age

In cases where based on the appearance of a person, the board or committee opines that he is under 18 years, they shall record such observation stating the age as nearly as maybe and proceed. However, if the board or committee has reasonable doubts regarding the child's age, it shall undertake the process of determination based on:

1) The birth certificate obtained from school, or a matriculation or equivalent certificate from the concerned examination board.
2) In the absence of (1), the birth certificate from the municipal authority, corporation or panchayat.

---

[70] Section 77, Act of 2015.

[71] Section 78, Act of 2015.

[72] Section 79, Act of 2015.

[73] Section 81, Act of 2015.

3) In the absence of (1) and (2), an ossification test or other medical age determination test may be conducted.

Juvenile Justice (Care and Protection of Children) Model Rules, 2016

The Juvenile Justice (Care and Protection of Children) Model Rules, 2016 were notified by the Ministry of Women and Child Development on 21 September 2016, in pursuance of the Juvenile Justice (Care and Protection of Children) Act, 2015.

An individual care plan has been defined in Section 2 (ix) of the Rules as a comprehensive development plan for a child based on age, gender-specific needs and his case history prepared in consultation with the child, in order to restore his self-esteem, dignity and self-worth and nurture him into a responsible citizen. It also addresses the following needs:

1) Health and nutrition needs.
2) Emotional and psychological needs.
3) Educational and training needs.
4) Leisure, creativity and play.
5) Protection from abuse, neglect and maltreatment.
6) Restoration and follow-ups.
7) Social mainstreaming.
8) Life skills training.

The social background report is prepared by the CWO outlining the background of the child in conflict with law.[74] Meanwhile, the social investigation report contains detailed information about the child's circumstances and situation based on economic, social, psycho-social and other relevant factors, and subsequent recommendations.[75]

Section 7 of the Rules of 2016 assigns several functions to the board in addition to those enumerated by the Act of 2015. These include provision of translators and interpreters; issuance of rehabilitated cards to juveniles; ordering the child's readmission to the school he was in prior to

[74] Section 2 (xvi), Rules of 2016.

[75] Section 2 (xvii), Rules of 2016.

institutionalisation or during the enquiry; working with boards in other districts to facilitate speedy enquiry and disposal of cases; inspections of childcare institutions; maintaining suggestion boxes or grievance redressal boxes; ensuring smooth functioning of children's committees; reviewing children's suggestion books at least once a month; and ensuring free legal services by responsible parties.

Section 8 details the pre-production actions of the police. It specifically states that no FIRs can be registered except in cases of heinous offences or where the offence is committed jointly with adults. The child must be placed under an SJPU or the CWPO immediately upon apprehension. In cases of petty or serious offences, the SJPU or CWPO shall record the particulars in the general diary followed by a social background report. The CWPO should be in plain clothes. The SJPU or CWPO shall immediately inform the parents or guardians of the child, the concerned probation officer and CWO. Under no circumstances can the child be remanded in a police lockup. The police may send the child to an observation home until he is brought before the board within 24 hours. The police cannot handcuff, fetter or chain a child, or use any form of coercion or force. The child must be informed of the charges levelled against him directly through his parents or guardian, and a copy of the FIR or police report must be provided to the parent or guardian. The child should not be compelled to confess his guilt and all interviews must be conducted at the SJPU or other child-friendly premises. The child must not be asked to sign any documents and be provided free legal aid.

The board must review the social background report, circumstances surrounding the apprehension and the nature of offence prior to passing orders.[76] In cases of heinous offences, where the child is above 16 years, the CWPO must submit statements of witnesses along with other relevant documents prepared during the investigation within one month of the child's first appearance before the board.[77] In cases of petty and serious offences, the final report must be filed at the earliest, not beyond a period of two months.[78] When witnesses are produced before the board, the enquiry must not be conducted in a strict adversarial manner. The board

[76] Section 10, Rules of 2016.

[77] Section 10(5), Rules of 2016.

[78] Section 10(6), Rules of 2016.

shall use the powers under Section 165 of the Indian Evidence Act, 1872[79] to interrogate the child and proceed with presumptions in favour of the child.[80] When recording a statement by the child, the board must address him in a friendly manner and encourage him to state the facts and circumstances without fear.[81]

Section 10A establishes procedures of preliminary assessment in cases of heinous offences by a child over 16 years. After determining his age, the board shall take the assistance of psychologists, psycho-social workers or other experts for the assessment. A presumption of innocence shall lie in favour of the child unless proven otherwise.

Upon receiving the preliminary assessment, the Children's Court may decide whether there is a need to try the child as an adult and record its reasons for doing so. In these cases, the trial must follow procedure under the Code of Criminal Procedure, 1973 while maintaining a child-friendly atmosphere. If the child is found to be involved in the commission of the offence, he should be sent to a place of safety until he turns 21 years old.

Section 25 of the rules highlights caring for children after they leave institutional care. It mandates states to prepare a programme for children who have to leave institutions upon turning 18, by providing for their education, giving them employable skills, and employment as well as places to stay to facilitate their reintegration into mainstream society. Children placed in aftercare programmes shall be provided funds for their essential requirements. Services provided may include:

1) Community group housing on a temporary basis.
2) Provision of stipends during vocational training or scholarships for higher education.
3) Arranging for skills training and placement.

---

[79] Section 165: Judge's power to put questions or order production. The judge may, in order to discover or obtain proper proof of relevant facts, ask any question he pleases, in any form, at any time, of any witness, or of the parties, about any fact relevant or irrelevant, and may order the production of any document or thing; neither the parties nor their agents shall be entitled to make any objection to any such question or order, nor, without the leave of the Court, to cross-examine any witness upon any answer given in reply to any such question.

[80] Section 10 (7), Rules of 2016.

[81] Section 10 (8), Rules of 2016.

4) Provision of counsellors to stay in regular touch.
5) Provision of creative outlets to channelise their energy.
6) Arranging loans and subsidies.
7) Encouraging children to sustain themselves without state intervention.

As per Section 26, all child care institutions with a capacity of a hundred children are suggested to maintain a minimum staff as follows:

Table 3.5: Suggested Staffing Pattern

No.	*Personnel/Staff*	*Number*
1.	Person-in-charge (superintendent)	1
2.	Probation officers/CWOs/case workers; a CWO may be designated as a rehabilitation-cum-placement officer	3
3.	Counsellors/psychologists/mental health experts	2
4.	House mothers/house fathers	4
5.	Educators/tutors	2 (part-time)
6.	Medical officer (physician)	1 (on call)
7.	Para-medical staff/staff nurse/nursing orderly	1
8.	Storekeeper-cum-accountant	1
9.	Art, craft and activity teacher	1 (part-time)
10.	PT instructor-cum-yoga trainer	1 (part-time)
11.	Cooks	2
12.	Helpers	2
13.	Housekeeping staff	2
14.	Driver	1
15.	Gardener	1 (part-time)

The requisite standards of physical infrastructure have been laid down in Section 29, which calls for a segregation of children based on age, giving due consideration to their physical and mental status and the nature of offence committed. The segregation should be preferably look like this—7–11 years, 12–16 years and 16–18 years—in observation homes, and 11–15 years and 16–18 years in special homes. All institutions should be child-friendly and not look like a jail or lockup. The section mandates that every institution should maintain copies of the Act and Rules for the staff and children.

A total built-up area of 8,495 square feet per institution is recommended, with designated areas for dormitories, classrooms, sick room, kitchen, dining hall, store, recreation room, library, five bathrooms, eight toilets, office rooms, counselling and guidance room, workshops, residence for person in charge, two rooms for juvenile justice board members and a playground.

Section 30 states that bedding and clothing should be provided as per climactic conditions (see Tables 3.6–3.8).

Table 3.6: Quantity of Bedding

No.	*Article*	*Quantity per child*
1.	Mattress	One at the time of admission and subsequently one after every year.
2.	Cotton *durry*	Two at the time of admission and subsequently two after every two years.
3.	Cotton bedsheets	Two at the time of admission and subsequently one after every six months.
4.	Pillow (cotton-stuffed)	One at the time of admission and subsequently one after every year.
5.	Pillow cover	One at the time of admission and subsequently one after every year.
6.	Cotton blankets/*khes*	Two at the time of admission and subsequently one after every two years.
7.	Cotton-filled quilt (in cold regions)	One at the time of admission and subsequently one after every two years.
8.	Mosquito net	One at the time of admission and subsequently one after every six months.
9.	Cotton towels	Two at the time of admission and subsequently one after every three months.

Table 3.7: Quantity of Clothing (Boys)

No.	*Article*	*Quantity per child*
1.	Shirts	Two at the time of admission and subsequently one after every six months.
2.	Shorts	Two at the time of admission and subsequently one after every six months for younger boys.
3.	Pants	Two at the time of admission and subsequently one after every six months for older boys.
4.	Age-appropriate undergarments	Three sets every quarter.
5.	Woollen jerseys (full-sleeve)	Two annually.
6.	Woollen jerseys (half-sleeve)	Two annually.
7.	Woollen caps	One in one year.
8.	Kurta pyjamas for nightwear	Two sets every six months.

Table 3.8: Quantity of Clothing (Girls)

No.	*Article*	*Quantity per child*
1.	Skirt and blouse, salwar kameez, or half sari with blouse and petticoat	Five sets per year for girls depending on age and regional preferences.
2.	Age-appropriate undergarments	Three sets every quarter.
3.	Sanitary towels	Twelve packs per year for older girls.
4.	Woollen sweaters (full-sleeve)	Two annually.
5.	Woollen sweaters (half-sleeve)	Two annually.
6.	Woollen shawls	One per year.
7.	Nightwear	Two sets every six months.

Section 31 sets the standards of hygiene and sanitation along the lines of the Rules of 2007, namely—sufficient treated drinking water; sufficient water for bathing, washing clothes, maintenance and cleanliness of institution; proper drainage system; garbage disposal; protection from mosquitoes; annual pest control; sufficient number of airy and well-lit bathrooms with at least one bathroom for ten children; sufficient space for washing and drying of clothes; washing machine; clean and fly proof kitchen with separate area for washing of utensils; sunning of bedding twice every month; maintenance of cleanliness in medical centre; proper washing of vegetables and fruits; clean and pest proof store for maintenance of food articles.

Section 32 calls for the preparation of a daily routine in consultation with the children's committee for a disciplined and regimented life, personal hygiene and cleanliness, physical exercise, yoga, educational classes, vocational training, organised recreation and games, moral education, group activities, prayer and special programmes for Sundays and other holidays.

The rules provide for a meticulous diet scale to be followed by the institutions under Section 33 (see Table 3.9).

Table 3.9: Diet and Nutrition Scale

Name of food product	*Scale per head per day*
Rice/Wheat/Ragi/Jowar	600 g (700 g for 16–18-year-olds), of which at least 100 g to be wheat, ragi or jowar.
Dal/Rajma/Chana	120 g
Edible oil	25 g
Onion	25 g
Salt	25 g
Turmeric	5 g
Coriander powder	5 g
Ginger	5 g
Garlic	5 g
Tamarind/Mango powder	5 g
Milk (at breakfast)	150 mL
Dry chillies	5 g
Vegetables: leafy/non-leafy	100 g/130 g

Name of food product	*Scale per head per day*
Curd or buttermilk	100 g/mL
Chicken (once a week) or eggs (four days a week)	115 g
Jaggery and groundnut seeds or paneer (vegetarians only)	60 g each (100 g paneer), once a week.
Sugar	40 g
Tea/coffee	5 g
Sooji/Poha	150 g
Ragi	150 g
For 50 children per day Pepper	 25 g
Jeera seeds	25 g
Black gram dal	50 g
Mustard seeds	50 g
Ajwain seeds	50 g
For 10 kg of chicken Garam Masala	 10 g
Copra	150 g
Khus-khus	150 g
Groundnut oil	500 mL
For sick children Bread	 500 g
Milk	500 mL
Khichdi	300 g
Other items LPG for cooking only	

Section 34 provides for rules to be followed by the institutions towards medical care. This includes medical examination of each child admitted to the institution within 24 hours; maintaining medical records of each child based on monthly check-ups; first-aid kits and trained staff; immunisation; preventive measures against outbreak of infectious diseases; sick children to be kept under constant medical supervision; counselling of every child and specific mental health interventions wherever needed; and referring children in need to drug deaddiction and rehabilitation programmes.

Section 35 emphasises the state of mental health of children. The institution should be free of abuse, allowing children to cope and regain their confidence. It calls for the provision of individual therapy and all institutions should have the services of trained counsellors, or collaborate with external agencies for specialised therapy for children.

Section 36 mandates all institutions to provide education to all children according to their age and ability. This includes opportunities in mainstream schooling, bridge schooling, open schooling, non-formal education and learning. Specialised trainers should be present for children with special needs, either physical or mental. Section 37 calls for the provision of vocational training in every institution, including occupational therapy, skill- and interest-based training, which should be certified, and suitable placements.

Section 39 calls for a management committee to manage the institution and progress of every child. It shall meet once a month to review the state of affairs and standard of care. It is also required to setup a children's suggestion box easily accessible by children to be checked every week by the chairperson of the committee.

Section 40 calls for the establishment of a children's committee for each age group to participate in the following areas:

1) Improving the institution.
2) Reviewing the standard of care.
3) Preparing daily routines and diet scales.
4) Developing vocational, educational and recreational plans.
5) Respecting and supporting each other in crises management.
6) Reporting abuse and exploitation by peers and caregivers.
7) Managing the institution through the management committee.

Duties of Officials and Agencies under the Rules

Section 61 enumerates the duties of the person-in-charge of the institution.

1) To ensure compliance with the provisions of the Act and the Rules.
2) To ensure compliance with orders of the board, committee and Children's Court.
3) Providing an environment of love, care and affection.
4) Striving for the development of children.
5) Supervising and monitoring the discipline of the children and staff.

6) Planning, implementing and coordinating all programmes, activities and operations.
7) Organising local and national festivals within the home.
8) Organising excursions and picnics.
9) Allocating duties to personnel.
10) Maintaining standard of care.
11) Employing appropriate security measures.
12) Ensuring proper maintenance of case files.
13) Organising meetings of the management committee.
14) Preparing budgets and maintaining control over financial matters.
15) Coordinating with State Child Protection Society and DCPU.
16) Ensuring the production of the child before the board, committee and Children's Court.

The duties of the house father/house mother are assigned via Section 63.

1) Handling children with love and affection.
2) Taking proper care of children and their welfare.
3) Providing the children with necessary supplies upon reception.
4) Replenishing necessary supplies as per requirement and scales.
5) Maintaining discipline among children.
6) Ensuring that children maintain proper hygiene and sanitation.
7) Ensuring well-maintained, sanitised and hygienic surroundings.
8) Implementing the daily routine effectively.
9) Looking after safety and security arrangements.
10) Escorting children whenever they go out of the institution.
11) Maintaining registers and relevant duties.

Chapter IV
Analysis of Judicial Trends

It has already been established that doctrinally, reformation and rehabilitation form the cornerstones of juvenile justice systems. All legislations, ranging from the Children's Act of 1960 to the Act of 2015, intended reformation and rehabilitation irrespective of the degree of progressiveness of the provisions. The Supreme Court of India has largely accepted and respected these principles as the basis of our juvenile justice system. Challenges, however, have been mounted time and again with respect to their application. This chapter seeks to examine how the Supreme Court has dealt with them.

Reformation and Rehabilitation

In the case of *Raghbir* v. *State of Haryana*,[1] while holding that the provisions of the Haryana Children Act supersede those of the Code of Criminal Procedure (CrPC), 1973, the Supreme Court observed: 'Section 22 of this (Central) Act is in pari materia with Section 21 of the Haryana Children Act. A perusal of the above and other provisions of the Act and those of the central Children Act shows that the procedure for trial, conviction and sentence under the Children Acts are simple, humane and by courts manned with persons with knowledge of child psychology and child welfare; but not so under the CrPCs of 1898 and 1973. The intention of the State Legislature of Haryana and of the Parliament in enacting the Children Acts was to make provisions for trial of delinquent

[1] 1982 SCR (1) 686.

children and dealing with them in accordance with such procedures, so that the delinquent children do not come in contact with accused persons who are not children and but are hardened criminals. The purpose undoubtedly was to reclaim delinquent children and rehabilitate them in such a way that they become useful citizens later in life.'

In *Sheela Barse* v. *Union of India*,[2] where the petitioner had filed a writ petition under Article 32 of the Constitution of India for the release of children under the age of 16 lodged in various adult prisons, the Supreme Court took serious note. It stressed that special provisions had been enacted in various statutes in relation to children for trial by juvenile courts to establish a special procedure intended to safeguard the interest and welfare of children. It was emphatically stated that even in case the juvenile was convicted, he should not be kept in prison under any circumstance. Furthermore, 'If a child is a national asset, it is the duty of the State to look after the child with a view to ensuring full development of its personality. That is why all the statutes dealing with children provide that the child shall not be kept in jail. Even apart from this statutory prescription, it is elementary that a jail is hardly a place where a child should be kept. There can be no doubt that incarceration in jail would have the effect of dwarfing the development of the child, exposing him to baneful influences, coarsening his conscience and alienating him from the society.'

The first serious challenge to the principle of reformation and rehabilitation came with *Salil Bali* v. *Union of India and Anr.*[3] The Supreme Court observed that there could be no question as to fact that children are one of the most vulnerable sections of society, and unless they were provided with proper opportunities, growing them into responsible citizens of tomorrow would slip out of the hands of the present generation. It examined legislative intent and found that the essence of the Juvenile Justice (Care and Protection of Children) Act, 2000 and the Rules of 2007 was restorative and not retributive, that is, they provided for the rehabilitation and reintegration of children in conflict with law into mainstream society. The court held the provisions of the Act of 2000 to be valid and stated: 'There are, of course, exceptions

---

[2] 1986 SCALE (2) 230.

[3] (2013) 7 SCC 705

where a child in the age group of 16–18 may have developed criminal propensities, which would make it virtually impossible for him/her to be reintegrated into mainstream society, but such examples are not of such proportions as to warrant any change in thinking, since it is probably better to try and reintegrate children with criminal propensities into mainstream society, rather than to allow them to develop into hardened criminals, which does not augur well for the future.'

In the case of *Hari Ram* v. *State of Rajasthan and Anr*,[4] the Supreme Court observed: 'The scheme of the Act (of 2000) is to give children, who have, for some reason or the other, gone astray, to realise their mistakes, rehabilitate themselves and rebuild their lives and become useful citizens of society, instead of degenerating into hardened criminals.'

In the matter of *Jitendra Singh* v. *State of U.P.*,[5] it stated, 'It is quite clear from the above that the purpose of the Act is to rehabilitate a juvenile in conflict with law with a view to reintegrate him into society. This is by no means an easy task and it is worth researching how successful the implementation of the Act has been in its avowed purpose in this respect.'

The Delhi High Court, speaking in the matter of *Court On its Own Motion* v. *Department of Women and Child Development, Govt. of N.C.T. of Delhi*,[6] noted that a child is a part of the society in which he lives, and on account his immaturity, easily motivated by what he sees around him. The court stated this is why a child is not supposed to be treated as an adult offender, adding that the basis of difference in justice systems is that juveniles are different from adults, less responsible for their transgressions and more amenable to rehabilitation. What's more: 'It cannot be overlooked that youth offenders often have psychological or social issues that need to be addressed as part of the rehabilitative process. Adult facilities/prison often lack the staff to address the needs of young incarcerated persons. In effect, what will happen is that if the youth is sent to an adult prison, then it is more likely for him to reoffend and escalate into violent behaviour than their peers who go to juvenile system, where rehabilitative services are far more extensive. Juveniles

[4] (2009) 13 SCC 211.

[5] (2013) 11 SCC 193.

[6] (2013) 2 RCR (Criminal) 362.

confined within an adult prison may not have social services they need but with constant access to criminal minds, there are more chances of them becoming recidivist.'

Going a step further, the Delhi High Court in the above-mentioned case declared the lodging of juveniles in adult prisons to be violative of their fundamental right to life and personal liberty guaranteed under Article 21 of the Constitution of India, 1950. It stated, 'There can be no cavil in saying that lodging juveniles in adult prisons amounts to deprivation of their personal liberty on multiple aspects.' The court reasoned that at the time of arrest of such persons, there is no proper age verification and had that been so, the juveniles would not have been subjected to the hardships of an adult criminal justice system.

However, post the ratification of the Act of 2015, its constitutional validity with regard to the prosecution of children aged 16–18 years in the adult criminal system upon committing heinous offences was challenged in the case of *Tehseen Poonawala* v. *Union of India*[7] on the grounds that it violated Article 14 of the constitution by creating a fictional classification between children aged 15 and below and those aged 16–18 years. Also, the imprisonment of a child was a violation of Article 21 in that it deprived him of his liberty. But the writ petition was not admitted by the Supreme Court, citing that the validity of the Act of 2015 couldn't become a subject matter of public interest litigation and could only be admitted if an aggrieved party came before the court.[8]

Implementation of Juvenile Justice Acts

The Supreme Court has time and again pointed at lapses in implementation of the provisions of the acts by lower judiciary, state governments as well as the central government. It has tried to resolve legal issues that bar said implementation, while simultaneously directing the administration to implement the provisions wherever the government was found to be lacking.

---

[7] W.P. No. 94 of 2016.

[8] LiveLaw News Network, 'SC refuses to entertain plea against new Juvenile Justice Act,' *LiveLaw.in*, 26 February 2016, http://www.livelaw.in/sc-refuses-to-entertain-plea-against-new-juvenile-justice-act-2/.

In the case of *Gopinath Ghosh* v. *State of West Bengal*,[9] contention with respect to the convict's age and applicability of juvenile justice legislation's benefits was raised for the first time in front of the Supreme Court instead of lower courts. While ordinarily the court would be reluctant to entertain a petition based on factual averments for the first time, it was equally hesitant to nullify the provisions of a very socially progressive statute by hiding behind a technicality. In its opinion, '... whenever a case is brought before the magistrate and the accused appears to be aged 21 years or below, before proceeding with the trial or undertaking an enquiry, an enquiry must be made about the age of the accused on the date of the occurrence. This ought to be more so where special acts dealing with juvenile delinquents are in force. If necessary, the magistrate may refer the accused to the medical board or the civil surgeon, as the case may be, for obtaining creditworthy evidence about age. The magistrate may as well call upon the accused also to lead evidence about his age. Thereafter, the learned magistrate may proceed in accordance with law. This procedure, if properly followed, would avoid a journey up to the apex court and the return journey to the grass-root court. If necessary and found expedient, the High Court may on its administrative side issue necessary instructions to cope with the situation herein indicated.'

While dealing with the writ petition in *Sheela Barse & Ors.* v. *Union of India & Ors.*,[10] the Supreme Court emphasised legislative and institutional impediments to the implementation of the provisions of the Children Act, 1960. It suggested that instead of each state having its own Children Act, the central government should initiate a parliamentary legislation to ensure universality of and complete uniformity in the provisions of the laws governing children throughout the country. The law so enacted should contain mandatory provisions for 'ensuring social, economic and psychological rehabilitation of the children who are either accused of offences or are abandoned or destitute or lost'. Further, it was clearly stated, '... it is not enough merely to have legislation on the subject, but it is equally, if not more, important to ensure that such legislation is implemented in all earnestness and mere lip sympathy is not paid

[9] 1984 (Supp.) SCC 228.

[10] 1986 SCALE (2) 230.

such legislation and justification for non-implementation is not pleaded on ground of lack of finances on the part of the State. The greatest recompense which the State can get for expenditure on children is the building up of a powerful human resource ready to take its place in the forward march of the nation.'

Going further, the Supreme Court directed state governments to set up requisite remand homes and observation homes, where the children accused of committing offences could be lodged pending investigation and trial. It emphatically said that under no conditions should a child be sent to adult prisons, and if state governments do not have enough infrastructure to lodge a child, he should be released on bail. Calling into scrutiny juvenile courts, the apex body said 'they are nothing but a replica of the ordinary criminal courts, only the label being changed'.

The Supreme Court also directed the state governments to established one juvenile court in each district, where the magistrates must have 'proper and adequate training for dealing with cases against juveniles, because these cases require a different type of procedure and qualitatively a different kind of approach'.

At this point, the researchers want to impress that while judgement in the *Sheela Barse* case was passed in 1986 and followed by two enactments—Act of 1986 and Act of 2000—the Supreme Court in 2011, acting on complaints about non-compliance with legislations regarding constituting juvenile justice boards and child welfare committees, had to direct state governments once again to set them up in each district (*Sampurna Behura* v. *Union of India*[11]). In the same matter, the court ordered, 'All the Juvenile Justice Boards should ensure that juveniles in conflict with law who are brought before them are provided immediate legal aid, and if there is any difficulty, to direct or instruct the respective District Legal Services Authority to provide such legal aid.'

It further directed the home departments of each state government as well as the Director-Generals of Police of each state to ensure that at least one police officer with aptitude, in every station, is given appropriate training and orientation and designated juvenile or child welfare officer. He will handle the juvenile or child in coordination with the police as provided under Sub-section (2) of Section 63 of the Act of 2000. The

[11] (2011) 9 SCC 801.

court also ordered the District Legal Services Authorities to conduct required training and orientation of police officers so designated, and that such training should occur under the State Legal Services Authority.

In the matter of *Court On its Own Motion* v. *Department of Women and Child Development, Govt. of N.C.T. of Delhi*,[12] the issue of juvenile incarceration in adult prisons came before the High Court of Delhi, despite directions given to respective governments in the Sheela Barse case as far back as 1986. The court proceeded to issue meticulous and extensive guidelines for all authorities while dealing with juveniles. A few select ones have been reproduced here to illustrate the determination and proactiveness of the judiciary.

1) For Commissioners of Police:

   The Commissioner of Police shall issue a standing order clarifying the roles and responsibilities of police officers, investigation officers, enquiry by Deputy Commissioners of Police (DCPs) in case of lapse, juvenile or child welfare officers, SHOs and DCPs in view of the provisions of the JJ Act and Rules made thereunder judgement of Hon'ble Delhi High Court in W.P. (C) 8889 of 2011 dated 21.03.2012 and any subsequent order/judgement as may be passed and to revise and modify such standing order in case of any change in law.

   The Commissioner of Police on receipt of half-yearly report suggested in Para C-3 from Nodal Head of Special Juvenile Police Unit (SJPU) shall pass necessary directions to give effect to the recommendations and to address the concerns as may be raised in such reports. An action taken report of the same shall also be forwarded to the Juvenile Justice Committee of the Hon'ble Delhi High Court.

2) For DCPs, in-charge of districts concerned:

   i. In case any person approaches a DCP with a complaint that police is not taking notice of juvenility of any offender and is refusing to take on record the documents being provided to suggest juvenility and instead treating a child as an adult, it shall be the duty of the DCP concerned to conduct an immediate enquiry into such complaint. Such enquiry shall be completed

[12] 2013 (3) RCR (Criminal) 362.

within 24 hours of having received such complaint and if the complaint turns out to have merit and truth, the DCP shall order the concerned police officers to immediately take corrective steps and initiate disciplinary action against erring police officials.

ii. In cases where any action is taken against an erring police officer, a quarterly report of the same containing the nature and reasons of such lapse and details of action taken shall be furnished by the DCP to the concerned Juvenile Justice Board (JJB) having jurisdiction over that district, along with a copy to the Nodal Head of SJPU for their record and intimation.

iii. DCPs shall, during regular monthly meetings with all the SHOs and Inspector–Investigations, brief them about their responsibilities, any new judgement or order from JJBs and courts, any practice direction, etc., and shall ensure that their subordinate police officers don't show children as adults, take all necessary steps to verify the age of accused persons and are in overall compliance with the provisions of JJ Act and Rules.

iv. .... On being intimated by the JJBs about any lapse committed on age investigation, the DCP concerned shall institute an enquiry and take such action as may be required or appropriate. An action taken report shall be submitted to the JJB by the DCP within a month of receipt of such intimation.

3) For Nodal Heads of SJPUs:

i. The Nodal Head shall conduct quarterly inspections of all police stations through an official not below the rank of Assistant Commissioner of Police in order to check that all police stations have put in place the required setup and obligations.

ii. ....

iii. The Nodal Head shall make a report on half-yearly basis and submit it to the Commissioner of Police with recommendations. A copy shall also be submitted to the Juvenile Justice Committee of the Hon'ble Delhi High Court.

iv. ....

4) For officers-in-charge of police stations:

   i. It shall be the duty of the officer-in-charge to ensure that police officers of his or her station have taken all WP(C) 8889/2011 Page 20 of 33 measures to ensure that proper enquiry or investigation on the point of age has been carried out, and that all required formalities and procedures have been carried out, and required documents have been prepared in this regard.

   ii. The officer-in-charge shall also ensure that a notice board, prominently visible, shall contain information in Hindi, Urdu and English apprising that persons below 18 years are governed under the provisions of the JJ Act and cannot be kept in police lockups and jails, and are not to be taken to the adult criminal courts. Such notice board shall also contain the names and contact details of juvenile welfare officers, probation officers and legal aid lawyers of Delhi State Legal Services Authority.

5) For investigation officers, or any police officer acting under the instruction of an investigation officer:

   i. Every police officer at the time of arresting/apprehending young offenders shall be under obligation to inform the alleged offender about his right to be dealt with under the provisions of JJ Act if he is below 18 years, and proper counselling shall be done on the point of age.

   ii. The investigation officer or any other police officer affecting the arrest/ apprehension shall also prepare the age memo. A copy of such age memo shall also be delivered to the alleged offender and his parents/guardians/relatives who have been intimated about his arrest.

   iii. ....

   iv. On completion of age enquiry, which shall be done preferably within one week of arrest/apprehension, the completed age memo shall be filed before the court concerned.

   v. At the time of first production of an offender, who is between 18 and 21 years as per the initial enquiry of the investigation officer, before the court, the investigation officer or police officer responsible for producing the offender shall produce alleged offender along with a copy of the FIR and age memo before the secretary of the respective District Legal Services Authority, irrespective of whether the alleged offender is being represented by a legal aid lawyer or not.

vi. If the alleged offender claims to be a juvenile and age documents to support such claim are not readily available and it is not possible for the investigation officer to obtain such documents within 24 hours of arrest, the accused shall be produced before the JJB.

....

6) For juvenile welfare officers:

i. It shall be the duty of the juvenile or child welfare officer to obtain the copy of age declaration done by JJB or child welfare officer and to forward such copy to the SJPU for entry into the record and to obtain a certificate that such entry has been done with SJPU and a copy of such certificate shall be deposited to the JJB or child welfare committee concerned.

ii. It shall be the duty of the juvenile welfare officer to ensure that any offender at the police station who might be a juvenile is not treated as adult and if he notices any such incident, he shall immediately report to the officer-in-charge of the police station concerned with an intimation to District SJPU.

....

7) For JJBs

The JJB shall conduct the proper age enquiry of each child brought before it as per the procedure laid down in Rule 12 of the Delhi Juvenile Justice (Care & Protection of Children) Rules 2009.

On every occasion, when the case of a juvenile is transferred from the adult court to the JJB and the juvenile is transferred from jail to the concerned observation home, the JJB shall interact with the juvenile and record his/her version on how he came to be treated as an adult. If, from the statement of the juvenile and after appropriate enquiry by the investigation officer, it appears that the juvenile was wrongly shown as an adult by the investigation officer, then the JJB shall intimate the concerned DCP. This intimation shall be done in all those cases, which are received from the JJB by way of transfer from

> the adult court, and shall be done even in all those cases in which the declaration of juvenility has been done by the adult court.
>
> JJBs shall determine the age of a person by way recording the evidence brought forth by the juvenile and the prosecution/ complainant and the parties shall be given an opportunity to examine, cross examine or re-examine witnesses of their choice.
>
> In case of medical age examination, the parties shall be given copies of the medical age examination report immediately by the JJBs. The parties shall have the right to file objection thereto, including the right to cross-examine before final age determination is done.
>
> While declaring the age, the order of age declaration shall also state the age as nearly as possible as on the date of commission of the offence.
>
> Before commencing the age enquiry, a notice thereof shall be served upon the complainant by the JJB or the court concerned, which shall also accord opportunity to the complainant of being heard on the issue including producing evidence; however, the age enquiry will be concluded within the stipulated time limit of one month.
>
> It shall be the duty of the board to ensure that every juvenile in whose respect age enquiry is being conducted is being represented by a counsel, and in those cases where there is no lawyer present before the board at the time of hearing of case, the board shall provide a legal aid lawyer.[13]

In *Chandrajeet Kumar* v. *State,*[14] where the Delhi High Court found that the accused had spent nine years in jail even after the offence was found have been committed while he was a child, the court directed the Delhi Judicial Academy to come up with a refresher course on law pertaining to juvenile justice, which would be organised and implemented in every district court for the benefit of the judges. It held that 'A Sessions Court has dealt with the case, completely oblivious of the valuable rights of a juvenile under the Juvenile Justice (Care & Protection) Act, ignorant of judicial precedents on the subject and the orders of the learned single judge of this court in this very case. This situation suggests a revisit to training in law relating to juveniles, procedural and substantive.'

---

[13] WP(C) NO. 8889 of 2011.

[14] Crl. A. 371/2015.

In May 2017, the matter of *Re: Exploitation of Children in Orphanages in the State of Tamil Nadu,*[15] the Supreme Court issued directions to union and state governments that pursuant to the provisions of the Act of 2015, the registration of all childcare institutions should be positively completed by 31 December 2017 the registration process should also include a database of all children in need of care and protection, which should be updated every month; the union and state governments, and governments of union territories must concentrate on the rehabilitation and social reintegration of children in need of care and protection, and several schemes of the Indian government including skill development, vocational training, etc. must be taken advantage of keeping in mind the need to rehabilitate such children; the process of preparing individual childcare plans is a continuing process and must be initiated immediately and an individual childcare plan must be prepared for each child in each childcare institution on or before 31 December 2017; the minimum standards of care as required by and in terms of the JJ Act and the Model Rules be positively enforced on or before 31 December 2017.

Minimum Age of Criminal Responsibility

In *Rohtas v. State of Haryana,*[16] the appellant accused had been charged under Section 302 of the Indian Penal Code (IPC). After the recording of evidence was concluded, it was pointed out that the Sessions Judge had no jurisdiction to try the appellant, as the appellant happened to fall under the provisions of the Haryana Children Act, 1974. On remand, the magistrate found that the appellant was a child and proceeded to try him under the Haryana Act. In a revision petition filed by the brother of the deceased, the High Court held that the provisions of CrPC, 1973, prevailed over the provisions of the Haryana Act. It pointed out that Section 5 of the CrPC, 1973, carves out a clear exception to the trial of an offence under any special or local law for the time-being in force, or any special jurisdiction or power conferred or any special form of procedure prescribed by any other law for the time-being in force. The Haryana Act was in force when the CrPC was passed and therefore, the

[15] W.P.N. 102 of 2007.

[16] 1980 SCR (1) 151.

Haryana Act, far from being inconsistent with Section 5 of the CrPC, appeared to be fully protected by its provisions.

Ever since the enactment of the Children Act, 1960, the Supreme Court has, in most cases, upheld the will of the legislature in construing provisions that seek to create a separate justice system for juvenile. Supporting the legislative intent, the court on several occasions has reasoned that the mind of a juvenile in not on a par with the mind of an adult. While answering a similar question in the context of the Rajasthan Children Act, the Supreme Court in *Umesh Chandra* v. *State of Rajasthan*[17] held that courts should rely upon a liberal construction of the provisions of the Act to advance its objectives, since the Act was piece of a social legislation meant for the protection of infants who commit criminal offences. It further noted: 'The Children Act was enacted to protect young children from the consequences of their criminal acts on the footing that their mind at that age could not be said to be mature for imputing mens rea as in the case of an adult.'

The same question arose in *Raghbir* v. *State of Haryana,*[18] whether a child who was 16 years old and charged with an offence under Section 302 of the IPC was entitled to the benefit of the Haryana Children Act, 1974. To answer, the Supreme Court relied upon a purposive construction and detailed the intent of legislators to conclude that the child should be tried in accordance with the Haryana Children Act: 'The purpose of the Haryana Legislature as well as of the Parliament in enacting the Haryana Children Act and the Central Children Act respectively was to give separate treatment to delinquent children in trial, conviction and punishment for offences including offences punishable with death or imprisonment for life.'

It would be correct to point out that the Supreme Court wasn't paying a mere lip service to the issue. In its application of the stated principle, the court has on several occasions gone beyond the provisions of the acts to ensure that no person is tried as an adult for an offence committed by him when he was a juvenile. In *Gopinath Ghosh* v. *State of West Bengal,*[19] where the accused had been tried and convicted by

---

[17] (1982) 2 SCC 802.

[18] 1982 SCR (1) 686.

[19] (1984) SUPP SCC 228.

lower courts for an offence under Section 302 of the IPC, the accused raised the argument of his juvenility at the time of the occurrence of the offence for the first time. After satisfying itself that the accused was indeed a juvenile at the time the offence was committed, the Supreme Court observed: 'In view of the underlying intendment and beneficial provisions of the Act read with clause (f) of Article 39 of the Constitution, which provides that the State shall direct its policy towards securing that children are given opportunities and facilities to develop in a healthy manner and in conditions of freedom and dignity and that childhood and youth are protected against exploitation and against moral and material abandonment, we consider it proper not to allow a technical contention that this contention is being raised in this Court for the first time to thwart the benefit of the provisions being extended to the appellant, if he was otherwise entitled to it.'

The apex court, however, has also been fastidious in its application of facts to law. Where it learned that the school certificate produced by the accused before the Sessions Court had been dismissed in light of the medical report, on the ground that it was not unusual for parents to understate the age of the children on school certificates for future purposes, the Supreme Court found that the school certificate could not have been brushed aside on the basis of surmises and in favour of medical reports, which were estimates. It upheld the conviction of the accused but quashed the sentence of life imprisonment in line with the judgement of the apex court in the case of *Jayendra and Anr.* v. *State of U.P.*[20]

In *Pradeep Kumar* v. *State of U.P.*,[21] where the accused had been convicted under Section 302 of the IPC, the Supreme Court considered the school leaving certificate of the accused as well as the medical report and concluded that the accused had not completed the age of 16 years at the time of the occurrence of the offence. He should have been tried under the U.P. Children Act instead of being sentenced to imprisonment.

In *Bhola Bhagat* v. *State of Bihar*,[22] the High Court rejected the contention of the accused that they were children—as defined in the Bihar Children Act, 1970—on the date of occurrence of the offence,

---

[20] (1981) 4 SCC 149.

[21] 1995 Supp (4) SCC 499.

[22] (1997) 8 SCC 720.

and that their trial along with the adult accused by the criminal court was not in accordance with law. The ground was that except for the age given by the appellants and the estimate of the court at the time of their examination under Section 313 of the CrPC, there was no other material in support of the appellants' claim that they were below 18 years of age. The apex court over ruled the judgement of the High Court and held: 'To us it appears that the approach of the High Court in dealing with the question of age of the appellants and the denial of benefit to them of the provisions of both the Acts was not proper. Technicalities were allowed to defeat the benefits of a socially oriented legislation like the Bihar Children Act, 1982 and the Juvenile Justice Act, 1986. If the High Court had doubts about the correctness of their age as given by the appellants and also as estimated by the trial court, it ought to have ordered an enquiry to determine their ages. It should not have brushed aside their plea without such an enquiry.'

In *Akbar Shaikh* v. *State of West Bengal*,[23] however, the Supreme Court considered the matter on facts and found that the claim of juvenility of the accused was unsustainable; no such question had ever been raised. Even where a similar point was raised by five other accused, no plea was filed even before the High Court on behalf of the accused. In support of juvenility, two documents were relied upon—statement recorded under Section 313 of the CrPC, and voters' list. The court observed that the recorded statement was not a decisive document and the voters' list had been drawn up much after the incident had occurred. Consequently, the court found no merit in the argument of the accused and did not order any enquiry as to the determination of age.

Consequent to the increase of the age of juvenility from 16 years to 18 years under the Act of 2000, a question arose before the Supreme Court—whether the accused should be tried under the Act of 1986 (where 16 years is the age of juvenility) or the Act of 2000 (where 18 years is the age of juvenility)—in the case of *Hari Ram* v. *State of Rajasthan and Anr.*[24] The High Court had considered testimony from Ram's father as well as medical reports, and concluded that at the time of the offence Ram was over 16 years, thereby excluding him from the juvenile justice

[23] (2009) 7 SCC 419.

[24] (2009) 13 SCC 211.

system. The accused appealed on the reasoning that by adopting such a technical approach to determining his age, the court had defeated the purpose of juvenile justice laws. Considering the amendments brought in by way of the Juvenile Justice (Care and Protection of Children) Amendment Act, 2006, the Supreme Court held that, 'The law as now crystallised on a conjoint reading of Sections 2(k), 2(l), 7-A, 20 and 49 read with Rules 12 and 98, places beyond all doubt that all persons who were below the age of 18 years on the date of commission of the offence even prior to 1-4-2001, would be treated as juveniles, even if the claim of juvenility was raised after they had attained the age of 18 years on or before the date of commencement of the Act and were undergoing sentence upon being convicted.'

In *Dayanand* v. *State of Haryana*,[25] the apex court found that the accused was aged 16 at the time of occurrence of the offence and hence could not be kept in prison in lieu of the order of the Sessions Court as affirmed by the High Court. The court set aside the sentence and ordered the accused to be released from prison. Similarly, where the accused had completed 16 years of age and were not juvenile under the Act of 1986 but were under 18 years and still juveniles under the Act of 2000, the Supreme Court gave the benefit of the Act of 2000 to the accused and ordered for them to be released forthwith.[26]

In the matter of *Shah Nawaz* v. *State of U.P. and Anr.*,[27] where the accused presented the school leaving certificate as proof of juvenility at the time of commission of offence, the Supreme Court made pertinent enquiries. Upon satisfaction, it referred to Rule 12 of the Rules of 2007 and stated that the provision gave preference to a school leaving certificate over a medical report. It set aside the order of the High Court.

In *Abuzar Hussain* v. *State of West Bengal*,[28] the Supreme Court summarised its position as:

39.1. A claim of juvenility may be raised at any stage even after final disposal of the case. It may be raised for the first time before this Court as well after final disposal of the case. The delay in raising the claim of

---

[25] (2011) 2 SCC 224.

[26] *Lakhan Lal* v. *State of Bihar*, (2011) 2 SCC 251.

[27] (2011) 13 SCC 751.

[28] (2012) 10 SCC 489.

juvenility cannot be a ground for rejection of such claim. The claim of juvenility can be raised in appeal even if not pressed before the trial court and can be raised for the first time before this Court though not pressed before the trial court and in appeal court.

39.2. For making a claim with regard to juvenility after conviction, the claimant must produce some material, which may prima facie satisfy the court that an enquiry into the claim of juvenility is necessary. Initial burden has to be discharged by the person who claims juvenility.

39.3. As to what materials would prima facie satisfy the court and/or are sufficient for discharging the initial burden cannot be catalogued nor can it be laid down as to what weight should be given to a specific piece of evidence, which may be sufficient to raise presumption of juvenility but the documents referred to in Rule 12 (3)(a)(i) to (iii) shall definitely be sufficient for prima facie satisfaction of the court about the age of the delinquent necessitating further enquiry under Rule 12.

The statement recorded under Section 313 of the Code is too tentative and may not by itself be sufficient ordinarily to justify or reject the claim of juvenility. The credibility and/or acceptability of the documents like the school leaving certificate or the voters' list, etc. obtained after conviction would depend on the facts and circumstances of each case and no hard and fast rule can be prescribed that they must be prima facie accepted or rejected. If such documents prima facie inspire confidence of the court, the court may act upon such documents for the purposes of Section 7A and order an enquiry for determination of the age of the delinquent.

39.4. An affidavit of the claimant or any of the parents or a sibling or a relative in support of the claim of juvenility raised for the first time in appeal or revision or before this Court during the pendency of the matter or after disposal of the case shall not be sufficient justifying an enquiry to determine the age of such person unless the circumstances of the case are so glaring that they satisfy the judicial conscience of the court to order an enquiry into determination of age of the delinquent.

39.5. The court where the plea of juvenility is raised for the first time should always be guided by the objectives of the 2000 Act and be alive to the position that the beneficent and salutary provisions contained in the 2000 Act are not defeated by hyper-technical approach and the persons who are entitled to get benefits of the 2000 Act get such benefits.

The courts should not be unnecessarily influenced by any general impression that in schools the parents/guardians understate the age of their wards by one or two years for future benefits or that age determination by medical examination is not very precise. The matter should be considered prima facie on the touchstone of preponderance of probability.

39.6. Claim of juvenility lacking in credibility or frivolous claim of juvenility or patently absurd or inherently improbable claim of juvenility must be rejected by the court at threshold whenever raised.[29]

In light of the 2012 Delhi gang rape case, where one of the accused was a juvenile, several writ petitions questioning the validity of the blanket exemption granted to all juveniles from prosecution in the adult criminal justice system were filed before the Supreme Court, which were clubbed together for hearing in the matter of *Salil Bali* v. *Union of India and Anr.*[30] The court took the view that the age of 18 years had been fixed based on the understanding of experts in child psychology and behavioural patterns that till such an age, children in conflict with law could still be redeemed and restored to mainstream society instead of becoming hardened criminals in future. While holding the provisions of the Act as valid, the Supreme Court observed that '... in the absence of any proper data, it would not be wise on our part to deviate from the provisions of the Juvenile Justice (Care and Protection of Children) Act, 2000, which represent the collective wisdom of Parliament. It may not be out of place to mention that in the Juvenile Justice Act, 1986, male children above the age of 16 years were considered to be adults, whereas girl children were treated as adults on attaining the age of 18 years. In the Juvenile Justice (Care and Protection of Children) Act, 2000, a conscious decision was taken by Parliament to raise the age of male juveniles/children to eighteen years.'

'In recent years, there has been a spurt in criminal activities by adults, but not so by juveniles, as the materials produced before us show. The age limit, which was raised from 16 to 18 years in the Juvenile Justice (Care

[29] (2012) 10 SCC 489.

[30] (2013) 7 SCC 705.

and Protection of Children) Act, 2000, is a decision which was taken by the Government, which is strongly in favour of retaining Sections 2(k) and 2(l) in the manner in which it exists in the Statute Book.'[31]

The question came up for consideration again in the case of *Dr Subramanian Swamy and Ors.* v. *Raju and Ors.*[32] It was contended that the act had to be read down since it results in over classification of all juveniles, irrespective of their level of mental maturity, when they are grouped in one class; furthermore, the Act replaces the criminal justice system in the country and therefore derogates a basic feature of the Constitution. Dr Swamy urged that the relevant provisions of the Act—that is, Sections 1(4), 2(k), 2(l) and 7—must be read to mean that juveniles (children below the age of 18) who are intellectually, emotionally and mentally mature to understand the implications of their actions and have committed serious crimes do not come under the Act's purview. Such juveniles should be liable to be dealt with by penal law and the regular hierarchy of courts under the criminal justice system administered in India.

The Supreme Court observed that in line with its earlier judgements,[33] while reading down a provision, 'courts must read the legislation literally in the first instance. If on such reading and understanding the vice of unconstitutionality is attracted, the courts must explore whether there has been an unintended legislative omission. If such an intendment can be reasonably implied without undertaking what, unmistakably, would be a legislative exercise, the Act may be read down to save it from unconstitutionality.'

The Court applied this principle of reading down and concluded: 'There is no ambiguity, much less any uncertainty, in the language used to convey what the legislature had intended. All persons below the age of 18 are put in one class/group by the Act to provide a separate scheme of investigation, trial and punishment for offences committed by them. A class of persons is sought to be created who are treated differently. This is being done to further/effectuate the views of the international

[31] (2013) 7 SCC 705.

[32] (2014) 8 SCC 390.

[33] *D.T.C.* v. *D.T.C. Mazdoor Congress and Ors.*, 1991 SCC Suppl. (1) 600.

community, which India has shared by being a signatory to the several conventions and treaties already referred to.'

Additionally, the Court reiterated that the Act's objective is to ensure the rehabilitation of the young offenders in society, and enable them become contributing members in their adult years. The legislative wisdom that led to the enactment of the Act of 2000 in its present form was the acceptance of the previously stated principle.

Post the Supreme Court judgement in the aforementioned cases, on 20 December 2015, the Delhi Commission of Women (DCW) chairperson Swati Maliwal[34]—in an attempt to ensure that the juvenile offender in the 2012 Delhi gang rape case wasn't released upon the completion of his term of stay—filed a Special Leave Petition with the Court. It was dismissed December 21 on the ground that there was no legislative sanction to retain the juvenile in the system.[35]

Following the Act of 2015's enactment, the minimum age of criminal responsibility has now been lowered to 16 years for heinous offences. In a much publicised case where a 17-year-old juvenile ran over a pedestrian while driving his father's luxury car, the JJB decided he was to be tried as an adult since 'he was in no manner lacking in mental and physical capacity to commit the offence. On the date of the offence, he had the ability to understand the consequence of the offence.'[36]

Retrospective Application of the Act

In the previous segment, pertaining to determination of age, the Supreme Court resorted to purposive construction to interpret provisions in light of legislative intent when technicalities arose, which can bar juvenile justice while implementing the legislations. However, in one instance,

---

[34] LiveLaw News Network, 'DCW moves SC at 1 AM to stall Nirbhaya case juvenile's release; SC agrees to hear on Monday,' *LiveLaw.in*, 20 December 2015, http://www.livelaw.in/dcw-moves-sc-at-1-am-to-stall-nirbhaya-case-juveniles-release-sc-agrees-to-hear-on-monday/.

[35] *Swati Maliwal Jaihind, Chairperson Delhi Commission of Women* v. *Raju through Juvenile Justice Board & Ors.* CRLMP No. 22044-22045 of 2015.

[36] K.M. Ashok, 'Hit and Run Case: Minor to be Tried as Adult by Applying New Juvenile Justice Act,' *LiveLaw.in*, 4 June 2016, http://www.livelaw.in/hit-run-case-minor-tried-adult-applying-new-juvenile-justice-act/.

retrospective application of the age of juvenility (provided as 18 in the Act of 2000) came into effect when the juvenile had crossed the age of 16 under the Act of 1986. It was legislature that had to bring in an amendment to clarify its position following the Supreme Court's judgement in *Pratap Singh* v. *State of Jharkhand and Anr.*[37]

Section 20 of the Act of 2000, as it stood unamended, read: '(Special provision in respect of pending cases) Notwithstanding anything contained in this Act, all proceedings in respect of a juvenile pending in any Court in any area on the date on which this Act comes into force in that area, shall be continued in that Court as if this Act had not been passed and if the Court finds that the juvenile has committed an offence, it shall record such finding and instead of passing any sentence in respect of the juvenile, forward the juvenile to the Board which shall pass orders in respect of that juvenile in accordance with the provisions of this Act as if it had been satisfied on enquiry under this Act that a juvenile has committed the offence.'

This section, on account of ambiguity in language, raised the question of whether the Act of 2000 would be applicable if proceedings had been initiated under the Act of 1986 and were pending when the Act of 2000 was enforced. The Supreme Court interpreted the section literally. It took into consideration the language of the expression, 'Notwithstanding anything contained in this Act, all proceedings in respect of a juvenile pending in any Court in any area on date of which this Act came into force', and stated: 'The proceedings in respect of a juvenile pending in any court referred to in Section 20 of the Act is relatable to proceedings initiated before the 2000 Act came into force and which are pending when the 2000 Act came into force. The term "any court" would include even ordinary criminal courts. If the person was a "juvenile" under the 1986 Act the proceedings would not be pending in criminal courts. They would be pending in criminal courts only if the boy had crossed 16 years or girl had crossed 18 years. This shows that Section 20 refers to cases where a person had ceased to be a juvenile under the 1986 Act but had not yet crossed the age of 18 years then the pending case shall continue in that court as if the 2000 Act has not been passed and if the court finds that the juvenile has committed an offence, it shall

---

[37] (2005) 3 SCC 251.

record such finding and instead of passing any sentence in respect of the juvenile, shall forward the juvenile to the Board which shall pass orders in respect of that juvenile.'

The Supreme Court went on to state that the provisions of the Act of 2000 would be applicable only to those cases that were initiated and pending trial/enquiry for offences committed under the Act of 1986, provided that the person had not completed 18 years of age as on 1 April 2001, when it came into effect. So, the apex body extended the benefits of the Act of 2000 only to those who weren't 18 years old on the date of the Act's passing as opposed to the application of the act to those who were 18 on the date of the commission of the offence. At this juncture, it is pertinent to note that the question of the relevant date for application of the Act is a separate aspect and has been dealt with in the subsequent segment of this chapter. While in the context of the aspect of the date of application, the Supreme Court (in the same case) took the correct view in holding that relevant date for the application of the Act would be the date of the commission of offence, in the answering of the present question of law, the Supreme Court faltered in not extending the benefits of the Act retrospectively to those who were 18 at the time of the commission of the offence and were being tried or had been sentenced under the provisions of the Act of 1986.

To correct the problem that led to the interpretation of Section 20 in such a manner, in 2006, the parliament added an explanation to the section, vide the Amendment Act of 2006. It stated in clear terms that with respect to all pending cases, the determination of age shall be in terms of the provision of the Act, that is, the person should be aged 18 at the time of the commission of offence. 'In all pending cases including trial, revision, appeal or any other criminal proceedings in respect of a juvenile in conflict with law, in any court, the determination of juvenility of such a juvenile shall be in terms of clause (l) of Section 2, even if the juvenile ceases to be so on or before the date of commencement of this Act and the provisions of this Act shall apply as if the said provisions had been in force, for all purposes and at all material times when the alleged offence was committed.'

However, even after the explanation had been added, which applied to cases of retrospective application of the law as well, the Supreme

Court did not immediately take notice of the amended section and stuck to its interpretation as in the Pratap Singh case. In the matter of *Jameel* v. *State of Maharashtra*,[38] citing the judgement in the Pratap Singh case, the apex court rejected the argument of the accused: 'So far as the submission of the learned counsel in regard to the applicability of the 2000 Act is concerned, it is not in dispute that the appellant on the date of occurrence had completed 16 years of age. The offence having been committed on 16.12.1989, the 2000 Act has no application. In terms of the Juvenile Justice Act, 1986, "juvenile" was defined to mean "a boy who had not attained the age of 16 years or a girl who had attained the age of 18 years".'

In the matter of *Ranjeet Singh* v. *State of Haryana*,[39] the Supreme Court relied on the Jameel case judgement and stated: 'Section 20 of the Act does not in any way help the appellant. It deals with cases where proceedings related to a period when 1986 Act was in force. What Section 20 provides is that the proceedings shall continue as if the Act (i.e. Act of 2000) is not in existence. To put it differently, even if the definition of "juvenile" has undergone a change by fixing the age to be 18 years the proceedings shall continue on the footing that the accused was a juvenile under the 1986 Act. What appellant contends is to reverse the situation, i.e. take the applicable age to be 18 years. That is not legally permissible.'

In a 2008 case, *Vimal Chadha* v. *Vikas Choudhary and Anr.*,[40] after the amendments had been brought to the notice of the court, the court accepted that there was scope of consideration of the amendments and model rules in any other case. However, it gave its verdict in light of its judgement in the Jameel case and the facts, and opined that the matter may be considered afresh under the provisions of Section 472 of CrPC.

Finally, in the case of *Hari Ram* v. *State of Rajasthan and Anr.*,[41] the Supreme Court reviewed its earlier position regarding the amendments and held that it was beyond doubt that all persons below 18 years on the date of commission of the offence even prior to 1 April 2001, would

---

[38] (2007) 11 SCC 420.

[39] (2008) 9 SCC 453.

[40] (2008) 8 SCALE 608.

[41] (2009) 13 SCC 211.

be treated as juveniles. This would be even if the claim of juvenility was raised after they had attained the age of 18 on or before the date of commencement of the Act and were undergoing sentence upon being convicted. It Court observed: 'The effect of the proviso to Section 7-A introduced by the Amending Act makes it clear that the claim of juvenility may be raised before any court, which shall be recognised at any stage, even after final disposal of the case, and such claim shall be determined in terms of the provisions contained in the Act and the Rules made thereunder, which includes the definition of "juvenile" in Section 2(k) and 2(l) of the Act even if the juvenile had ceased to be so on or before (emphasis supplied) the date of commencement of the Act. The said intention of the legislature was reinforced by the amendment effected by the said Amending Act to Section 20 by introduction of the Proviso and the Explanation thereto, wherein also it has been clearly indicated that in any pending case in any court the determination of juvenility of such a juvenile has to be in terms of clause 2(l) even if the juvenile ceases to be so "on or before the date of commencement of this Act" (emphasis supplied) and it was also indicated that the provisions of the Act would apply as if the said provisions had been in force for all purposes and at all material times when the alleged offence was committed.'

The consequence of this decision can be observed in *Amit Singh* v. *State of Maharashtra and Anr.*,[42] where it was contended that the accused was a juvenile at the time of the commission of offence and hence should be tried by the board. The Supreme Court applied the ratio from the *Hari Ram* case and held that Section 20 as amended extended even to juveniles who had completed 18 years as on 1 April 2001.

In *Kalu* v. *State of Haryana*,[43] the Supreme Court noted: 'The Explanation to Section 20 makes it clear that in all pending cases, which would include not only trials but even subsequent proceedings by way of revision or appeal, the determination of juvenility of a juvenile would be in terms of Clause (l) of Section 2, even if the juvenile ceased to be a juvenile on or before 1.4.2001, when the Juvenile Act came into force, and the provisions of the Juvenile Act would apply as if the said provision

---

[42] (2011) 13 SCC 744.

[43] (2012) 8 SCC 34.

had been in force for all purposes and for all material times when the alleged offence was committed.'

Relevant Date of Application of the Act

Apart from technical challenges in determining age and retrospective application of the law, another detail brought before the Supreme Court was with regard to the date of application of the Act; that is, whether the relevant date to apply the Act should be the date of commission of offence or the date of production of the offender before the magistrate. Once again, the Supreme Court relied upon legislators' intent to resolve the question.

In *Umesh Chandra* v. *State of Rajasthan*,[44] the Supreme Court took the view that the date of application of the Act should be the date of the commission of the offence. After examination of Sections 3[45] and 26[46] of the Children Act, it concluded that both clearly pointed towards the date of occurrence of the offence to be the relevant date. It reasoned that the Children Act was enacted with the intent 'to protect young children from the consequences of their criminal acts on the footing that their mind at that age could not be said to be mature for imputing mens rea as in the case of an adult. This being the intendment of the Act, a clear finding has to be recorded that the relevant date for applicability of

---

[44] (1982) 2 SCC 802.

[45] Section 3, Children Act, 1960: **Continuation of enquiry in respect of child who has ceased to be child.** Where an enquiry has been initiated against a child and during the course of such inquiry the child ceases to be such, then, notwithstanding anything contained in this Act or in any other law for the time being in force, the enquiry may be continued and orders may be made in respect of such person as if such person had continued to be a child.

[46] Section 26, Children Act, 1960: **Special provision in respect of pending cases.** Notwithstanding anything contained in this Act, all proceedings in respect of a child pending in any court in any area on the date on which this Act comes into force in that area, shall be continued in that court as if this Act had not been passed and if the court finds that the child has committed an offence, it shall record such finding and, instead of passing any sentence in respect of the child, forward the child to the children's court, which shall pass orders in respect of that child in accordance with the provisions of this Act as if it had been satisfied on enquiry under this Act that the child has committed the offence.

the Act is the date on which the offence takes place. It is quite possible that by the time the case comes up for trial, growing in age being an involuntary factor, the child may have ceased to be a child.'

However, in the case of *Arnit Das* v. *State of Bihar*,[47] when a similar question of law came up, the two-judge bench of the Supreme Court took a curious approach towards a solution. During the proceedings, it asked U.R. Lalit, the senior counsel of the appellant: 'What happens if a boy or a girl of just less than 16 or 18 years of age commits an offence and then leaves the country or for any reasons neither appears nor is brought before the competent authority until he or she attains the age of, say 50 years? If the interpretation suggested by the learned senior counsel for the appellant were to be accepted, he shall have to be sent to a juvenile home, special home or an observation home or entrusted to an aftercare organisation where there would all be boys and girls of less than 16 or 18 years of age. Would he be required to be dealt by a Juvenile Welfare Board or a Juvenile Court?'

While this logic of the Court viewed can hardly be faulted, its decision to choose the date of production of the accused before a magistrate as the relevant date for application of the Act certainly can be. In the case, the Supreme Court used intrinsic aids of interpretation to analyse the language of the Act to the come to its conclusion.

Additionally, it used Section 3 of the Act of 1986[48] to infer legislative intent, stating: 'It provides for an enquiry initiated against the juvenile being continued and orders made thereon even if such person had ceased to be a juvenile during the course of such enquiry. There would have been no need of enacting Section 3 if only the age of the juvenile would have been determinable by reference to the date of the offence.'

---

[47] (2000) 5 SCC 488.

[48] Section 3, Juvenile Justice Act, 1986: **Continuation of enquiry in respect of juvenile who has ceased to be a juvenile.** Where an enquiry has been initiated against a juvenile and during the course of such enquiry the juvenile ceases to be such, then, notwithstanding anything contained in this Act or in any other law for the time being in force, the enquiry may be continued and orders may be made in respect of such person as if such person had continued to be a juvenile.

Through an examination of Section 32,[49] the court concluded that the use of the expressions 'brought before it' and 'juvenile' indicates that it gains jurisdiction to enquire into the age of the juvenile only when he is brought before it. Further, the court reasoned that Section 8[50] comes into play only when the person appears or is brought before a magistrate not empowered to exercise the authority of the board or juvenile court. While studying Section 20,[51] the court again took into consideration the use of the expression, 'is produced before a Juvenile Court', for the provision to spring into action. On the basis of these analyses, the court held that the crucial date for determining whether a person is a juvenile is the date when he is brought before the competent authority.

The issue was once again brought up in *Pratap Singh* v. *State of Jharkhand and Anr.*,[52] pertaining to whether the date of occurrence will

---

[49] Section 32, Juvenile Justice Act, 1986: **Presumption and determination of age.** (1) Where it appears to a competent authority that a person brought before it under any of the provisions of this Act (otherwise than for the purpose of giving evidence) is a juvenile, the competent authority shall make due enquiry as to the age of that person and for that purpose shall take such evidence as may be necessary and shall record a finding whether the person is a juvenile or not, stating his age as nearly as may be. (2) No order of a competent authority shall be deemed to have become invalid merely by any subsequent proof that the person in respect of whom the order has been made is not a juvenile, and the age recorded by the competent authority to be the age of the person so brought before it shall, for the purposes of this Act, be deemed to be the true age of that person.

[50] Section 8, Juvenile Justice Act, 1986: **Procedure to be followed by a Magistrate not empowered under the Act.** (1) When any Magistrate not empowered to exercise the powers of a Board or a Juvenile Court under this Act is of opinion that a person brought before him under any of the provisions of this Act (otherwise than for the purpose of giving evidence) is a juvenile, he shall record such opinion and forward the juvenile and the record of the proceeding to the competent authority having jurisdiction over the proceeding. (2) The competent authority to which the proceeding is forwarded under Sub-section (1) shall hold the enquiry as if the juvenile had originally been brought before it.

[51] Section 20, Juvenile Justice Act, 1986: **Enquiry by Juvenile Court regarding delinquent juveniles.** Where a juvenile having been charged with an offence appears or is produced before a Juvenile Court shall hold the enquiry in accordance with the provisions of Section 39 and may, subject to the provisions of this Act, make such order in relation to the juvenile as it deems fit.

[52] (2005) 3 SCC 251.

be the reckoning date for determining the age of the alleged offender as a juvenile, or the date when he is produced in court/before a competent authority. The Supreme Court finally settled the issue in favour of the judgement of the Court in the Umesh Chandra case. It held that Section 3 and Section 26 of the Act of 1986 were in pari materia with Section 3 and Section 26 of the Rajasthan Children Act, 1970. Referring to the legislative intendment of the Act after considering its preamble, aims, objectives and provisions, it was noted that 'the legislature intended to provide protection, treatment, development and rehabilitation of neglected or delinquent juveniles and for the adjudication thereof'.

The three-judge bench of the Supreme Court in the Umesh Chandra case held that the Act being a piece of social legislation is meant for the protection of infants who commit criminal offences and, therefore, such provisions should be liberally and meaningfully construed to advance the objectives of the Act. It further observed that contrary to the Umesh Chandra case, the decision in the Arnit Das case had been rendered by a two-judge bench that had not considered earlier judgement. Thus, the Supreme Court stated that the judgement in the Arnit Das case couldn't be said to be good law and upheld the *Umesh Chandra* decision.

Sentencing and Quantum of Punishment

The point raised by the Supreme Court in the Arnit Das case can also be examined in lieu of earlier judgments where the Court was faced with such a situation, and how it was handled in terms of sentencing and quantum of punishment.

In *Jayendra* v. *State of U.P.*,[53] the conviction of the accused was upheld though he was a child under the Uttar Pradesh Children Act, 1951. The accused' age being 23 years, he was not sent to an 'approved school'. Instead the Court quashed his sentence and directed him to be released. Similarly, in *Bhoop Ram* v. *State of U.P.*,[54] while the Court upheld the conviction of the appellant who was aged 28 at the time, his sentence

[53] (1981) 4 SCC 149.

[54] (1989) 3 SCC 1.

was quashed. A similar policy of upholding convictions but quashing sentences was followed in a plethora of cases.[55]

The second method used by courts saw the upholding of convictions but modifying sentences to the period of detention already undergone. In the case of *Dharambir* v. *State of N.C.T. of Delhi*,[56] the Supreme Court upheld the conviction, but as the appellant had already undergone two years and four months in detention, it quashed the sentence. Similarly, in *Satish Dhanna* v. *State of Madhya Pradesh*,[57] the Court upheld the conviction of the appellant but modified the sentence to the period of detention already undergone.

The third way of dealing with such cases has been to allow the appeal and remit the case to the JJB for disposal. This was done in *Hari Ram* v. *State of Rajasthan*[58] and *Dayanand* v. *State of U.P.*[59] Directions were issued for the appellant to be produced before the JJB for passing appropriate orders in accordance with the provisions of the Act of 2000.

The Court now seems to be exercising a fourth method as well. In *Ashwani Kumar Saxena* v. *State of Madhya Pradesh*,[60] the conviction of the appellant was upheld, however the sentence awarded by the lower court was set aside and all records remitted to the JJB for suitable punishment. This rule was also followed in *Jitendra Singh* v. *State of U.P.*,[61] 'It is clear that the case of the juvenile has to be examined on merits. If it found that the juvenile is guilty of the offence alleged to have been committed, he simply cannot go unpunished. However, as the law stands, the punishment to be awarded to him or her must be left to the Juvenile Justice Board constituted under the Juvenile Justice (Care and Protection of Children) Act, 2000. This is the plain requirement of Section 20 of the Juvenile Justice (Care and Protection of Children) Act, 2000.'

---

[55] *Pradeep Kumar* v. *State of U.P.*, 1995 Supp 4 SCC 419; *Upendra Kumar* v. *State of Bihar*, (2005) 3 SCC 592; *Gurpreet Singh* v. *State of Punjab*, (2005) 12 SCC 615; *Vijay Singh* v. *State of Delhi*, (2012) 9 SCC 768.

[56] (2010) 5 SCC 344.

[57] (2009) 14 SCC 187.

[58] (2009) 13 SCC 211.

[59] (2011) 2 SCC 224.

[60] (2012) 9 SCC 750.

[61] (2013) 11 SCC 193. See also, *Kamlendra Singh* v. *State of Madhya Pradesh*, AIR 2013 SC 1783; *Ketankumar Gopalbhai Tandel* v. *State of Gujrat*, (2013) 9 SCALE 487.

This is still not a rule of thumb, though. In *Bharat Bhushan* v. *State of Himachal Pradesh*,[62] where the appellant was not a juvenile under the Act of 1986 since he had crossed 16 years, the Court observed: 'The case, however, was pending before the High Court in appeal on the date the 2000 Act came into force and had, therefore, to be dealt with under Section 20 of the Act which required the High Court to record a finding about the guilt of the accused but stop short of passing an order of sentence against him. Inasmuch as the High Court convicted the appellant, it did not commit any mistake for the power to do so was clearly available to the High Court under the provisions of Section 20. What was not permissible was passing of a sentence for which purpose the High Court was required to forward the juvenile to the Juvenile Board constituted under the Act.' Irrespective, the Court held that a reference to the board at this point was irrelevant and unnecessary because the appellant was already 36 years old and a father of three children. Given that he had already undergone three years of his sentence of imprisonment, a reference to the JJB at this stage in his life would serve no purpose.

In the case of *Mumtaz* v. *State of Uttar Pradesh*,[63] the Supreme Court interpreted Section 25 of the Act of 2015 in light of the judgement of the court in the Jitendra Singh case and sent the matter back to the board for determination of quantum of fine to be imposed on the accused, and compensation payable to the deceased after setting aside the sentence of life imprisonment.

---

[62] (2013) 11 SCC 274.

[63] 2016 SCC OnLine SC 653.

Chapter V

Juvenile: Pre-Institutionalisation

It is imperative to ascertain the geographical, economic, social, political, familial and legal factors that conditioned the interviewees prior to their institutionalisation. In the course of data collection, the researchers enquired about the backgrounds of the inmates. This information shall be reverted to in subsequent chapters by way of cross-tabulation to gain clarity about status quo. A rigorous analysis is sine qua non for this book.

This chapter deals with data on the background of the juveniles—their age, education and occupation before institutionalisation. It analyses information related to family such as dependency on family members and occupation of providers. It also offers information on addiction to substances and their sociability. Cross-tabs were formulated among different variables indicating trends across combinations, giving an idea of the situation of juveniles.

Demographic Data

Table 5.1: Demographic Information of the Respondents

Variable	*Category*	*Frequency*	*Percentage*
State	New Delhi	66	21.9
	Haryana	112	37.1
	Punjab	124	41.1
	Total	302	100

Variable	*Category*	*Frequency*	*Percentage*
City	Ambala	31	10.3
	Delhi	66	21.9
	Faridabad	31	10.3
	Faridkot	18	6.0
	Hisar	50	16.6
	Hoshiarpur	57	18.9
	Ludhiana	49	16.2
	Total	302	100
Age of the respondents	11–13	10	3.3
	14–15	60	19.9
	16–17	143	47.3
	18>	89	29.5
	Total	302	100
Level of education	Illiterate	59	19.5
	Primary school	67	22.2
	Middle school	83	27.5
	Secondary school	66	21.9
	Senior secondary school	22	7.3
	Graduate	5	1.7
	Total	302	100
Preoccupation of the inmates prior to institutionalisation	Student	131	43.4
	Employee	78	25.8
	Neither	93	30.8
	Total	302	100

Data was collected from homes in three states—Delhi, Haryana and Punjab—and the sample included 302 respondents. The maximum number of respondents were from Punjab (41.1 per cent) and the minimum were from Delhi (21.9 per cent). Haryana offered 37.1 per cent of the respondents. The sample was constituted from across seven cities in these states—Faridkot, Ludhiana and Hoshiarpur in Punjab, Faridabad, Ambala and Hisar in Haryana, and the city of New Delhi.

The maximum number of respondents were from New Delhi (21.9 per cent), followed by Hoshiarpur (18.9 per cent); the least were from Faridkot (6 per cent).

The minimum age set was 11 years. The majority of the inmates (47.4 per cent) were 16–17 years old, while 29.5 per cent were 18 years old and above. More than 75 per cent of the respondents for this study were 16 years and above, while only 3.3 per cent were 11–13 years old. Thus, most respondents were over 14 years old. This data matches the National Crime Records Bureau (NCRB)[1] report for 2016, which stated that the majority of juveniles in conflict with law (73 per cent) were in the age group of 16–18 years. Delhi had 7 per cent of the total number of juvenile cases reported in the country, Haryana had 3.3 per cent and Punjab had 3 per cent in 2016. Delhi ranked third in incidences of juveniles in conflict with law, Haryana ranked eleventh and Punjab ranked twenty-first.[2] In light of existing literature that demonstrates a curvilinear relationship between offending and age, where the offending increases in early adolescence with maximum in early adulthood and declines afterwards.[3]

The data from this study somewhat supports this hypothesis as the maximum percentage of respondents were 16–17 years old. However, the expected increase in respondents who were delinquents of 18 years and above was not found. Keeping in mind these findings based on NCRB data and the findings of previous literature, the age group from early adolescence seems to be more vulnerable to delinquency than younger ones; intervention programmes for this age group onwards could be worked out with schools to prevent juvenile delinquency.

It was observed that more than 80 per cent of delinquents had some form of education, and only 19.5 per cent were illiterate. Around 22.2

---

[1] 'Crime in India 2016: Statistics,' National Crime Records Bureau, accessed 22 March 2019, http://ncrb.gov.in/StatPublications/CII/CII2016/pdfs/NEWPDFs/Crimeper cent20inper cent20Indiaper cent20-per cent202016per cent20Completeper cent20PDFper cent20291117.pdf.

[2] 'Crime in India 2016: Statistics,' NCRB.

[3] Lisa Stolzenberg and Stewart J. D'Alessio, 'Co-Offending and the Age-Crime Curve,' *Journal of Research in Crime and Delinquency*, Vol. 45, no. 1 (February 2008): 65–86.

per cent had studied until the fifth grade and 21.9 per cent had studied until the tenth grade. The middle school category had the maximum number of respondents (27.5 per cent), while the least belonged to the graduate level (1.7 per cent) followed by senior secondary (7.3 per cent). This indicated that higher education was less prevalent among the juveniles, although a considerable percentage of them had had some level of education. Around 71.5 per cent of respondents had attended primary, middle or secondary school. According to NCRB data (pan-India), 12.3 per cent of juveniles in conflict with law were illiterate, 32.8 per cent were primary educated, 45.3 per cent had education above the primary level and below matriculation, and 9.6 per cent were educated to matriculation and above.[4] Doubtless, there are parallels in this study's findings and NCRB data.

In both the cases, the percentage of illiterate juveniles is less compared to the literate. One may consider the literature review, where a link was established between academic performance and delinquency. Although the maximum number of delinquents were literate, higher education was found to be less prevalent among delinquents. Thus, it is important to check dropout rates in schools to prevent delinquency. In schools, the youth can focus on career advancement and future employment, but truancy can become gateways to delinquent activities, which, in turn, can cause stigma and provoke disciplinary action preventing them from staying in schools. Moreover, academic performance must be overseen as well. Students should be encouraged to learn and perform well in a cordial environment in schools. Higher academic performance is linked with lower delinquency, as previously discussed.

Also, peer influence plays a significant role in delinquent behaviour. Teachers and other school authorities as well as parents can monitor the company children keep and take action to dissociate delinquent cliques.

The respondents were placed in three categories with respect to their occupation prior to institutionalisation. Most respondents were students (43.5 per cent), 25.8 per cent were employed and around 30.8 per cent were neither studying nor employed. Ann Dryden Witte observed that early childhood education, with intervention from parents, can reduce

[4] Stolzenberg and D'Alessio, 'Co-Offending,' 65–86.

juvenile delinquency.[5] However, education and training with high-risk youths did not show any long-term impact. He also discussed the lack of consistent evidence among quasi-experimental studies for education programmes in reducing crime. David Farrington[6] found that an important predictor of aggression and violence at eight to 10 years of age was school failure, low parental interest and low attainment. Farrington et al.[7] found that crime committed by youth during a period of unemployment was more likely than when they were employed. Available data suggested that the youth might have committed crimes for financial needs and that unemployment was closely related to crime for younger children (15–16 years).

As the maximum number of respondents in this study were either studying or working, they can be encouraged to continue respectively after their time in the homes. However, we don't know of their regularity at the school or workplace, their level of performance, relationship with peers and response to relevant authorities. Thus, not only is there a need to keep the juvenile engaged after release, he must also be encouraged to perform well and have a cordial relationship with peers and the authorities. It is important for the juvenile to be engaged in sustainable work or education and continuing can deter them from walking out and associating with wrong cliques or engaging in deviant behaviour.

On cross-tabulating data under 'age' and 'education' (Annexure III, Table 5.4), we find that the percentage of literates in each age group was higher than the percentage of illiterates—60 per cent of 11–13-year-old respondents were literate and 68.3 per cent of 14–15-year-olds were literate. About 81.8 per cent respondents in the age group of 16–17 years were literate and 88.8 per cent of those 18 years and above were literate. The last group had the greatest number of literate inmates. Among the illiterate respondents, the maximum percentage came from the age group

[5] Ann Dryden Witte, 'Crime,' in *The Social Benefits of Education*, ed. J. Behrnman and N. Stacey (Ann Arbor: University of Michigan Press, 1997), 219–46.

[6] David P. Farrington, 'Early Predictors of Adolescent Aggression and Adult Violence,' *Violence and Victims*, Vol. 4, no. 2 (1989): 79–100.

[7] David P. Farrington et al., 'Are There Any Successful Men from Criminogenic Backgrounds?' *Psychiatry*, Vol. 51, no. 2 (1988): 116–30.

16–17 years (44.1 per cent), but also, this group contained the greatest number of primary-educated respondents (53.7 per cent).

A cross-tabulation of the variables 'state of the inmates' and 'level of education' (Annexure III, Table 5.5) indicated that Punjab had highest percentage of illiterate respondents (55.9 per cent), while Haryana had the lowest (15.3 per cent). However, as far as primary and middle school education go, Punjab also had highest percentage (43.3 per cent and 37.3 per cent respectively). Among those who had studied at secondary and senior secondary levels, Haryana had the highest numbers (57.6 per cent and 63.6 per cent). In terms of graduates, Delhi had the highest number (60 per cent). There were no graduates from Punjab.

According to the row percentages for states, most of Delhi's respondents had middle-school education, followed by primary, illiterate, secondary and graduates. Haryana had the maximum percentage of respondents at the secondary level, followed by middle school, primary, senior secondary, illiterates and graduates. Punjab's maximum respondents were illiterate, followed by middle school, primary, secondary and senior secondary-educated. NCRB[8] data points out that 27.9 per cent juveniles in conflict with law from Delhi were illiterate, 40.5 per cent had primary education, 29.5 per cent were below matriculation level, and 2.1 per cent had matric education and above. But in the current study, the maximum percentage had attended up to middle school. For Haryana, 12.44 per cent were illiterate, 24.4 per cent had had primary education, 49.8 per cent were between primary and matric-level educated, and 13.4 per cent were over the matriculation level. The maximum percentage of respondents lay in the primary-matric category, not unlike NCRB data where the most juveniles were educated beyond the primary level. For Punjab, 15.9 per cent were illiterate, 25.5 per cent had primary education, 52.2 per cent were between primary and matric-level educated, and 6.4 per cent were over the matric level. In this study, the maximum percentage of respondents from Punjab were illiterate unlike according to NCRB data, where the maximum percentage were educated above the primary level.[9]

---

[8] 'Crime in India 2016: Statistics,' NCRB.

[9] 'Crime in India 2016: Statistics,' NCRB.

Cross-tabulating inmates' age and occupation prior to institutionalisation (Annexure III, Table 5.6) indicated that maximum respondents across the age groups were studying; others were working or doing neither. In the case of the 11–13 age group, 50 per cent were studying, of the 14–15-year-olds, 46.7 per cent were studying, of the 16–17-year-olds, 43.4 per cent were studying, and 40.4 per cent of those 18 years and above were studying.

The highest percentage of juveniles who were employed were in the age group of 16–17 years (43.6 per cent), as well as the highest percentage of students (47.3 per cent), and those who were doing nothing (50.5 per cent). About 40 per cent of children aged 11–13 years were employed, indicating child labour among juvenile delinquents, although they constituted only 5.1 per cent of the total number of employed respondents.

An analysis of 'level of education' crossed with 'preoccupation prior to institutionalisation' (Annexure III, Table 5.7) roughly suggested that with an increase in the level of education, the percentage of respondents employed decreased. For example, of those who were employed 43.6 per cent were illiterate, whereas 1.3 per cent and 2.6 per cent had secondary and senior secondary respectively. None of the graduates were employed. Of those who were neither studying nor working, the highest percentage (35.5 per cent) had primary education, while among students, the highest percentage had secondary education (48.1 per cent). The maximum number of respondents with middle school, secondary, senior secondary and graduate education were studying, whereas the illiterate or primary-level respondents were more likely to be employed, or neither employed nor studying.

A cross-tabulation of 'state' and 'preoccupation prior to institutionalisation' (Annexure III, Table 5.8) indicated that in Delhi, the highest percentage of respondents was neither studying nor employed (40.9 per cent); in Haryana, the highest percentage was studying (53.6 per cent) while in Punjab, the most respondents (38.7 per cent) were studying.

Most respondents who were studying before institutionalisation were from Haryana (45.8 per cent), while the maximum number of respondents who were working, and neither working nor studying, were from Punjab (48.7 per cent and 40.9 per cent respectively).

Information about Family/Significant Others

Table 5.2: Frequency Table for Information about Family/Significant Others

Title	*Category*	*Frequency*	*Percentage*
Provider for inmate	Self	27	8.9
	Mother	24	7.9
	Father	229	75.8
	Brother	16	5.3
	Others	6	2.0
Occupation of provider	Daily wage labourer	90	29.8
	Skilled labourer	141	46.7
	Businessperson	30	9.9
	Salaried worker	19	6.3
	Not specified	22	7.3

The maximum percentage of respondents were dependent on their fathers (75.8 per cent), while 7.9 per cent were dependent on their mothers; 89.1 per cent depended on their immediate family like father, mother or brother, but only 2 per cent were dependent on others like relatives. About 8.9 per cent of respondents provided for themselves. The data demonstrates the role of fathers in financially providing for the juveniles. Richard Johnson[10] found that the role of fathers in causing delinquency was greater than the role of mothers. For both sexes, distance from the father was related to delinquency, however, Johnson also suggested that having positive recall regarding parental love and respect was more closely related to law violation than spending more time with parents. Joan McCord[11] noted that good parenting by mothers protected their children from criminogenic influences even in neighbourhoods where delinquency was higher, and that a father's interaction with his family was less relevant than a mother's role, having greater bearing as the child matured. These studies indicate the importance of parents in the life of a child and the role they play in preventing juvenile delinquency. Thus, it is important to educate

---

[10] Richard E. Johnson, 'Mother's versus Father's Role in Causing Delinquency,' *Adolescence*, Vol. 22, no. 86 (Summer 1987): 305–15.

[11] Joan McCord, 'Family Relationships, Juvenile Delinquency, and Adult Criminality,' *Criminology*, Vol. 29, no. 3 (August 1991): 397–417.

parents about their roles and good parenting skills so they can be involved in their child's development. These skills can be discussed by schools or social workers involved in rehabilitating juveniles.

According to NCRB data on juveniles' family backgrounds, in Delhi, 83 per cent were with families, 10.6 per cent with guardians and 6.4 per cent homeless. In Haryana, 90.3 per cent juveniles lived with families, 3.8 per cent with guardians and 5.9 per cent were homeless. In Punjab, 96.1 per cent lived with families, 2.5 per cent with guardians and 1.2 per cent were homeless. So, pan-India, 86.2 per cent juveniles lived with families, 10.3 per cent with guardians and 3.5 per cent homeless.[12] Haryana data shows that there were more homeless juveniles than those living with their guardians. Ann Masten et al.[13] found that housing status was not one of the main predictors of child behavioural problems; rather parental distress and recent life events were major predictors. This explains why most juvenile delinquents were found to be living with families. It is possible they were exposed to stressful events and tensions that could have caused delinquency. Rolf Loeber and Magda Stouthamer-Loeber[14] concluded that parental rejection was strongly linked to juvenile delinquency, while parents' marital relations and criminality were moderately linked. Thus, following NCRB data and aforementioned studies, homelessness may not be a cause of delinquency. If the juvenile is staying with a family that is disruptive with wrong parenting, it is more likely to provoke delinquent behaviour.

Data was also collected on the occupation of the providers for the respondents in this study. In the majority of cases (46.7 per cent), the provider for the juvenile was engaged in skilled labour as a factory worker, carpenter, car mechanic, farmer, plumber, etc. In 29.8 per cent cases, the provider was a daily wage labourer, 9.9 per cent providers were engaged in commercial activities such as mom-and-pop shops, vegetable and fruit vending, etc., while

---

[12] 'Crime in India 2016: Statistics,' NCRB.

[13] Ann S. Masten et al., 'Children in Homeless Families: Risks to Mental Health and Development,' *Journal of Consulting and Clinical Psychology*, Vol. 61, no. 2 (January 1993): 335–43.

[14] Rolf Loeber and Magda Stouthamer-Loeber, 'Family Factors as Correlates and Predictors of Juvenile Conduct Problems and Delinquency,' *Crime and Justice*, Vol. 7 (1986): 29–149.

7.3 per cent didn't specify the occupation of the primary breadwinners. This data sheds light on the socioeconomic demographic to which the majority of inmates belonged, given that only 6.3 per cent had salaried workers for providers, forming part of the supposedly upward mobile middle class.

Several studies have been undertaken by researchers on the link between socioeconomic status and delinquency, but findings have varied. Bradley Wright et al.[15] analysed and found that both low and high socioeconomic status (SES) were linked to delinquency, and that low SES promoted delinquency by increasing individuals' alienation, financial strain and aggression, and decreasing educational and occupational aspirations. High SES promoted individuals' delinquency by increasing risk-taking and social power and decreasing conventional values.[16]

Our data shows that most juvenile providers were skilled or daily wage labourers. A cross-tabulation of the variables 'age of the inmates' and 'provider of the inmates' (Annexure III, Table 5.9) demonstrated that the maximum percentage of respondents across the age groups were dependent on their fathers—90 per cent among 11–13-year-olds, 78.3 per cent among 14–15-year-olds, 69.2 per cent among 16–17-year-olds and 83.1 per cent in the age group 18 years and above. The highest percentage of self-dependent respondents came from the 16–17 age group (48.1 per cent), followed by those 18 years and above (37 per cent). Hence, 85.1 per cent of self-dependent respondents were 16 years old or more.

Of those dependent on their mothers, fathers and brothers, the maximum percentage of respondents were in the age group 16–17 years (54.2 per cent, 43.2 per cent and 87.5 per cent respectively). Also, for respondents 18 years old and above, the maximum number were dependent on their fathers, followed by self-dependent (11.2 per cent).

Cross-tabulating the variables 'provider for the inmate' and 'occupation of the provider' (Annexure III, Table 5.10) indicated that more than half of those who were self-dependent were daily wage labourers (51.9 per cent) followed by skilled labourers (37 per cent). In case of mothers as well, the maximum percentage were daily wage labourers (37.5 per cent). This was

---

[15] Bradley R. Entner Wright et al., 'Reconsidering the Relationship between SES and Delinquency: Causation But Not Correlation,' *Criminology*, Vol. 37, no. 1 (February 1999): 175–94.

[16] Wright et al., 'Reconsidering the Relationship,' 176.

not observed for fathers, more than half of whom (52.4 per cent) were skilled labourers. For brothers too, the maximum percentage fell in the category of skilled labourers (50 per cent). Among the skilled labourers, the maximum percentage was fathers (85.1 per cent); ditto for daily wage labourers (71.1 per cent). This was followed by self (15.6 per cent). Among salaried workers, the maximum percentage was also fathers (73.7 per cent). Thus, a higher percentage of salaried workers were fathers. However, among all the fathers, only 6.1 per cent were salaried workers. Thus, although the maximum percentage of the salaried workers were fathers, fewer respondents had their providers as father. None of those who were self-dependent were salaried workers, while 26.3 per cent were mothers. Among those who were doing business, 86.7 per cent were fathers, followed by brothers (10 per cent). The self-dependent did not depend on any kind of business.

Psycho-Social Factors

Table 5.3: Frequency Table for Psycho-Social Factors

Title	*Category*	*Frequency*	*Percentage*
Sociability	Yes	165	54.6
	No	137	45.4
Addiction	Tobacco	22	7.3
	Alcohol	24	7.9
	Cannabinoids	7	2.3
	Narcotics	23	7.6
	None	226	74.8

The sociability of respondents was studied on two parameters—whether they had friends inside the home, and outside it. It was observed that a majority of the juveniles (54.6 per cent) were social, while 45.4 per cent had difficulty making friends.

Addiction to intoxicating substances prevalent among the inmates came from tobacco (cigarettes, bidis or chewing tobacco), alcohol, cannabinoids (charas, hash and ganja), and narcotics (smack, heroin, etc.). More than quarter of the juveniles had developed addictions. Almost 7.3 per cent were addicted to tobacco, 7.9 per cent to alcohol, 2.3 per cent to cannabinoids, and 7.6 per cent to narcotics. But a majority

(74.8 per cent) of the inmates, that is 226 respondents, did not have any addictions. In this sample, almost similar percentages were addicted to alcohol, tobacco and narcotics, and a lower percentage was addicted to cannabinoids. Thus, even though the percentage of addicts was low, addiction was present, which is a cause of concern because it indicates exposure to addictive substances at an early age and lack of social control in preventing juveniles from forming addictions. Also, different forms of addiction were seen, such as to tobacco and alcohol, which are more readily and openly available, and to narcotics and cannabinoids, which aren't so. Addiction to substances that are less readily and openly available is also concerning as it may indicate juveniles' contact with peddlers, making them vulnerable to drug-related crimes. The data does not reveal whether the inmates consumed the addictive substances with others or alone, which could have shed light on their socialisation patterns and the company they keep.

Rajita Sinha and Caroline Easton[17] noted: 'With marijuana abuse increasing significantly among adolescents and young adults, it is not surprising that among youth referred to juvenile court those who test positive for cannabinoids commit twice as many felonies as those who test negative.'[18] Based on their analysis, Rolf Loeber et al.[19] found a strong link between persistence substance abuse and persistence delinquency. In their study, the preadolescent group showed concurrence between substance abuse and delinquency, and half of the samples showed internalising problems such depression and withdrawn behaviour.

A cross-tabulation of the variables 'age of inmates' and 'addiction to intoxicants' (Annexure III, Table 5.11) indicated addiction to narcotics among 11–13-year-olds, demonstrating they had exposure to narcotics and had formed addictions. This formed 20 per cent of this age group (two respondents). Of the total respondents addicted to narcotics, this age group formed 8.7 per cent. Thus, more than 8 per cent of narcotic

---

[17] Rajita Sinha and Caroline J. Easton, 'Substance Abuse and Criminality,' *The Journal of the American Academy of Psychiatry and the Law*, Vol. 27, no. 4 (February 1999): 513–26.

[18] Sinha and Easton, 'Substance Abuse and Criminality,' 515.

[19] Rolf Loeber et al., 'Developmental Aspects of Delinquency and Internalising Problems and Their Association with Persistent Juvenile Substance Use between Ages 7 and 18,' *Journal of Clinical Child Psychology*, Vol. 28, no. 3 (September 1999): 322.

addicts were less than 14 years old. Among the age group of 14–15 years, six respondents (maximum number) were narcotic addicts, two respondents were addicted to cannabinoids, and one was addicted to tobacco. None were addicted to alcohol. Among inmates aged 16–17 years, the maximum number of addicts were addicted to tobacco (14 respondents), followed by alcohol (10 respondents), unlike the younger age groups. For inmates who were 18 years and above, the maximum number of the addicts were addicted to alcohol (14 respondents), followed by narcotics (eight respondents).

If we look at the data for tobacco addicts, 63.6 per cent and 31.8 per cent were 16–17 years and 18 years and above, thus, 94.5 per cent of tobacco addicts were over 16 years. Among alcoholics, 41.7 per cent were 16–17 years and 58.3 per cent were 18 years and above; 100 per cent of alcoholics were over 16 years. However, in the case of cannabinoids, there was some form of addiction found among 14–15-year-olds (28.6 per cent of total cannabinoid addicts), with no addicts in the age group of 11–13 years. About 71.4 per cent cannabinoid addicts were over 16 years old, as were 65.2 per cent of narcotic addicts. Thus, for all forms of addictions, the maximum percentage of addicts were over 16 years.

It is, however, very important to note that in all the age groups, the percentage of non-addicts was far more than addicts (80 per cent for 11–13 years, 85 per cent for 14–15 years, 76.2 per cent for 16–17 years, and 65.2 per cent for 18 and above years). The numbers decreased for 16–17-year-olds and 18 and above in this study. But it is to be remembered that among every age group, some form of addiction is present.

Michael Windle found that 'that early-adolescent general delinquency, rather than simply substance involvement, increases the risk for late-adolescent substance abuse and related alcohol problems'.[20]

A cross-tabulation of the variables 'state' and 'addiction to intoxicants' (Annexure III, Table 5.12) demonstrated that Punjab had the maximum percentage of addicts (15.2 per cent), followed by Haryana (7 per cent) and Delhi (3 per cent). For each state, the percentage of non-addicts was higher. For example, in Delhi, non-addicts constituted 86.4 per cent, in

[20] Michael Windle, 'A Longitudinal Study of Antisocial Behaviours in Early Adolescence as Predictors of Late Adolescent Substance Use: Gender and Ethnic Group Differences,' *Journal of Abnormal Psychology*, Vol. 99, no. 1 (March 1990): 90.

Haryana, 81.3 per cent, and in Punjab 62.9 per cent. Trends in addiction for each state were also highlighted by this sample. In Delhi, the greater addiction was to cannabinoids and narcotics (three respondents each), followed by alcohol (two respondents) and tobacco (one respondent). In Haryana, the maximum percentage of respondents were addicted to alcohol and tobacco (eight respondents each), then narcotics (four respondents) and cannabinoids (one respondent). In Punjab, the greater addiction was to narcotics (16 respondents), followed by alcohol (14 respondents), tobacco (13 respondents) and cannabinoids (three respondents). The most narcotic addicts were from Punjab (69.6 per cent). Among cannabinoid addicts, the maximum percentage were from Delhi and Punjab (42.9 per cent); the majority of tobacco and alcohol addicts were from Punjab (59.1 per cent and 58.3 per cent respectively).

Cross-tabulating the variables 'level of education' and 'ability to socialise' showed that among all education levels (except senior secondary), the percentage of respondents who were sociable was more than respondents who were not. In the case of senior secondary respondents, only 40.9 per cent were sociable, while the rest were not. Among the graduates, around 60 per cent were found to be sociable, and among the illiterate, 59.3 per cent were. These were the extreme ends of the education level in our data schematic and indicated similar percentages of sociable respondents. There was no data to support that lower levels of education was related to lower sociability or otherwise.

A cross-tabulation of the variables 'level of education' and 'addiction to intoxicants' (Annexure III, Table 5.14) indicated that among the illiterate, the maximum number were narcotic addicts (13 respondents). Among those with primary education, the maximum respondents were addicted to tobacco (seven respondents), while among those with middle school education, the maximum were narcotic addicts (six respondents). Amid secondary, senior secondary and graduate level respondents, maximum addicts abused alcohol (three, four and one respectively). However, the percentage of non-addicts was greater than addicts across each education level—the illiterate, 50.8 per cent; primary level, 68.7 per cent; middle school, 81.9 per cent; secondary level, 92.4 per cent; senior secondary level, 77.3 per cent; and graduate level, 80 per cent. Thus, the minimum percentage of non-addicts was found among the illiterate, followed primary level respondents (68.7 per cent), indicating that more addicts were found among these two groups.

Among tobacco addicts, the maximum percentage were illiterate or studying at the primary level (40.9 per cent each), while among alcoholics, the maximum percentage were primary-educated (29.2 per cent) followed by the illiterate (20.8 per cent). Among cannabinoid addicts, the maximum percentage of respondents were also from the same groups (28.6 per cent each). Among narcotic addicts, the maximum percentage were illiterate (56.5 per cent) followed by middle school students (26.1 per cent). Thus, the educational levels that had the highest percentage of addicts were illiterates or primary; of all the respondents, 16.6 per cent had some form of addiction and had had education below the fifth grade.

Cross-tabulating the variables 'addiction to intoxicants' and 'ability to socialise' (Annexure III, Table 5.15) indicated that fewer cannabinoid and narcotic addicts were sociable, that is, 56.5 per cent narcotic addicts and 57.1 per cent cannabinoid addicts were non-sociable. This phenomenon needs further exploration before drawing any conclusions. About 50 per cent of alcohol addicts were unsociable, but also only 55.8 per cent of non-addicts were sociable. Among sociable respondents, 76.4 per cent were non-addicts, though interestingly, 73 per cent of unsociable respondents were not addicted to any intoxicating substances.

Diane Santesso et al.[21] noted that among the Canadian samples, low sociability and shyness were related to high substance abuse. K.J. Sher and T.J. Trull[22] observed that there was some evidence linking alcohol consumption and low extraversion. However, there is also contrary evidence, as Roman Kotov et al.[23] found in their meta-analysis—that

---

[21] Diane L. Santesso et al., 'Are Shyness and Sociability Still a Dangerous Combination for Substance Use? Evidence from a US and Canadian Sample,' *Personality and Individual Differences*, Vol. 37, no. 1 (July 2004): 5–17.

[22] K.J. Sher and T.J. Trull, 'Personality and Disinhibitory Psychopathology: Alcoholism and Antisocial Personality Disorder,' *Journal of Abnormal Psychology*, Vol. 103 (1994): 92–102.

[23] Roman Kotov et al., 'Linking "Big" Personality Traits to Anxiety, Depressive, and Substance Use Disorders: A Meta-Analysis,' *Psychological Bulletin*, Vol. 136, no. 5 (2010): 768–821.

substance abuse disorder was not correlated with extraversion, and anti-social personality disorder had average association with extraversion.

A cross-tabulation of the variables 'addiction to intoxicants' and 'preoccupation prior to institutionalisation' indicated that the maximum percentage of those addicted to tobacco were employed (59.1 per cent) and the maximum percentage of those addicted to alcohol were studying (45.8 per cent). The maximum percentage of cannabinoid addicts were also employed (57.1 per cent) while the maximum percentage of narcotic addicts were neither employed nor studying (56.5 per cent). The most number of non-addicts were studying (51.5 per cent). Although this sample's data demonstrates that the maximum percentage of addicted respondents were either employed or studying except for narcotics, one cannot overlook the negative impact addiction has on one's performance while working and studying. Current data does not explore the performance of addicts while working or studying. However, the maximum percentage of students and employees were non-addicts (88.5 per cent and 60.3 per cent respectively). At the same time, the maximum percentage of those neither studying nor working were also non-addicts.

Stephen Heishman et al.[24] studied the effects of alcohol and marijuana on mood, memory and performance and found that both impaired performance on word recall tests, and alcohol impaired performance on number recognition test. Thus, both alcohol and marijuana impact memory. Moderate to heavy alcohol consumption among adolescent boys and girls has been linked to negative impact on neurocognitive functioning. Stephen Porter and John Pryor[25] noted that heavy alcohol drinkers among university students had lower GPA. It had a strong effect on student-faculty interaction and heavy drinkers were less likely to be engaged with their faculty.

---

[24] Stephen J. Heishman et al., 'Comparative Effects of Alcohol and Marijuana on Mood, Memory, and Performance,' *Pharmacology Biochemistry and Behaviour*, Vol. 58, no. 1 (September 1997): 93–101.

[25] Stephen R. Porter and John Pryor, 'The Effects of Heavy Episodic Alcohol Use on Student Engagement, Academic Performance, and Time Use,' *Journal of College Student Development*, Vol. 48, no. 4 (July 2007): 455–67.

Chapter VI

Juvenile: In Conflict with the Law

In this chapter, the researchers seek to examine the experiences of juveniles when they first came in conflict with law. The first point of contact is the police. The minds of juveniles being impressionable, their experiences can shape and mould thought processes in ways that may either support or be inimical to the aims of the Juvenile Justice (Care and Protection) Act of 2000 as well as the Juvenile Justice (Care and Protection of Children) Act of 2015.

This chapter provides data on the nature of offences, whether the offence was committed alone or with others, and recidivism. It also provides information on juveniles' interaction with the criminal justice system including police officers and courts, as well as their negotiation with confinement and the provision of legal aid.

Table 6.1: Information about Delinquent Behaviour

Title	*Category*	*Frequency*	*Percentage*
Nature of offence	Petty	38	12.6
	Serious	21	7
	Heinous	243	80.5
Company at the time of offence	None	121	40.1
	Other juveniles	59	19.5
	Adults	100	33.1

Title	*Category*	*Frequency*	*Percentage*
	Juveniles at behest of adults	22	7.3
Recidivism	Yes	33	10.9
	No	269	89.1

The percentage of juveniles charged with heinous offences was maximum (80.5 per cent) followed by those charged with petty offences (12.6 per cent) and serious offences (7 per cent). Most of the respondents committed offences categorised as heinous by the Act. This can provide direction to the type of intervention efforts that are to be undertaken to check recidivism. All forms of offences were found among the delinquents. However, one needs to consider whether there is a variation in the response of the police, courts and the justice system as a whole to these offenders based on the nature of the offence.

Most juveniles committed the offence alone (40.1 per cent) whereas 33.1 per cent committed the offence with adults; 19.5 per cent juveniles committed the offence with other juveniles, and 7.3 per cent did so at the behest of adults. This data gives some idea about peer influence on delinquent behaviour. The majority of the juveniles committed the offence alone, and only a fraction did so with other juveniles. Hence, one may say that maximum percentage of juveniles were not directly influenced by peers in committing the offence. The data in this study indicated that across all age groups, the maximum percentage was of those who committed the crime alone. However, this is not to ignore the impact peer influence has on juvenile delinquents. K.C. Mohanan et al.[1] found a correlation between delinquent behaviour and antisocial peer influences, while H.L. Chung and L. Steinberg[2] noted that adolescents who did not receive proper parenting and emotional support had more antisocial friends and indulged more in antisocial behaviour. While E.S. Scott

[1] K.C. Monahan et al., 'Affiliation with Antisocial Peers, Susceptibility to Peer Influence, and Antisocial Behaviour during the Transition to Adulthood,' *Developmental Psychology*, Vol. 45, no. 6 (2009): 1520–30.

[2] H.L. Chung and L. Steinberg, 'Relations between Neighbourhood Factors, Parenting Behaviours, Peer Deviance, and Delinquency among Serious Juvenile Offenders,' *Developmental Psychology*, Vol. 42, no. 2 (2006): 319–31.

and Steinberg[3] suggested that most juveniles committed crimes in groups, whereas adults were more involved in crimes committed alone, L. Stolzenberg and S.J. D'Alessio found that 'solo offending is the primary form of offending among all ages including juveniles'.[4] They added that solo offending was dominant even among children aged 10 years and concluded that co-offending was not the initiating cause of delinquent behaviour; the data in this study supports their findings. Moreover, data shows that 33.1 per cent of juveniles—the second-highest number—committed the offence with adults. This indicates adult influence on juveniles in committing crimes, far greater than juvenile influence (19.5 per cent).

Most of the juveniles (89.1 per cent) were first-time offenders, and 10.9 per cent were recidivists, that is, they had been charged and convicted for other offences earlier. Pan-India data[5] sourced from the National Crime Records Bureau (NCRB) indicated that 5.2 per cent juveniles were recidivists and 94.8 per cent were apprehended for the first time. The similarity between data from NCRB and this study was that the maximum percentage of respondents were first-time offenders. Albert J. Reiss, Jr. and D.P. Farrington[6] found that recidivism was less common if a crime was committed alone, than in the company of others. However, this was not dependent on age and serial number of offences. C.C. Cottle et al.[7] also noted that those who had delinquent peers were more at risk of recidivism; their meta-analysis indicated a link between socioeconomic backgrounds and reoffending as well, where those from poorer backgrounds were at a greater risk of reoffending. They also

[3] E.S. Scott and L. Steinberg, 'Adolescent Development and the Regulation of Youth Crime,' *The Future of Children*, Vol. 18, no. 2 (2008): 15–33.

[4] L. Stolzenberg and S.J. D'Alessio, 'Co-Offending and the Age-Crime Curve,' *Journal of Research in Crime and Delinquency*, Vol. 45, no. 1 (2008): 80.

[5] National Crime Records Bureau, 'Crime in India: 2016 Statistics,' accessed 25 March 2019, http://ncrb.gov.in/StatPublications/CII/CII2016/pdfs/NEWPDFs/Crime%20in%20India%20-%202016%20Complete%20PDF%20291117.pdf.

[6] Albert J. Reiss, Jr. and David P. Farrington, 'Advancing Knowledge about Co-offending: Results from a Prospective Longitudinal Survey of London Males,' *Journal of Criminal Law and Criminology*, Vol. 82 (1991): 360–95.

[7] C.C. Cottle et al., 'The Prediction of Criminal Recidivism in Juveniles: A Meta-Analysis,' *Criminal Justice and Behaviour*, Vol. 17 (2001): 367–94.

found that those who had committed a serious offence were more at risk of recidivism, and that substance abuse was significantly related to recidivism. Factors such as significant family problems and being raised in a single-parent home were also linked to high risk of recidivism.

In their study on the risk factors of recidivism and severity of recidivism among serious offenders, E. Mulder et al. found that factors such as past criminal behaviour, poor parenting, physical and emotional abuse in the family and delinquent peers were risky for recidivism.[8] Criminal behaviour in the family was linked to serious violent offending, and recidivism mostly took place within two years. Mulder et al. also noted that 79.9 per cent of their sample had reoffended in the Netherlands after leaving the institute. Intervention efforts may vary with the juveniles who are recidivists and non-recidivists. Recidivism indicates a presence of habit formation in committing delinquent crime, family failure in preventing crime, and a non-responsive attitude towards authorities. It also indicates the need to improve how the justice system treats delinquents. It is possible that recidivists may find reintegration with the society more difficult than non-recidivists with frequent interruption of the justice system in their lives and greater supervision by the police.

A cross-tabulation of the variables 'age of inmates' and 'nature of offence' (Annexure III, Table 6.3) indicated that for each age group, the maximum percentage of the type of offence committed were heinous—70 per cent respondents for 11–13 years, 63.3 per cent respondents for 14–15 years, 83.2 per cent for 16–17 years, and 88.8 per cent for those aged 18 years and above. About 65.6 per cent respondents who were 16 years and above had committed heinous offences, and the maximum percentage belonged to the 16–17 age group (49 per cent). A comparative analysis of the age groups indicated that there was a decline in the percentage of respondents committing petty offences with increase in age; 30 per cent in the 11–13 group, 23.3 per cent respondents in the 14–15 group, 12.6 per cent in the 16–17 group, and 3.4 per cent in the 18 years and above group. Of those who committed serious offences, the maximum number came from the age group of 14–15 years (38.1 per cent),

[8] E. Mulder et al., 'A Classification of Risk Factors in Serious Juvenile Offenders and the Relation between Patterns of Risk Factors and Recidivism,' *Criminal Behaviour and Mental Health*, Vol. 20, no. 1 (2010): 23–28.

while of those who committed petty offences, the maximum percentage were in the 16–17 age group (47.4 per cent). Among those who committed heinous offences, the maximum percentage were in the age group of 16–17 years (49 per cent). One observes that among juveniles who were 18 years old and above, only a tiny percentage committed petty offences, while the majority committed heinous offences.

Cross-tabulating the variables 'age of inmates' and 'company at the time of commission of offence' (Annexure III, Table 6.4) indicated that for all age groups, the maximum number of respondents committed the offence alone. About 50 per cent of the 11–13-year-old respondents committed the offence alone, followed by those who were with other juveniles (40 per cent), and lastly with adults (10 per cent). No respondent in this group committed an offence at the command of adults. For the 14–15-year-olds, the maximum percentage of respondents committed the offence alone (41.7 per cent), followed by those who were with adults (35 per cent), then other juveniles (18.3 per cent), and lastly at the behest of adults (5 per cent). For the age group 16–17 years, the maximum percentage committed the offence alone (39.9 per cent), then with adults (35 per cent), other juveniles (17.5 per cent) and at the commands of adults (7.7 per cent). In the 18 years and above group, the maximum percentage of respondents committed the offence alone (38.2 per cent), then with adults (31.5 per cent), other juveniles (21.3 per cent), and lastly at the command of adults (9 per cent). Thus, the percentage of those committing crimes alone declined with increase in age. More respondents 14 years and over committed crimes with adults; the maximum percentage (50 per cent) belonged to the 16–17 age group, followed by those 18 years and above (28 per cent).

The 16–17 age group had the highest percentage of respondents who committed crimes alone (47.1 per cent), with other juveniles (42.4 per cent), and with adults (50 per cent). In the age group 18 years and above, 36.4 per cent of respondents committed crimes at the command of adults. Thus, children of this age range were vulnerable to adults directing them to commit offence, or offending with adults or other juveniles.

Monahan et al.[9] found evidence that delinquent behaviour was correlated to deviant peers; that with increasing age from adolescence to

[9] Monahan et al., 'Affiliation with Antisocial Peers.'

young adulthood, the relationship between affiliating with antisocial peers and delinquent behaviour becomes weak. They noted that peer influence by antisocial peers decreases in late adolescents. However, some individuals in late adolescence, who are more influenced by peers, may be slow in resisting it and continue indulging in delinquent behaviour. The data of this study, however, does not match this finding; it is observed that with increasing age, the percentage of those committing crimes alone decreased, but across all age groups, the maximum percentage committed offended alone.

Reiss and Farrington[10] observed that with age, males declined in co-offending, although most of them somewhat continue co-offending. They did not suggest that individuals only co-offend or only commit crime alone, though some may have done one type of offending more than other. Stolzenberg and D'Alessio[11] also noted that solo offending was dominant in all age groups.

A cross-tabulation (Annexure III, Table 6.5) of the variables 'age of inmates' and 'recidivism' showed that the maximum percentage of respondents in each group were first-time offenders. The percentage was quite high for each category, the minimum being 84.3 per cent for those 18 years and above. The percentage of recidivist respondents increased with age—3 per cent for the 11–13 group, and 42.4 per cent each for 16–17-year-olds and 18 years and above. About 84.8 per cent of all recidivists were 16 years and above.

Analysing the variables 'state' and 'recidivism' (Annexure III, Table 6.6) suggested that in all the three states, the maximum percentage of respondents were non-recidivists, that is, the population of non-recidivists was much higher than the repeat offenders. A comparative analysis of the states suggests that Delhi had the maximum percentage of recidivists (16.7 per cent) followed by Punjab (9.7 per cent) and Haryana (8.9 per cent). NCRB data[12] suggests that 7 per cent of apprehended juveniles in Delhi were recidivists and 93 per cent were apprehended for the first time. In Haryana, only 2.3 per cent juveniles were recidivists, and in Punjab,

---

[10] Reiss and Farrington, 'Advancing Knowledge,'

[11] Stolzenberg and D'Alessio, 'Co-Offending,' 65–86.

[12] NCRB, 'Crime in India: 2016 Statistics.'

this number stood at 1.9 per cent. Thus, in Delhi, the percentage of recidivists was highest based on NCRB data and this study's findings.

A cross-tabulation of the variables 'level of education' and 'nature of offence' (Annexure III, Table 6.7) indicated that for each level of education, the percentage of those who committed heinous offences was maximum. Among those with middle level education, 91.6 per cent committed heinous crimes, and among secondary-level respondents, the number was 92.4 per cent. For those with senior secondary education, 86.4 per cent committed heinous offences, with graduates clocking the maximum percentage (100 per cent). Among the illiterate, 54.2 per cent committed heinous offences, while 74.6 per cent of primary educated juveniles did the same. As per the comparative analysis of educational levels, the percentage of petty offences decreased with the increase in education, with 44.7 per cent illiterates committing petty offences and none of the respondents in the secondary, senior secondary and graduate level committing petty offences. Among those who had committed serious offences, the maximum percentage were the illiterate (47.6 per cent), of those who had committed heinous offences, the maximum percentage was middle schoolers (31.3 per cent). Among those who had committed heinous crimes, 2.1 per cent respondents were graduates. Graduates and senior secondary level respondents formed the least percentage of respondents committing the total percentage of heinous offences.

An analysis of 'level of education' and 'recidivism' (Annexure III, Table 6.8) indicated that the maximum percentage of respondents for each education level were non-recidivists, including 100 per cent graduates. The percentage of recidivists for each education level was less compared to non-recidivists. About 78.8 per cent recidivists had middle school education or lower, demonstrating that the percentage of recidivists from senior secondary and graduate groups was low (9.1 per cent). Respondents with middle school education had the maximum percentage of recidivists (33.3 per cent); as observed, this was also the group with the highest incidence of committing heinous offences. Thus, more respondents from this group committed heinous offences and were recidivists than graduates, none of whom were recidivists and formed the least percentage of those who committed heinous offences. However, of the total percentage of non-recidivist respondents, those with middle school education constituted the highest percentage (26.8 per cent). About 45.5 per cent recidivists had been educated up to the fifth grade or lower. We can refer to the study by Cottle et al.[13] as well, which suggested that there wasn't a significant relationship between school attendance and school reports of academic achievement, with recidivism.

A cross-tabulation of the variables 'ability to socialise' and 'nature of offences' (Annexure III, Table 6.9) indicated that a higher percentage of respondents who had committed petty offences (60.5 per cent) had the ability to socialise compared to those who did not (39.5 per cent). In case of serious offenders, a higher percentage of respondents were not sociable (61.9 per cent), while among respondents who committed heinous offences, the percentage of those who were sociable (55.1 per cent) was more than those who weren't sociable.

Then, cross-tabulating the variables 'ability to socialise' and 'recidivism' (Annexure III, Table 6.10) indicated that for both sociable and unsociable categories, the maximum percentage of respondents were non-recidivists, 89.7 per cent and 88.3 per cent respectively. Among recidivists, a higher percentage of respondents were sociable (51.5 per cent) than not, although the difference isn't much. Among the non-recidivists, more respondents were sociable (55 per cent) than those who were unsociable (45 per cent). C. Van Dam et al.[14] found that offenders were less extroverted than students, and that extroversion was more common in recidivists than non-recidivists.

A cross-tabulation of 'nature of offence committed by the juveniles' and 'addiction to intoxicating substances' (Annexure III, Table 6.11) showed that the maximum percentage of the respondents for each category of offences were non-addicts—68.4 per cent petty offenders, 57.1 per cent serious offenders, and 77.4 per cent heinous offenders. Among the respondents who committed petty offences, the maximum were addicted to narcotics (six) and among respondents who committed serious offences, the maximum were addicted to narcotics and alcohol (three respondents each). Among those who committed heinous offences, the maximum were addicted to alcohol (21 respondents).

---

[13] Cottle et al., 'The Prediction of Criminal Recidivism.'

[14] C. Van Dam et al., 'PEN, Big Five, Juvenile Delinquency and Criminal Recidivism,' *Personality and Individual Differences,* Vol. 39, no. 1 (2005): 7–19.

Across all the categories of intoxicants, the maximum percentage of respondents committed heinous crimes—72.7 per cent tobacco addicts, 87.5 per cent alcoholics, 57.1 per cent cannabinoid addicts, and 60.9 per cent narcotic addicts. Among non-addicts 83.2 per cent committed heinous crimes. Thus, heinous offences were dominant irrespective of addiction, although it's wise to refer to R. Loeber and others'[15] study associating delinquency and substance abuse.

Table 6.2: Interaction with the Justice System

Title	*Category*	*Frequency*	*Percentage*
Behaviour of the police officer	Supportive	59	19.5
	Hostile	160	53
	Indifferent	83	27.5
Approached by the police officer in uniform	Yes	267	88.4
	No	35	11.6
Presence of family members during proceedings	Yes	282	93.4
	No	20	6.6
Confinement to judicial/ police custody	Yes	200	66.2
	No	102	33.8
Authority before which claim for the minority was made	Police	228	75.5
	Judge	74	24.5
Stigmatising semantics during proceedings	Yes	302	100
	No	0	0
Provision of legal aid	Yes	57	18.9
	No	245	81.1

[15] R. Loeber et al., 'Oppositional Defiant and Conduct Disorder: A Review of the Past 10 Years, Part I,' *Journal of the American Academy of Child and Adolescent Psychiatry*, Vol. 39, no. 12 (December 2000): 1468–84.

In more than 50 per cent cases, the respondents said the behaviour of the police was hostile (53 per cent) and a majority reported being subjected to torture. Supportive police officers were found in fewer cases (19.5 per cent), and in 27.5 per cent cases they were indifferent to the plight of the juveniles. Anthony Petrosino et al.[16] observed that labelling a child delinquent may cause him to be under more police surveillance, and result in him being arrested more often than other juveniles. The behaviour of police is important in forming juveniles' perceptions about the justice system. Hostile treatment can leave a scar in his mind, affecting him psychologically. The involvement of family members by the police is important. Essentially, the police need to respond sensitively to the juvenile and prevent harsh treatment and labelling.

Data was also collected to find out the number of instances where juveniles were approached by officials in uniform at any point, from the time of arrest to court or Board proceedings. An overwhelming majority (88.4 per cent) juveniles reported being approached by uniformed officials, while only 11.6 per cent stated they weren't. Approaching the juvenile in police uniform can be detrimental to his overall rehabilitation of the juvenile.

In a majority of cases, the family of the juvenile was present during proceedings (93.4 per cent) Anne Rankin Mahoney[17] discussed a study where 73 per cent of the youth felt the behaviour of parents did not change after the court hearing and was largely negative, while 27 per cent suggested there was change in the family status.[18] Involvement of family members can be crucial in the rehabilitation process of the juvenile. The family needs to be present throughout the process and can contribute to checking recidivism. Additionally, the family might need counselling. Disrupted families have been linked to delinquency, and they may be facing a lot of stress already, with juvenile delinquency becoming

[16] Anthony Petrosino et al., 'Formal System Processing of Juveniles: Effects on Delinquency,' *Crime Prevention Research Review*, no. 9 (2013), U.S. Department of Justice.

[17] Anne Rankin Mahoney, 'The Effect of Labelling Upon Youths in the Juvenile Justice System: A Review of the Evidence.' *Law & Society Review*, Vol. 8, no. 4 (1974): 583–614.

[18] Mahoney, 'The Effect of Labelling.'

another burden. Families may require support in not only ameliorating the condition of the juvenile, but of the family as a whole.[19]

A vast majority (66.2 per cent) of juveniles in this study said they had been confined in police or judicial custody before being sent to the home. In only 33.8 per cent of the cases were they sent directly to the home. In an overwhelming majority (75.5 per cent), the claim for juvenility was made before the police, while in 24.5 per cent cases it was made before the court/Board.

Data indicated that accusatory terms such as accused, charge-sheet, remand, warrant, trial and prosecution etc. were used around all the respondents during the proceedings. Inmates received legal aid from the state in only 18.9 per cent cases while in 81.1 per cent cases, no aid was provided.

A cross-tabulation of 'age of inmates' and 'confinement in judicial/police custody' (Annexure III, Table 6.12). suggested a direct relationship between the two variables, that is increased confinement to custody with increase in age. It is appalling that 50 per cent juveniles in the age group of 11–13 years were kept in police/judicial custody; however, this only formed 2.5 per cent of respondents kept in custody. About 58.3 per cent of those 14–15 years old were kept in the police/judicial custody, the number hitting 77.5 per cent for those aged 18 years and above. Of those kept in police/judicial custody, the maximum percentage of respondents were in the age group of 16–17 years (45.5 per cent), followed by 18 years and above (34.5 per cent).

An analysis of the variables 'age of inmates' and 'behaviour of police officers' (Annexure III, Table 6.13) indicated that the percentage of respondents in each age group reporting support from the police declined with age. For example, a comparative analysis indicated that 50 per cent of juveniles in the 11–13 group, 20 per cent in the 14–15 group, 19.6 per cent in the 16–17 group, and 15.7 per cent in the 18 and above group found police supportive. Of those who suggested the police were supportive, the maximum percentage of respondents were 16–17 years old (47.5 per cent), followed by 18 years and above (23.7 per cent). Of respondents who reported that the police were hostile, the maximum

---

[19] Roland J. Chilton and Gerald E. Markle, 'Family Disruption, Delinquent Conduct and the Effect of Subclassification.' *American Sociological Review*, Vol. 37, no. 1 (1972): 93–99.

percentage were 16–17 years old (43.1 per cent), followed by children 18 years and above (33.1 per cent). Only 3.1 per cent of 11–13-year-olds suggested the police were hostile. Among those who reported the police were indifferent, the maximum percentage of respondents were 16–17 years old (55.4 per cent), followed by those 18 years and above (26.5 per cent). Based on existing research, W.H. Barton cited that older juveniles receive harsher treatment from the police.[20]

A cross-tabulation of 'age of inmates' and 'provision of legal aid' (Annexure III, Table 6.14) suggested that among all age groups, the maximum percentage of respondents didn't get legal aid, including none from the age group 11–13 years. About 63.3 per cent of 14–15-year-olds, 83.9 per cent of 16–17-year-olds and 86.5 per cent 18-year-olds and above weren't provided legal aid, highlighting that a large percentage of respondents aged 16 years and above were not given aid. Among those provided with legal aid, 16–17-year-olds had the highest percentage of respondents (40.4 per cent), while 21.1 per cent were 18 and above.

Analysing 'age of inmates' and 'approached by the police in the uniform' (Annexure III, Table 6.15) indicated that across all age groups, the maximum percentage of the respondents were approached by police in uniform. A comparative analysis brought to light that 16–17-year-olds had the least percentage of the respondent (87.4 per cent) compared to others approached by uniformed police. The numbers were slightly higher for 11–13-year-olds (90 per cent) and 14–15-year-olds (91.7 per cent). Only 11.6 per cent of the total respondents were not approached by police in uniform; only 10 per cent juveniles in the 11–13 age group were not approached by officers in uniform. Out of those who weren't approached by uniformed officers, the 16–17 group had the maximum percentage of respondents (51.4 per cent), followed by 18-year-olds and above (11.6 per cent).

Cross-tabulating the variables 'state' and 'authority before which claim for minority was made' (Annexure III, Table 6.16) showed that across all the states, claims of minority for the maximum number of respondents were made before the police. A comparative analysis of the three states suggests that in Haryana, claim for juvenility for 80.4 per cent

---

[20] W.H. Barton, 'Discretionary Decision-Making in Juvenile Justice,' *Crime & Delinquency*, Vol. 22, no. 4 (1976): 470–80.

respondents was made before the police, compared to 75.8 per cent in Delhi and 71 per cent in Punjab. Also, claims for juvenility before a judge were maximum in Punjab (29 per cent) followed by Delhi (24.2 per cent) and (19.6 per cent).

While tabulating data for the variables 'confinement in judicial/ police custody' and 'authority before which claim for minority was made' (Annexure III, Table 6.17), it came to light that a higher percentage of those presented before the police and judge were confined to custody—that's 61.8 per cent of those who made claims to the police, and 79.7 per cent of those who presented before a judge. In both cases, more respondents were sent to custody than not. It was also observed that of the confined respondents, a higher percentage were presented before the police (70.5 per cent) than judges (29.5 per cent). However, when we look at the respondents who weren't confined, again, more respondents were presented before the police (85.3 per cent) than judges (14.7 per cent). Overall, a higher percentage of respondents were presented before the police (75.5 per cent).

A cross-tabulation of 'state' and 'behaviour of the police officer' (Annexure III, Table 6.18) indicated that of the supportive police officers, the maximum percentage were from Haryana (52.5 per cent) followed by Punjab (27.1 per cent) and Delhi (20.3 per cent). Among respondents who suggested the police was hostile, the maximum percentage were from Punjab (45.6 per cent), followed by Haryana (29.4 per cent) and Delhi (25 per cent), while of the respondents who said the police was indifferent, the maximum percentage, again, were from Punjab (42.2 per cent), followed by Haryana (41 per cent), then Delhi (16.9 per cent). Across all the states, the maximum respondents suggested the police was hostile, followed by those who found the police indifferent, and the least said they were supportive.

While analysing the variables 'state' and 'provision of legal aid' (Annexure III, Table 6.19), it was found that of the three states, Delhi had the maximum percentage of respondents provided with legal aid (47 per cent) followed by Punjab (12.9 per cent) and Haryana (8.9 per cent). The percentage difference between Delhi and the other two states was high, suggesting that more respondents were provided legal aid in

Delhi. Among the ones who were given legal aid, 54.4 per cent were from Delhi, 28.1 per cent from Punjab and 17.5 per cent from Haryana.

Cross-tabulating 'education' and 'authority before which claim of minority was made' (Annexure III, Table 6.20) indicated that except graduates, the maximum percentage of respondents claimed juvenility before the police. In the case of graduates, 80 per cent were presented before a judge and the rest before the police. For 81.4 per cent illiterate respondents, 79.1 per cent primary level juveniles, 75.9 per cent middle schoolers, 75.8 per cent secondary students, and 59.1 per cent senior secondary level educated children were presented before police. However, one sees a decline in the percentage of respondents presented from the senior secondary and graduate groups. It is possible that age might have affected the decision; juveniles belonging to these educational levels may look older and hence may have been presented before a judge. Of the respondents presented to the police as well as a judge, the maximum percentage were those with middle school education (27.6 per cent and 27 per cent respectively). There is an observable direct relationship between the level of education and claims made before a judge, that is, the higher the level of education, the higher the percentage of claims made before a judge. About 20.9 per cent of all educated up to primary level, 24.1 per cent of middle schoolers, 24.2 per cent of respondents educated up to tenth grade, 40.9 per cent of senior secondary students, and 80 per cent of graduates chose to make their claims of minority before the court instead of the police.

A cross-tabulation of 'level of education' and 'confinement to police/judicial custody' (Annexure III, Table 6.21) showed that for all educational levels, the maximum percentage of respondents were sent to police/judicial custody; middle schoolers were the maximum (27.5 per cent). All the graduates were sent to confinement, yet they formed 2.5 per cent of the group. Of those not sent to confinement, secondary-level students were the highest (31.4 per cent). Of respondents sent to confinement, primary or lower level students formed 43.5 per cent.

An analysis of the variables 'level of education' and 'behaviour of police' (Annexure III, Table 6.22) indicated that the maximum percentage of respondents across educational levels, except the senior secondary, found the police hostile. About 80 per cent graduates mentioned the same, as did 64.2 per cent respondents with primary education. Of juveniles who said the police was hostile, the middle schoolers constituted the highest percentage (27.5 per cent). Those educated up to primary school or less formed 46.9 per cent of the total percentage of respondents who found the police hostile. None of the graduates said the police were supportive. Among the respondents who said that the police were supportive, those having middle level of education formed the maximum percentage (32.2 per cent). Those having primary level education (16.9 per cent) or less (15.3 per cent) together formed another 32.2 per cent of this group. Thus, respondents with primary education or less constituted a smaller percentage suggesting the police were supportive. Most of the illiterate said the police were hostile (54.2 per cent), with only 15.3 per cent of this group experiencing police support. For those who said the police were indifferent, secondary-level students formed the maximum percentage (25.3 per cent); 38.6 per cent were educated up to the primary level or lower.

Analysing the occupation of the provider for the juvenile and the behaviour of police officials towards the juvenile (Annexure III, Table 6.23) suggested that within those who reported hostile treatment, the providers of 28.8 per cent were daily wage labourers, and for 48.1 per cent, skilled labourers. Among all provider occupations, hostile treatment by the police was dominant, ranging from 43.3 per cent to 59.1 per cent. The highest percentage of those reporting supportive behaviour from the police had skilled labourers (44.1 per cent) for providers, as did those reporting indifferent behaviour (45.8 per cent). Of respondents having salaried workers for providers, very few said the police were supportive (5.3 per cent). In this context, Barton found no relationship between social class of the juvenile and the severity with which the police treated the juvenile.[21]

A cross-tabulation of 'occupation of the provider' and the 'provision of legal aid' (Annexure III, Table 6.24) suggested, across most occupations other than the category 'not specified', the maximum percentage of respondents did not receive legal aid. Among respondents with salaried workers as their providers, 89.5 per cent did not receive legal aid, neither did 87.9 per cent respondents with skilled labourers for providers, nor 74.4 per cent juveniles with daily wage labourers for providers. This

[21] Barton, 'Discretionary Decision-Making.'

number is at 86.7 per cent for respondents with businesspersons as providers. In case of the 'not specified' category, 50 per cent respondents did not receive legal aid. Among those receiving legal aid, daily wage labourers (40.4 per cent) and salaried workers (3.5 per cent) constituted the highest and lowest category brackets. Among those who didn't receive aid, skilled labourers (50.6 per cent) formed the maximum percentage of providers.

Analysing the variables 'preoccupation of the juvenile prior to institutionalisation' and 'provision of legal aid' (Annexure III, Table 6.25) demonstrates that in all categories of preoccupation, the maximum percentage of respondents did not get legal aid. About 84.7 per cent juveniles who were studying, 80.8 per cent of those employed and 76.3 per cent of those doing nothing, received no legal aid. Of those who got legal aid, respondents who neither studying nor working formed the maximum percentage (38.6 per cent). Juveniles who were pursuing education prior to institutionalisation constituted the maximum percentage of those who didn't get aid (45.3 per cent).

Tabulating data on 'incidence of presence of family members during proceedings' and 'age of inmates' (Annexure III, Table 6.26) suggested that across the age groups, the highest percentage of respondents had family members present during proceedings. This includes all children of the 11–13 group, 93.3 per cent respondents from the 14–15 group, 93.7 per cent from the 16–17 group, and 92.1 per cent of those aged 18 and above. The last group also had the maximum percentage of respondents (7.9 per cent) where the family was absent, though not very different for other age groups.

A cross-tabulation of 'presence of family members during proceedings' and 'state' (Annexure III, Table 6.27) found that in Delhi, 95.5 per cent of the respondents' families were present; in Haryana, this number was 92.9 per cent, and in Punjab, 92.7 per cent. Clearly, in all the states, the percentage of respondents whose families were present was high.

Analysing data on 'presence of family members during proceedings' and 'preoccupation of juveniles prior to institutionalisation' (Annexure III, Table 6.28) indicated that of those whose families were present, the maximum percentage were studying (44.3 per cent), and among respondents whose families were absent, the maximum were employed

(50 per cent). About 95.4 per cent juveniles who were studying before institutionalisation had their family members present, as did 87.2 per cent of those who had been employed. In cases where the respondent was neither working nor studying, 95.7 per cent had their families present.

Tabulating data on 'presence of family members during proceedings' and 'incidences of the confinement to judicial/police custody' (Annexure III, Table 6.29) indicated that confinement was dominant both where family was present (65.6 per cent) and absent (75 per cent) as compared to cases where confinement did not take place. Altogether, though, there were fewer cases where family was absent (6.6 per cent).

A cross-tabulation of 'presence of family members during proceedings' and 'nature of offence' (Annexure III, Table 6.30) demonstrated that for all categories of offence, the maximum percentage of respondents had their families present—84.2 per cent for petty offenders, 85.7 for serious offenders and 82.3 per cent for those charged with heinous offences.

Similarly, tabulating data on 'state' and 'approached by policemen in uniform' (Annexure III, Table 6.31) indicated that across all states, the maximum percentage of respondents were approached by policemen in uniform—87.9 per cent in Delhi, 85.7 per cent in Haryana and 91.1 per cent in Punjab. Of those approached by uniformed police, Punjab had the majority of respondents (42.3 per cent); of respondents not approached, Haryana had the maximum percentage of cases (45.7 per cent).

A cross-tabulation of 'state' and 'use of accusatory terms or stigmatising semantics during proceedings' (Annexure III, Table 6.32) suggested that in all instances in Delhi, Haryana and Punjab, terms such as arrest, warrant, accused, charge-sheet, remand, trial and prosecution, etc. were used in the course of proceedings. Also, cross-tabulating data on 'nature of offence' and 'use of accusatory terms or stigmatising semantics during proceedings' (Annexure III, Table 6.33) showed that irrespective of the offence committed by the juvenile, terms such as arrest, warrant, accused, charge-sheet, remand, trial and prosecution, etc. were used.

There is clear scope for improvement in how police officers treat juveniles by adjusting behaviour, approaching them in civil dress, using non-stigmatising terms, and so on. Further, progress should be made with regard to providing legal aid to juveniles and reducing their rate of judicial confinement.

Chapter VII

Juvenile: Inside the Home

With rehabilitation being one of the stated aims along with the proper care, protection and treatment of juveniles, by catering to their development needs, it's imperative to examine whether the establishments created under the Act have been successful in achieving the same. In this chapter, the researchers based their queries upon the model rules, which lay down the standards for care and protection to be accorded to juveniles, and judge the observation homes and special homes by this yardstick.

Table 7.1: Information about Homes and the Quality of Services

Title	*Category*	*Frequency*	*Percentage*
Type of home	Special home	73	24.2
	Observation home	229	75.8
Likeability of environment in home	Like	206	68.2
	Dislike	96	31.8
Segregation of residential facilities on the basis of age	No segregation	302	100
Requirement of better infrastructure	Yes	290	96
	No	12	4
Quality of pest/insect control	Poor	13	4.3

Title	*Category*	*Frequency*	*Percentage*
	Below average	117	58.6
	Average	106	35.1
	Good	6	2
Quality of clothing/ bedding	Poor	4	1.3
	Below average	53	17.5
	Average	242	80.1
	Good	3	1
Quality of water	Poor	2	0.7
	Below average	52	17.2
	Average	239	79.1
	Good	9	3
Quality of bathrooms and their sufficiency for inmates	Poor	29	9.6
	Below average	154	51
	Average	113	37.4
	Good	6	2
Quality of kitchen (hygiene)	Poor	0	0
	Below average	7	2.3
	Average	206	68.2
	Good	89	29.5
Quality of kitchen (meals)	Poor	32	10.6
	Below average	115	38.1
	Average	142	47
	Good	13	4.3
Number of meals	Three meals	302	100
Routine	Yes	302	100
Existence/awareness of children's committee	Yes	74	24.5
	No	98	32.5
	No committee present	130	43

Title	*Category*	*Frequency*	*Percentage*
Extension of cooperation from staff to children's committee	Aware (Yes)	26	35.1
	Aware (No)	48	64.9
	Total	74	100
	Not aware/ committee not present	228	75.5
Monthly medical check-up	Yes	26	8.6
	No	276	91.4
Availability of first-aid kits	Yes	302	100
Availability of recreational facilities	Yes	302	100
Grant of leave/parole	Yes	5	1.7
	No	297	98.3
Availability of suggestion box	Unaware	302	100
Permission to meet family/parents	Yes	302	100
Quality/quantity of staff	Poor	39	12.9
	Below average	101	33.4
	Average	133	44
	Good	29	9.6
House mother/house father	Yes	172	57
	No	130	43

Infrastructure

The data collected from special and observation homes showed that more respondents lived in the latter (75.8 per cent). National Crime Records Bureau data suggests that in Delhi, 16.6 per cent juveniles held guilty were sent to special homes; in Haryana, this number is 27.7 per cent, and in Punjab, 69.3 per cent. Other categories of outcome for those held guilty included sending children home after advice or admonition, release on probation and placement under the care of parents or childcare institutes, and fines.[1]

The percentage of juveniles held guilty in Delhi was 90 per cent, in Haryana, 81.1 per cent, and in Punjab, 76.1 per cent. Therefore, comparatively, the percentage of juveniles held guilty was maximum in Delhi.[2] As per this study, most respondents liked the environment in the home (68.2 per cent) although 96 per cent children also suggested the need for better infrastructure.

Quality of Services

In no home was there any segregation of children on the basis of age, that is, all children aged 11–18 years and above were housed together. The level of satisfaction about the quality of pest/insect control was low, where only 2 per cent respondents mentioned the service was good. A majority said it was below average (58.6 per cent) and around 35.1 per cent suggested it was average. The level of satisfaction about the quality of clothing also was not high—only 1 per cent said it was good, where 80.1 per cent deemed quality of clothing to be average, 17.5 per cent said it was below average and 1.3 per cent called it poor.

Again, 79.1 per cent inmates responded that the quality of water was average; 17.2 per cent said it was below average, 0.7 per cent said it was poor and only 3 per cent said quality was good. The response to quality and sufficiency of bathrooms was largely average (51 per cent), followed by below average (37.4 per cent). Again, a few respondents said it was good (2 per cent). However, the response to the quality of kitchen (hygiene) was better—68.2 per cent respondents deemed it average and 29.5 per cent said it was good; 2.3 per cent respondents said it was below average.

---

[1] National Crime Records Bureau, 'Crime in India: 2016 Statistics,' accessed 25 March 2019, http://ncrb.gov.in/StatPublications/CII/CII2016/pdfs/NEWPDFs/Crime%20in%20India%20-%202016%20Complete%20PDF%20291117.pdf.

[2] NCRB, 'Crime in India: 2016 Statistics.'

Again low satisfaction was experienced by the respondents with regard to quality of food. A high percentage called it average (47 per cent), 38.1 per cent reported below average, and 10.7 deemed it poor and deplorable. Only 4.3 per cent stated the quality of food was good. Also, it was found that in all the homes, three meals per day per inmate were provided, as opposed to the mandated four.

All inmates had to follow a routine, however where they did not attend vocational training or formal education, the routine tended to revolve around the meal timings.

Medical Needs

A majority of juveniles (91.4 per cent) stated that no medical check-ups were done on a monthly basis. All respondents stated that first-aid kits were available in the homes for immediate treatment of minor wounds and ailments.

Awareness about Children's Committee

There was no children committee in homes (43 per cent) in a majority of instances. Only 24.5 per cent respondents were aware of a children's committee in their home, while 32.5 per cent were unaware. Of the aware respondents, 64.9 per cent stated that the committee received no cooperation from the staff, and 35.1 per cent stated committees did.

Other Needs

Recreational facilities in one form or another were present in every observation and special home. In an overwhelming majority of cases (98.3 per cent), irrespective of their nature of offence, no leave/parole was granted to the juveniles. None of the respondents were aware of the existence of a suggestion box within the premises of the homes through which they could give infrastructure, recreation, vocation or education-related suggestions to the authorities. All interviewees were allowed to meet their family/parents on designated days as per the rules of the juvenile homes.

Staffing

About 44 per cent (highest) juveniles found the quality and quantity of staff within the home to be average; 33.4 per cent stated quality and quantity were below average, while 12.9 per cent replied it was poor. Only 9.6 per cent respondents stated that quality was good. In 57 per cent cases, a house mother or house father were present, while in the rest, the positions were vacant.

A cross-tabulation of the age of inmates and the type of home they were lodged (Annexure III, Table 7.2) indicated that the maximum percentage of those 17 years and below were in observation homes, but the maximum 18-year-olds and above were in special homes (56.2 per cent). All children aged 11–13 years were in observation homes irrespective of the nature of offence, as were 98.3 per cent of 14–15-year-olds. Among the respondents lodged in special homes, the maximum percentage were 18 years and above (68.5 per cent), while the maximum percentage of juveniles in observation homes were in the 16–17 age group (52.8 per cent). Thus, more children between 11 and 17 years were lodged in observation homes, and more interviewees 18 years and above were in special homes.

Analysing data on the nature of offence and the type of home they were housed in (Annexure III, Table 7.3) suggested that the maximum percentage of respondents, irrespective of the nature of offence, were in observation homes—97.4 per cent petty offenders, 76.2 per cent serious offenders, and 72.4 per cent of heinous offenders. There was a decline in the percentage of respondents lodged in observation homes, with the seriousness of the offence.

Cross-tabulating data on state and the type of home the juvenile was sent to (Annexure III, Table 7.4) indicated that the maximum percentage of respondents across all states were in observation homes—75.8 per cent in Delhi, 72.3 per cent in Haryana and 79 per cent in Punjab. Clearly, more respondents in each state were in observation homes compared to special homes. Among respondents in special homes, Haryana had the highest percentage (42.5 per cent), followed by Punjab (35.6 per cent) and Delhi (21.9 per cent). Of those lodged in observation homes, the maximum percentage were in Punjab (42.8 per cent) then Haryana (35.4 per cent), and Delhi (21.8 per cent).

An analysis of information on the state of the juvenile and the prima facie likeability of the environment inside the home (Annexure III, Table 7.5) indicated that in all the states, the maximum respondents liked the environment—72.7 per cent in Delhi, 61.6 per cent in Haryana and 71.8 per cent in Punjab. Among those who liked the environment, Punjab had the maximum percentage of respondents (43.2 per cent), while among those who disliked the environment, Haryana had maximum respondents (44.8 per cent). However, based on data on states and segregation of residential facilities on the basis of age inside the home (Annexure III, Table 7.6) it's clear that in no state was any age-centric segregation done.

A cross-tabulation of states and the requirement of better infrastructure inside the home as perceived by the juvenile (Annexure III, Table 7.7) showed that in all the states, the percentage of respondents stating such requirement was far higher than those who said there was no such requirement—86.4 per cent in Delhi, 98.2 per cent in Haryana, and 99.2 per cent in Punjab. Of those respondents stating there was a requirement, the percentage of respondents from Delhi was minimum (19.7 per cent) whereas the percentage in Punjab (42.4 per cent) was the highest; Haryana clocked in 37.9 per cent such respondents. Overall, urgent requirement for better infrastructure was found in all the states.

Cross-tabulating data on states and the quality of pest/insect control inside the home (Annexure III, Table 7.8). showed that maximum percentage of respondents in all states thought quality was below average—71.2 per cent in Delhi, 54.5 per cent in Haryana, and 55.6 per cent in Punjab. The percentage of interviewees who stated quality to be good was just 1.5 per cent in Delhi, 0 in Haryana and 4 per cent in Punjab. Among those who stated below average, the maximum percentage was from Punjab (39 per cent), while those who said quality was good, again, 83.3 per cent were from Punjab. Among those who said quality was poor, the maximum were from Delhi (53.8 per cent). A comparative analysis suggested that Delhi had the highest percentage of respondents who said quality was poor or below average (81.8 per cent), followed by Punjab (58.1 per cent) and Haryana (57.1 per cent).

An analysis of data on state and quality of clothing/bedding provided in the home (Annexure III, Table 7.9) suggested that the maximum percentage of respondents in all three states found quality of bedding average; Haryana accounted for 85.7 per cent of the respondents, Punjab, 84.7 per cent, and Delhi 62.1 per cent. None of the respondents from Delhi and Haryana said that quality was good, while 2.4 per cent respondents from Punjab did. About 37.9 per cent of respondents in Delhi, 14.3 per cent in Haryana and 12.9 per cent in Punjab said that quality was poor or below average.

A cross-tabulation of state and the quality of water for drinking and sanitation inside the home (Annexure III, Table 7.10) suggested that maximum respondents in each state found the quality average, with 56.1 per cent from Delhi, 78.6 per cent from Haryana and 91.9 per cent from Punjab. Very few respondents mentioned that quality was good—4.5 per cent in Delhi, 0 in Haryana and 4.8 per cent in Punjab. In Delhi, 39.4 per cent respondents stated quality was below average; in Haryana, 21.4 per cent stated it was poor or below average, and in Punjab, 3.2 did. Thus, most respondents deemed the quality of water average, with few stating it was good.

Cross-tabulating state and the quality and quantity of bathrooms provided within the home (Annexure III, Table 7.11) indicated that maximum percentage of respondents in each state found the quality below average—that's 60.6 per cent in Delhi, 49.1 per cent in Haryana and 47.6 per cent in Punjab. None of the respondents from Delhi and Haryana stated that quality was good while 4.8 per cent respondents from Punjab found quality good. Of those stating that the quality was below average, the maximum percentage of respondents were from Punjab (38.3 per cent). However, none of the respondents from Punjab stated quality to be poor, with 86.2 per cent of such respondents from Haryana.

An analysis of data on states and the quality of kitchens in terms of hygiene (Annexure III, Table 7.12) suggested that maximum respondents in all three states found quality average, with 68.2 per cent respondents in Delhi, 75.9 per cent in Haryana and 61.3 per cent in Punjab. However, one can observe that compared to the other crosstabs, a higher number of respondents in this analysis found quality to be good. Thus, the quality of the kitchen in terms of hygiene was better than other services.

A comparative examination of the states showed that Punjab had the maximum percentage of respondents who stated that kitchen hygiene was good (38.7 per cent) compared to Haryana (24.7 per cent) and Delhi (21.3 per cent). Only 2.3 per cent of the total respondents stated that the quality was below average.

Cross-tabulates between the state and quality of kitchen in terms of meals (Annexure III, Table 7.13) suggested that the maximum respondents in Delhi (53 per cent) and Haryana (49.1 per cent) found quality below average, whereas the maximum percentage of respondents in Punjab (68.5 per cent) stated that the quality was average. Few respondents (3 per cent) in Delhi and none in Haryana stated that quality was good, whereas 8.9 per cent respondents in Punjab stated so. Thus, in Delhi and Haryana, more respondents suggested that quality was below average whereas in Punjab, more respondents found quality to be average. Again, more respondents in Delhi (7.6 per cent) and Haryana (21.4 per cent) than Punjab (2.4 per cent) suggested that meal quality was poor. Comparatively, it appears the situation was better in Punjab with regard to meals than other states.

Analysing state and the existence of and/or awareness about children's committee (Annexure III, Table 7.14) data showed that 56.1 per cent respondents in Delhi and 49.2 per cent in Punjab were unaware. Of those who were aware, 60.8 per cent were from Punjab and 39.2 per cent from Delhi, with Haryana having none. No observation or special home in Haryana had any children's committee.

A cross-tabulation of state and the extension of cooperation from the staff to the children's committee (Annexure III, Table 7.15) suggested that in Delhi (58.6 per cent) and Punjab (68.9 per cent) maximum respondents stated the committee did not receive any cooperation from staff. Among respondents who mentioned that committees received cooperation, more respondents were from Punjab (53.8 per cent). This data is tabulated only for those who said they were aware of the children committee, that is 74 respondents in total.

Cross-tabulating data on state and the requirement to follow a routine within the home (Annexure III, Table 7.16) demonstrated that in all observation and special homes across Delhi, Haryana and Punjab, children were required to follow a routine. Then, an analysis of details on states and the frequency of monthly medical check-ups as reported by juveniles (Annexure III, Table 7.18) suggested that maximum respondents across all states did not get regular monthly check-ups. That includes all in Punjab, 99.1 per cent in Haryana and 62.1 per cent in Delhi. Of those who said there weren't regular check-ups, Punjab had the maximum percentage of respondents (44.9 per cent) followed by Haryana (40.2 per cent) and Delhi (14.9 per cent). In fact, Delhi had the maximum percentage of respondents who said there were routine medical check-ups (37.9 per cent). Furthermore, analysing information on states and the availability of first-aid kits within the home (Annexure III, Table 7.19) showed that in all homes across Delhi, Haryana and Punjab, first-aid kits were present in the homes to tackle any medical emergencies or minor medical needs of the juveniles.

A cross-tabulation of data on state and the availability of recreational facilities inside the home (Annexure III, Table 7.20) showed that all juveniles were exposed to recreational facilities in one form or another.

Then, an analysis of details on state and the grant of leave/parole to juveniles (Annexure III, Table 7.21) suggested that the maximum percentage of respondents across all three states did not receive such grants—0 in Haryana, 99.2 per cent in Punjab and 93.9 per cent interviewees in Delhi did not receive leave/parole. Of these, Punjab had the maximum respondents (41.4 per cent) followed by Haryana (37.7 per cent) and Delhi (20.9 per cent). Only 6.1 per cent of respondents from Delhi received leave/parole with none from Haryana and only one respondent from Punjab. Overall, the situation regarding the grant of leave/parole across all the states was grim.

A cross-tabulation of state and availability of suggestion box within the homes (Annexure III, Table 7.22) showed that in all homes across all states, juveniles were unaware of the existence of any suggestion box within the premises of the home. Analysing data on state and the permission to meet family/parents (Annexure III, Table 7.23) showed that respondents across all states were allowed to meet family/parents on designated days.

Tabulating information on state and quality/quantity of staff inside the homes (Annexure III, Table 7.24) suggested that in Delhi and Haryana, maximum respondents thought quantity/quality to be below average—51.5 per cent and 41.1 per cent respectively. In Punjab, the maximum percentage of respondents suggested that quantity/quality of staff was average (57.3 per cent). Of those who suggested that staffing was poor, Haryana had maximum respondents (59 per cent) followed by Delhi (23.1 per cent) then Punjab (17.9 per cent). In comparative analysis of those who suggested that staffing was poor or below average, Delhi showed 65.2 per cent respondents, Haryana, 61.6 per cent, and Punjab, 22.6 per cent. Thus, Punjab fared better than other states in this comparison. Of those who suggested that staff was good, 86.2 per cent were from Punjab, 10.3 per cent from Delhi and 3.4 per cent from Haryana.

A cross-tabulation of state and the presence of house father/house mother within the home (Annexure III, Table 7.25) demonstrated that while all respondents in Delhi said they were present, all respondents in Haryana mentioned that house father/house mother were absent. In Punjab, 85.5 per cent respondents mentioned that the house mother and house father were present.

Based on these findings, it's clear that there is scope for improvement in juvenile services in terms of quality of pest control, clothing, water, kitchen, food, monthly medical check-ups and staff. Also, segregation of inmates based on age needs to be done. Infrastructure is to be better as well.

Chapter VIII

Juvenile: Post-Release Prospects

The successful re-entry of the juvenile into the mainstream society after his stay at the juvenile home depends largely upon the success of the reformation techniques and programmes in the home. In this chapter, the researchers have sought to examine and analyse the impact and implementation of such programmes.

Data was collected on plans the inmate had post-release, vocational training and education, therapy and utility of the therapy, and attitude of the staff in provision of these services. The findings of the researchers have been tabulated below.

Table 8.1: Information Regarding Post-Release Plan

Title	*Category*	*Frequency*	*Percentage*
Inmate's plan	Continue schooling	142	47
	Continue previous job	56	18.5
	Find new job	63	20.9
	Don't know	41	13.6
Awareness about institute's post-release plan/ institute care plan	No	302	100

Title	*Category*	*Frequency*	*Percentage*
Awareness about date of release/ appearance	Yes	273	90.4
	No	29	9.6
Provision of vocational training	Yes	50	16.6
	No	42	13.9
	No provision	210	69.5
Need for other options in vocational training	Agree	24	7.9
	Indifferent	19	6.3
	Disagree	8	2.6
	Missing	251	81.3
Vocational training as a post-release aid	Agree	17	5.6
	Neutral	12	4
	Disagree	21	7
	Strongly disagree	1	0.3
	Missing	251	83.1
Attitude/performance of trainers/educators/ teachers	Caring	1	0.3
	Helpful	119	39.4
	Indifferent	142	47
	Incompetent	37	12.3
	Missing	3	1
Attendance of formal education	Yes	162	53.6
	No	140	46.4

Title	*Category*	*Frequency*	*Percentage*
Encouragement in engaging in voluntary service/open school	Yes	3	1
	No	299	99
Attendance of therapy sessions	Yes	34	11.3
	No	215	71.2
	Once	53	17.5
Type of therapy	Individual	51	16.9
	Group	34	11.3
	Both	2	0.7
	Missing	215	71.2
Utility of therapy sessions	Yes	16	5.3
	To some extent	26	8.6
	No	45	14.9
	Missing	215	71.2
Use of positive reinforcement	Yes	167	55.3
	No	49	16.2
	Unaware	86	28.5
Attitude and performance of the counsellor	Poor	1	0.3
	Below average	23	7.6
	Average	49	16.2
	Good	14	4.6
	Missing	215	71.2

The inmates were asked about their personal plans post their release. The highest percentage intended to pursue and complete their education (47 per cent), followed by those who wanted to look for a new job (20.9 per cent), and those who wanted to continue in their previous job

(18.5 per cent). About 13.6 per cent of respondents did not know what to do. Thus, there is a need for rehabilitation services for juveniles. They can be provided appropriate opportunities post-release; those who did not have any idea of what to do can be provided with career counselling. The career counsellor can also provide information on potential courses juveniles could take while staying in the centre, as well as recommend organisations the inmates can connect with post-release.

When asked about a juvenile's awareness of the institution's post-release plan/individual care plan, all respondents unanimously answered that they were unaware of any such plan being drawn up for them. Clearly, there is a need to sensitise staff on existing laws and rules that are to be followed. They should be trained in making plans with juveniles, and factor in available resources, educational backgrounds, skills, etc. Initiative should be taken to put such plans in place with the juveniles.

Data on awareness of the juveniles with regard to their date of release and/or next appearance before the Juvenile Justice Board suggested that in 90.4 per cent cases, juveniles were aware, but in 9.6 per cent cases, they weren't. However, in several instances, even when the juveniles were aware of such dates of appearance, lack of manpower in the police force/among staff to accompany them to the hearing rendered the knowledge futile.

According to data on the frequency of provision and attendance of vocational training within the home, in a large majority of cases (69.5 per cent), there was no provision. Of the 30.5 per cent cases where such training was available, only 16.6 per cent of inmates attended it, while 13.9 per cent did not attend any vocational training. The data suggests that the percentage of cases where vocational training was not available was quite high and this needs to be looked into. Vocational training should be provided at all facilities for better rehabilitation of the juvenile. Also, inmates are to be encouraged to attend such training and be monitored in terms of their attendance and performance.

The respondents were questioned about whether there was a need for other options in vocational training; 7.9 per cent said there was, 6.3 per cent were indifferent and 2.6 per cent disagreed. A large percentage of data (83.1 per cent) was missing, thus affecting the analysis for this variable.

Data on efficacy of the vocational training programme as a post-release aid pointed at 5.6 per cent respondents who found it helpful, 4 per cent were neutral and 7 per cent did not agree. Again, a large percentage of data was missing (83.1 per cent), thus affecting the analysis for this variable as well.

Based on data on respondents' view of the performance of trainers/teachers/educators, the maximum percentage of respondents (47 per cent) found their attitude towards the children to be indifferent. Around 39.4 per cent of juveniles found the trainers to be helpful, 12.3 per cent stated the trainers were incompetent and a very low percentage of respondents (0.3 per cent) found them to be caring. Only 1 per cent of the sample did not respond to the query. The data indicates the need to improve the performance of trainers and encourage them to be caring and more helpful towards the juveniles.

It was found that the majority of the inmates (53.6 per cent) were continuing their formal education while in the institution, whereas 46.4 per cent were not following any formal education courses. Inmates could be linked with open schools and provided with a variety of courses that could help develop skills and keep them engaged.

Only 1 per cent children received any encouragement to engage in voluntary service/open schools, while the remaining didn't. This indicates a need to train staff to be sensitive to the needs of juveniles and who would encourage them to engage in activities that would build their future.

The attendance of therapy sessions by juveniles was limited. Few respondents (11.3 per cent) were in attendance on a regular basis, while the majority (71.2 per cent) did not attend therapy at all. About 17.5 per cent of juveniles had only attended one session during their stay in the home. It is not just attendance that matters, but also the quality and effectiveness of the therapy. The right handling of juveniles is important, and therapy should help them become better at adapting and coping in the institution, and once they are released. The regularity of attending therapy is also significant as one may require more than one session, and ongoing support to overcome the barriers and troubles he or she may be facing.

Three types of therapy sessions existed for juveniles—individual, group or both. About 16.9 per cent of respondents attended individual sessions, 11.3 per cent group sessions and 0.7 per cent attended both. Very few attended both types of sessions, whereas more respondents attended individual sessions. It is necessary to reiterate here that 71.2 per cent of juveniles did not attend any therapy.

The data on the usefulness of therapy sessions, that is, whether the juveniles found them helpful or not, showed that only 5.3 per cent (lowest) of juveniles felt the sessions were helpful, while 8.6 per cent felt that they were helpful to some extent. Around 14.9 per cent felt they were not helpful. This data indicates the need to improve the quality of therapy sessions. However, one also needs to maintain the therapist-patient ratio, where the therapist is not overburdened with cases.

Where the use of positive reinforcement to inculcate and encourage good behaviour among juveniles goes, the maximum percentage of respondents (55.3 per cent) stated that positive reinforcement was used by the staff. A lower percentage suggested it was not (16.2 per cent) the case. Around 28.5 per cent of the respondents were unaware.

Data on the views of respondents on the attitude and performance of counsellors suggested that around 16.2 per cent found it average and 7.6 per cent, below average. But 4.6 per cent respondents mentioned it was good. One respondent mentioned that the attitude and performance of counsellors were poor. It is to be noted that 71.2 per cent of the respondents did not attend any therapy sessions.

A cross-tabulation of the preoccupation of juveniles prior to institutionalisation and the attendance of formal education within the home (Annexure III, Table 8.2) showed that of those who were studying prior to coming to the institution, a higher percentage (64.1 per cent) were attending formal training than those who weren't (35.9 per cent). In case of the gainfully employed, before coming to the home, the respondents attending formal education were less than those not attending, that is 56.4 per cent of those who were employed were not attending formal education. In case of those who were doing neither, more respondents were not attending formal education, that is 52.7 per cent. Comparative analysis suggests that more students who studied before were attending formal education, than those who had studied before but were not attending formal education. However, this trend was not observed for those who were working or doing neither before coming to the institution. Of the respondents attending formal education, the maximum percentage was of those who had studied (51.9 per cent), followed by those who were doing neither (27.2 per cent), and then those who were previously employed (21 per cent).

Cross-tabulating the nature of offence and attendance of therapy sessions (Annexure III, Table 8.3) indicated that for all the offences, the maximum percentage of juveniles did not attend therapy. Thus, in the case of petty offences, 65.8 per cent did not attend therapy, and in the case of serious and heinous offences, 71.4 per cent and 72 per cent of respondents respectively did not attend therapy at all. In fact, therapy sessions were not being attended at all by most juveniles (71.2 per cent). Of the respondents attending therapy regularly, the maximum percentage were those who had committed heinous offences (70.6 per cent); also, 18.1 per cent of respondents who had committed heinous offences had received therapy once.

A cross-tabulation between the state and the inmates' plan post-release (Annexure III, Table 8.4) indicated that in all the states, the maximum percentage of respondents wanted to continue their schooling—37.9 per cent (Delhi), 60.7 per cent (Haryana) and 39.5 per cent (Punjab). Of those who wanted to continue studying, the maximum percentage were from Haryana (47.6 per cent). Among those who wanted to find a new job, the maximum percentage were from Punjab (55.6 per cent), while of those who wanted to continue their previous jobs, the maximum percentage were also from Punjab (51.8 per cent). It is worthy to note that a cross-tabulation between the states and awareness of institutes' individual care plan/post-release plan (Annexure III, Table 8.5) suggested that none of the inmates were aware of any such plans drawn up by the administration on their behalf and for them.

Cross-tabulating data on states and the juvenile's awareness about his date of release and/or next hearing (Annexure III, Table 8.6) indicated that the maximum percentage of the respondents in all states were duly aware; 98.5 per cent in Delhi, 99.1 per cent in Haryana and 78.2 per cent in Punjab. Among those who were aware, Haryana had the maximum percentage of respondents (40.7 per cent), followed by Punjab (35.5 per cent) and Delhi (23.8 per cent). Punjab had the highest percentage of unaware respondents.

An analysis of data on states and the provision of vocational training in the homes (Annexure III, Table 8.7) suggested that in Haryana and Punjab, more respondents mentioned there was no provision. For example, in Haryana, 100 per cent respondents said there was no provision, while in

Punjab, 79 per cent respondents said the same. No respondent from Delhi suggested lack of provision, and 60.6 per cent of respondents in the state attended training. Of those who said there was vocational training and attended it, 80 per cent were from Delhi and 20 per cent from Punjab; none were from Haryana. For Delhi, all respondents mentioned provision of training, and for Haryana, all respondents mentioned no provision. Of all those who suggested no provision of training, 53.5 per cent were from Haryana and 46.7 per cent from Punjab.

A cross-tabulation of states with the performance and attitude of trainers/teachers (Annexure III, Table 8.8) indicated that in Delhi, the maximum percentage of respondents suggested the trainers were helpful (68.3 per cent). In Haryana and Punjab, the maximum percentage of respondents suggested they were indifferent (50 per cent and 54.8 per cent respectively). Of those who said the trainers were helpful, the maximum percentage (38.7 per cent) were from Punjab, 36.1 per cent were from Delhi and the least were from Haryana (25.2 per cent). Of those who suggested the trainers were indifferent, the maximum percentage were from Punjab (47.9 per cent), 39.4 per cent from Haryana and 12.7 per cent from Delhi. Comparative analysis indicated that more respondents in Delhi said the trainers were helpful than in other states.

Analysing data on states and the attendance of formal education in the home (Annexure III, Table 8.9) suggested that a higher percentage of respondents in Delhi (65.2 per cent) and Haryana (54.5 per cent) were attending formal education than not. However, in Punjab this was not the trend—53.2 per cent of respondents did not attend formal education as compared to 46.8 per cent who did. Of those who attended formal education, the maximum percentage were in Haryana (37.7 per cent), then in Punjab (35.8 per cent) and lastly, Delhi (26.5 per cent).

A cross-tabulation between states and the encouragement of children to engage in voluntary services and open schooling (Annexure III, Table 8.10) indicated that most respondents in Delhi (95.5 per cent) and all respondents in Punjab and Haryana had experienced no such encouragement. Only 1 per cent of the total respondents said there was such encouragement.

Then, cross-tabulating data on states and regularity in and attendance of therapy sessions (Annexure III, Table 8.11) indicated that for Delhi, the maximum percentage were attending sessions regularly (47 per cent) whereas in Haryana and Punjab, the majority (88.4 per cent and 78.2 per cent respectively) were not. Of those attending regularly, the maximum percentage were from Delhi (91.2 per cent). Among those who had attended once, the majority were from Punjab (47.2 per cent). Of those who did not attend any sessions, the majority were from Haryana (46 per cent), and a slightly less percentage (45.1 per cent) were from Punjab.

An analysis of data on states and types of therapy sessions (Annexure III, Table 8.12) suggested that the maximum percentage of those who responded in Delhi had group sessions (59.6 per cent). In Haryana and Punjab, the maximum percentage of respondents had individual sessions (84.6 per cent and 85.2 per cent respectively). Again, this data only includes those respondents who had attended sessions.

A cross-tabulation of details on states and the utility and efficacy of therapy sessions as perceived by the juveniles (Annexure III, Table 8.13) indicated that the maximum percentage of respondents across the states found no usefulness—44.7 per cent from Delhi, 61.5 per cent from Haryana and 59.3 per cent from Punjab. None of the respondents who responded to this question from Haryana said that there any use at all.

Cross-tabulating states with the attitude and performance of counsellor/therapist as perceived by juveniles (Annexure III, Table 8.14) indicated that of the total respondents, in each state, the maximum percentage of children said that the attitude and performance of counsellors were average (53.2 per cent in Delhi, 76.9 per cent in Haryana and 51.9 per cent in Punjab). This was followed by a below average response for Delhi (31.9 per cent) and Haryana (23.1 per cent), and a good response for Punjab (29.6 per cent).

A cross-tabulation between addiction to intoxicants among juveniles and their attendance of therapy sessions (Annexure III, Table 8.15) indicated that the higher percentage of addicts and non-addicts (except those addicted to cannabinoids) did not attend any sessions. That is, 70.8 per cent of non-addicts, 52.2 per cent of narcotic addicts, 87.5 per cent alcoholics, and 90.9 per cent of tobacco addicts were not attending the sessions. This percentage was more than those in attendance or those who had attended once. However, in the case of cannabinoid addicts 57.1 per cent had attended the session once; this percentage was higher than those who had not, or those who had attended the sessions. Among those who attended the sessions, the maximum percentage of attendees were non-addicts (85.3 per cent). Among those who had not attended, the maximum percentage was also non-addicts (74.4 per cent). Thus, there is need for more therapy sessions for both addicts and non-addicts, including ongoing sessions. For addicts, support for quitting their addictions is required.

Cross-tabulating the sociability of juveniles and the regularity in and attendance of therapy sessions by (Annexure III, Table 8.16) indicated that irrespective of the ability to socialise, the maximum percentage of respondents were non-attendees. Thus, 64.2 per cent of the sociable and 79.6 per cent of the unsociable were non-attendees. In total, 71.2 per cent of the respondents did not attend any sessions. Of those who did, the maximum percentage were those who were sociable (70.6 per cent). Of those who attended once, the maximum percentage were sociable (66 per cent).

An analysis of data on the type of home and regularity in and attendance of therapy sessions (Annexure III, Table 8.17) indicated that in both special and observation homes, the maximum percentage of respondents did not attend any sessions. This includes 74.7per cent respondents in observation homes and 60.3 per cent in special homes. The trend indicated that maximum percentage of respondents, irrespective of homes, did not attend therapy. Of those who did attend regularly, and who attended once 82.4 per cent and 56.6 per cent were in observation homes. However, of those who did not attend the sessions, the maximum percentage were in observation homes as well (79.5 per cent). The percentage of respondents receiving therapy in both types of homes was less, that is, 8.2 per cent (special homes) and 12.2 per cent (observation homes).

A cross-tabulation of age of inmates and their attendance of therapy sessions (Annexure III, Table 8.18) indicated that irrespective of age, the maximum percentage of respondents did not attend—90 per cent of 11–13-year-olds, 53.3 per cent of 14–15-year-olds, 74.1 per cent of 16–17-year-olds, and 76.4 per cent of those 18 years and above. Of the respondents attending the sessions, the maximum percentage were 14–15 years old and 16–17 years old (44.1 per cent each). Of those attending regularly, only 2.9 per cent were 11–13 years old, while of those who attended the sessions once, the maximum were in the age group of 16–17 years (41.5 per cent).

Analysing data on the type of home and provision of vocational training (Annexure III, Table 8.19) indicated that the maximum percentage of respondents in either home did not have any provision, that is, respondents in special homes (42.5 per cent) and those in observation homes (78.2 per cent) did not have any vocational training provisions. Comparatively, a higher percentage of respondents from observation homes did not have any provision of training (13.1 per cent) compared to 27.4 per cent respondents in special homes. From this, one may infer that the provision of training in special homes was more prevalent compared to in observation homes.

Cross-tabulating age of juveniles with the provision of vocational training (Annexure III, Table 8.20) indicated that irrespective of age, the maximum respondents fell in the category of 'no provision'. Of these, the highest percentage belonged to 16–17 category (53.3 per cent), followed by 18 years and above (29.5 per cent). Of those who did attend training, the highest percentage of respondents were 16–17 years old (50 per cent). Of those who did not attend, the highest percentage of respondents were from the 14–15 age group, and the 18-and-plus category (42.9 per cent each).

From this data one may conclude that there is a need to sensitise staff in encouraging and helping the juveniles; improve vocational training and educational facilities; and improve the regularity of therapy sessions. Also, these sessions need to be made more effective and useful to the juveniles.

Chapter IX
Major Findings

Juvenile: Pre-Institutionalisation

This section presents the researchers' major findings with respect to demographics and other details of inmates prior to their institutionalisation. The findings have been arranged according to the variables for ease of understanding, and can be used to develop an intervention programmes or strategies for juvenile delinquents. Various factors were studied, from demographics and family backgrounds to the quality of service provided by the institutes. The research also explored aspects of vocational training and treatment provided to juveniles, as well as their interaction with the justice system.

Age of the Juveniles

A large majority of inmates (76.8 per cent) were aged 16 years and above; 3.3 per cent fell within the age bracket of 11–13 years, 19.9 per cent were aged 14–15 years, a significant 47.4 per cent were 16–17 years old, and 29.5 per cent were 18 and above. This is somewhat similar to the NCRB 2016[1] data, where the majority of juveniles were in the age group of 16–18 years (73.8 per cent). According to L. Stolzenberg and

[1] National Crime Records Bureau, 'Crime in India 2016 Statistics,' accessed 24 March 2019, http://ncrb.gov.in/StatPublications/CII/CII2016/pdfs/NEWPDFs/Crime%20in%20India%20-%202016%20Complete%20PDF%20291117.pdf.

S.J. Alessio,[2] previous research has shown the relationship between age and crime to be curvilinear. That is, crime increases during adolescence, is maximum during early adulthood and falls from there. The data for this study somewhat supports the hypothesis, with the maximum percentage of respondents aged 16 years and above, but declining in the group 18 years old and above. Crime maximising during early adulthood is not seen in our sample of inmates who're 18 years old and above.

State of the Juveniles

A majority of interviewees were from Punjab (41.4 per cent); 37.1 per cent were from Haryana, and 21.9 per cent were from homes in Delhi.

Level of Education

There are several studies connecting crime and education, where crime is linked to school attendance, school achievements and other factors.[3] In his article, J.S. Vacca found that a ninth-grade-level juvenile delinquent studies at the fourth-grade level. Mercer Sullivan[4] discussed that juvenile delinquents who, after confinement, return to education, may face difficulty in terms of stigmatisation, previous disciplinary problems with the school and falling behind in their education.

In this study, a simple majority of the inmates (27.5 per cent) were educated until middle school, that is between sixth and ninth grades, while only 1.7 per cent had graduated college. About 22.2 per cent were educated only up to fifth grade, 21.9 per cent had completed their matriculation, and 7.3 per cent had completed their senior secondary schooling. The NCRB (2016)[5] data showed that 45.3 per cent juveniles in conflict with law had education between the primary and matriculation levels—the maximum percentage for the categories. According to this

---

[2] L. Stolzenberg and S.J. D'Alessio, 'Co-Offending and the Age-Crime Curve,' *Journal of Research in Crime and Delinquency*, Vol. 45, no. 1 (2008): 65–86.

[3] J.S. Vacca, 'Crime Can be Prevented if Schools Teach Juvenile Offenders to Read,' *Children and Youth Services Review*, Vol. 30 (2008): 1055–106.

[4] Mercer L. Sullivan, 'Youth Perspectives on the Experience of Reentry,' *Youth Violence and Juvenile Justice*, Vol. 2 (2004): 56–71.

[5] NCRB, 'Crime in India 2016 Statistics.'

study, the maximum percentage (27.5 per cent) of interviewees fell in the middle school category.

A bulk (44.1 per cent) of the illiterate were 16–17 years old, while all the graduates and a majority (68.2 per cent) of those who completed schooling were over 18 years. About 40 per cent of 11–13-year-old inmates were illiterate, as were 31.3 per cent of the 14–15 year-olds. It was observed that 80.5 per cent respondents had some form of education, while around 19.5 per cent were completely illiterate. NCRB (2016)[6] data indicated that 12.3 per cent of the juveniles in conflict with law were illiterate.

About 57.6 per cent (highest) and 63.6 per cent (highest) of inmates who had completed their matriculation and schooling respectively were from Haryana. A majority of the illiterate (55.9 per cent) and 43.3 per cent of those educated only up to the primary level were from Punjab. Meanwhile, 60 per cent of the graduates were from Delhi and the rest from Haryana. NCRB (2016) data indicated that 65.5 per cent of literate juveniles in conflict with law were from Haryana, 84.1 per cent from Punjab and 73.5 per cent from Delhi.[7]

Providers for Inmates

For a vast majority of juveniles (75.8 per cent), the father was the primary income earner, while in 8.9 per cent of the cases the juvenile fended for himself. About 7.9 per cent and 5.3 per cent inmates had mothers and brothers respectively responsible for family income, while in 2 per cent cases, other family members such as uncles and grandparents provided for the juvenile.

In 46.7 per cent cases, the provider for the juvenile was engaged in skill labour as a factory worker, carpenter, car mechanic, farmer, plumber, etc, while in 29.8 per cent cases the provider was a daily wage labourer. About 9.9 per cent providers were engaged in commercial activities such as running mom-and-pop shops, vegetable and fruit vending, etc., while 7.3 per cent interviewees didn't specify the occupation of the primary breadwinners. This data sheds light on the socioeconomic demographic

[6] NCRB, 'Crime in India 2016 Statistics.'

[7] NCRB, 'Crime in India 2016 Statistics.'

the majority of the inmates belonged to, given that the providers of only 6.3 per cent inmates were salaried workers forming part of the supposedly upward mobile middle class. Both high and low socioeconomic status have been found to be linked with delinquency.[8] Charles Tittle and Robert Meier,[9] in their analysis of previous empirical studies, found that SES and delinquency are linked, but didn't support that negative SES and delinquency is common and prevalent.

Nearly 14.4 per cent inmates who provided for themselves belonged to the 14–15 years age group; 48.1 per cent were 16–17 years and 37 per cent were 18 years and above.

In 54.1 per cent cases where the juvenile was providing for himself, he was engaged as a daily wage labourer, and 37 per cent were employed as skilled labourers. In a majority (37.5 per cent) of cases where the mother was the primary breadwinner, she was employed as a daily wage labourer, while in the majority of cases where the father or brother was the primary provider, they were skilled labourers (52.4 per cent and 50 per cent respectively).

Preoccupation of the Inmate

About 43.4 per cent (highest) of the juveniles were studying/schooling, while 25.8 per cent were employed for the purpose of remuneration, and 30.8 per cent were neither employed nor pursuing studies. Nearly 40 per cent of the 11–13 years group were employed for remuneration. While 43.4 per cent of 16–17-year-olds were studying, a staggering 32.9 per cent were neither studying nor employed; 40.4 per cent of those 18 years and above were studying, 31.5 per cent were employed and 28.1 per cent were neither employed nor studying.

About 34.8 per cent of the inmates interviewed from Delhi were studying prior to institutionalisation while 40.8 per cent were neither studying nor employed. The highest number (45.8 per cent) of all inmates pursuing schooling, as well as 30.8 per cent of employed inmates were

---

[8] Bradley R.E. Wright et al., 'Reconsidering the Relationship between SES and Delinquency: Causation But Not Correlation,' *Criminology,* Vol. 37 (1999): 175–94.

[9] Charles R. Tittle and Robert F. Meier, 'Specifying the SES-Delinquency Relationship,' *Criminology*, Vol. 28 (1990): 271–99.

from Haryana. In Punjab, a majority (48.7 per cent) of the inmates were employed while 36.6 per cent were pursuing their education.

Of the illiterate, 57.6 per cent were employed gainfully while 42.4 per cent were neither employed nor studying. About 6 per cent of those educated up to primary level were still studying, 44.8 per cent were employed in the service of others, and 49.3 per cent were neither studying nor employed. Of the inmates educated up till middle school, 51.8 per cent were still studying, 13.3 per cent were employed, and 34.9 per cent were doing neither. A massive 95.5 per cent of interviewees who had completed their matriculation were still studying, as were 72.2 per cent of senior secondary students and 100 per cent of the graduates.

Ability to Socialise

In their article for *Youth and Society* journal, R. Lotz and L. Lee[10] noted that lonely adolescents were less likely to be delinquent. More peer engagement can result in deviant activities especially during the adolescence when peer influence is dominant. They also said that adolescents are more likely to have delinquent peer influence.[11] In this study, a majority of juveniles (54.6 per cent) were social while the rest had difficulty in making friends easily.

Among the illiterate, 40.7 per cent did not have friends outside or inside the homes, while 59.3 per cent were found to be sociable. About 59.1 per cent of interviewees who had completed their schooling were asocial and only 40.9 per cent had friends inside and outside the home. Furthermore, 48.5 per cent and 43.3 per cent of those who had completed matriculation and middle school respectively were found to be asocial, while 60 per cent graduates had friends inside and outside the home.

This study revealed the connection between sociability and addiction, indicating that more respondents addicted to narcotics (56.5 per cent) and cannabinoids (57.1 per cent) were unsociable, as were 50 per cent of alcohol addicts. On the other hand, 55.8 per cent of non-addicts were

---

[10] R. Lotz and L. Lee, 'Sociability, School Experience, and Delinquency,' *Youth and Society*, Vol. 31 (1999): 199–223.

[11] Lotz and Lee, 'Sociability, School Experience.'

sociable. K.J. Sher and T.J. Trull[12] discussed that there were different models relating to antisocial personality disorder. Some demonstrated that personality traits resulted in an individual engaging in substance abuse or antisocial behaviour, whereas according to others, the personality was being affected by the disorder.

Addiction to Intoxicants

J.S. Vacca, in his study, pointed out that one of the characteristics of an average juvenile delinquent in correctional facilities was that in addition to other aspects—such as coming from a broken home—they were drug users.[13] Drug use, particularly marijuana, has been associated with self or parents' delinquent behaviour.[14]

More than quarter of the juveniles had developed an addiction to intoxicants, and nearly similar numbers were addicted to alcohol, narcotics and tobacco. Fewer respondents were addicted to cannabinoids. Almost 7.3 per cent juveniles were addicted to tobacco, 7.9 per cent to alcohol, 2.3 per cent to cannabinoids, and 7.6 per cent to narcotics. The majority (74.8 per cent) comprised of non-addicts.

Addiction was more rampant in Punjab than the other states per this study, and it had the maximum percentage of narcotic addicts (69.6 per cent), tobacco (59.1 per cent) and alcohol addicts (58.3 per cent). Delhi and Punjab had the maximum percentage of respondents addicted to cannabinoids. Overall, while 86.4 per cent inmates from Delhi and 81.3 per cent from Haryana reported not being addicted to any substance, the figure for Punjab stands at 62.9 per cent, indicating a more serious drug abuse problem and associated crimes.

Nearly 8.7 per cent of inmates addicted to narcotics were between 11 and 13 years; 42.9 per cent of regular cannabinoid users and 41.7 per cent of alcoholics belonged to the 16–17 age group. About 58.3 per cent of those addicted to alcohol were 18 years and above, while a vast majority

---

[12] K.J. Sher and T.J. Trull, 'Personality and Disinhibitory Psychopathology: Alcoholism and Antisocial Personality Disorder,' *Journal of Abnormal Psychology*, Vol. 103 (1994): 92–102.

[13] Vacca, 'Crime Can be Prevented.'

[14] K.N. Dietrich et al., 'Early Exposure to Lead and Juvenile Delinquency,' *Neurotoxicology and Teratology*, Vol. 23 (2001): 511–18.

(63.6 per cent) of nicotine and tobacco addicts were 16–17 years old. As per this study, the maximum percentage of respondents for all forms of addiction were 16 and above. Some form of addiction was present in the 11–13 age group (narcotics) as well as the 14–15 age group (tobacco, cannabinoids and narcotics).

The illiterate or primary educated constituted 40.9 per cent each (highest) of tobacco addicts, while of those addicted to narcotics, 56.5 per cent were illiterate and 26.1 per cent had been educated up to middle school. Among cannabinoid users, 28.6 per cent (each) were either illiterate or educated up till primary level; also, the same two groups made up 50 per cent of alcoholics. However, the percentage of non-addicts at each education level was greater than addicts, although among the illiterate and primary educated, the percentage of non-addicts was lesser compared to other education levels. Overall, the incidence of addiction was higher among those less educated or illiterate.

About 63.6 per cent tobacco addicts, 50 per cent alcohol addicts, 42.9 per cent cannabinoid users and 43.5 per cent narcotic addicts were sociable. Of the non-addicts, 55.8 per cent were sociable and the rest were asocial.

About 59.1 per cent of juveniles addicted to tobacco were employed, 40.9 per cent were neither employed nor studying, and none addicted to tobacco were studying. Among alcoholics, 45.8 per cent were studying, 25 per cent were employed, and 29.2 per cent were neither; among cannabinoid users, 57.1 per cent were employed and 28.6 per cent were studying. About 56.5 per cent of narcotic addicts were neither studying nor employed, 34.8 per cent were employed gainfully and only 8.7 per cent were students. This data indicated that the maximum percentage of addicted respondents were either studying or working, except in case of narcotic users who were doing neither. The study does not explore the performance of respondents while studying or being employed. Hence, we don't know the extent to which their work, study or scholastic achievements were possibly affected by addiction.

Observations

1) The majority of respondents were 16 years and above.
2) The majority of respondents were literate, though those with higher education were few.

3) The majority of respondents were dependent on their fathers.
4) The majority of providers were engaged in skilled or daily wage labour.
5) The majority of respondents were studying prior to joining the institute.
6) There was not much difference between the social and asocial.
7) More addicts were from Punjab.

Juvenile: In Conflict with the Law

Nature of Offence

About 12.6 per cent of the juveniles had been charged with petty offences, 7 per cent with serious offences, and an overwhelming majority (80.5 per cent) had been charged under sections that constituted heinous offences (per the definition under Act of 2015). Nearly 70 per cent and 63.3 per cent of inmates aged 11–13 years and 14–15 years respectively had been charged with offences deemed heinous by the Juvenile Justice (Care and Protection of Children) Act, 2015. Similarly, overwhelming majorities (83.2 per cent and 88.8 per cent respectively) of inmates aged 16–17 years and 18-plus were charged with heinous offences. Overall, 81.5 per cent of all inmates charged with heinous offences were liable to tried as adults under the provisions of the new Act.

Of those charged with petty offences, 7.9 per cent were 18 years and above, 47.4 per cent fell in the 16–17 age bracket, 36.8 per cent were 14–15 years old, and 7.9 per cent were 11–13 years old. A comparative analysis indicated that there was a decline in petty offences with increase in age—30 per cent (11–13 years), 23.3 per cent (14–15 years), 12.6 per cent (16–17 years) and 3.4 per cent (18 years and above).

About 91.6 per cent of those educated up to middle school, 92.4 per cent of those who had matriculated, 86.4 per cent of school pass-outs, and all graduates had been charged under sections covering heinous offences. Of those charged with serious and petty offences, 47.6 per cent and 44.7 per cent respectively were illiterate—the maximum percentage—while the most number of inmates charged with heinous offences were in middle school.

For petty (60.5 per cent) and heinous offences (55.1 per cent), the maximum percentage of the respondents were sociable, but in case of serious offences, more respondents were unsociable (61.9 per cent). Heinous offences formed 81.2 per cent of the offences sociable juveniles were charged with, while 61.5 per cent of all serious offences and 44.9 per cent of all heinous offences were committed by juveniles who weren't sociable.

About 72.7 per cent of tobacco addicts, 87.5 per cent of alcoholics, 57.1 per cent of cannabinoid addicts and 60.9 per cent of narcotic had been charged with heinous offences. Among the narcotic addicts, 26.1 per cent had been charged with petty offences and 28.6 per cent of those addicted to cannabinoids had been charged with serious offences. Addiction to narcotics was more prevalent in case of petty and serious offences, but in case of heinous offences, alcohol addiction was more prevalent.

Company at the Time of Commission of Offence

About 19.5 per cent juveniles were in the company of other juveniles at the time of the offence. In 33.1 per cent cases, the respondents were in the company of adults, whereas in 7.3 per cent cases they were in the company of other juveniles who committed the offence at the behest of adults. The majority of respondents (40.1 per cent) did not have any company and were alone while committing the offence irrespective of age group. A comparative analysis suggested that this percentage fell within the increasing age group. None of the 11–13-year-olds committed the offence at the command of others, but those aged 14 years and above were more vulnerable to commit crimes with adults and at the command of adults. Of those who committed offences at the behest of adults, 50 per cent and 36.4 per cent were 16–17 years and 18-plus respectively. In the 16–17 age group, 42.4 per cent were in the company of other juveniles and 50 per cent were with adults when committing the offence. Overall, only 7.3 per cent juveniles reported to have committed offences at the behest of adults.

In existing literature, delinquency is often concluded to occur with other peers. However, it is observed that with an increase in age, the strength of relationships with other delinquent peers reduces as does the offending.[15] In this study, the percentage of respondents aged 18 years and above who committed offences with other juveniles (32.2 per cent) was less than the respondents who were 16–17 years and offended with other juveniles (42.4 per cent). Thus, with age there was a slight decline in offending with other juveniles. Stolzenberg and Alessio, in their study, found that solo offending was more prevalent among juveniles of all age groups, which matches this study's findings.[16]

Recidivism

About 10.9 per cent inmates were recidivists, that is they had been charged and convicted for other offences earlier, while 89.1 per cent were first-time offenders. Nearly 84.8 per cent of all recidivists were 16 and above; 90 per cent of all non-recidivists belonged to the 11–13, 14–15 and 16–17 groups, each, and this number fell only marginally to 84.3 per cent for 18-year-olds and above. Among the recidivists, more respondents were 16–17 years old, and 18 years and above (42.4 per cent each), with its occurrence rising with age.

Among recidivists, 33.3 per cent were from Delhi, 30.3 per cent from Haryana and 36.4 per cent from Punjab. Overall, 83.3 per cent inmates from Delhi, 90.3 per cent from Punjab, and 91.1 per cent from Haryana were not recidivists. A comparative analysis of state-based data from the NCRB report[17] suggested that Delhi had the maximum percentage of recidivists.

About 33.3 per cent (highest) of all recidivists had been educated only up to middle school while none of the graduates were recidivists; 21.2 per cent were illiterate and 24.2 per cent had been educated only till the primary level. About 45.5 per cent had studied only up to the fifth grade or lower, while 78.8 per cent had middle school or lower levels of education.

A slight majority of recidivists (51.5 per cent) did not have any difficulty in making friends while the remaining 48.5 per cent weren't as sociable. Meanwhile, 55 per cent of all non-recidivists were found to be sociable.

---

[15] Stolzenberg and D'Alessio, 'Co-Offending.'

[16] Stolzenberg and D'Alessio, 'Co-Offending.'

[17] NCRB, 'Crime in India 2016 Statistics.'

R. Loeber and T. Dishion's 1983 study, as discussed by C.C. Cottle et al., pointed out that a child with a history of lying and stealing was a strong predictor of recidivism.[18] In their meta-analysis, Cottle et al. found that males, of low socioeconomic status, those who had committed crime at an early age, engaged in more serious offences, battling significant family problems, and with delinquent peers were at an increased risk of recidivism.[19]

Confinement in Police/Judicial Custody

A vast majority (66.2 per cent) of juveniles had been confined in police or judicial custody before being sent to a home. In only 33.8 per cent of cases did the inmates state that they were sent directly to the home. The researchers observed a direct relationship between two variables—an more common trend of confinement to custody with higher age. Fifty per cent of juveniles (lowest) aged 11–13 years reported being sent to judicial/police custody, while 58.3 per cent (aged 14–15 years) were sent to custody. The figures stand at 63.6 per cent for 16–17-year-olds, and 77.5 per cent for those 18 years old and above.

Where the inmates had been confined to police/judicial custody, they made their claims before the police in 70.5 per cent of the cases and before courts in 29.5 per cent of the cases. Juveniles were sent to judicial/police custody in 79.7 per cent instances where the claims were made before a judge, as compared to 61.8 per cent cases where claims were made before the police.

Across all education levels, the maximum percentage of respondents were sent to confinement. Those with middle school education were the highest (27.5 per cent); 20.5 per cent of those sent to confinement were illiterate, 23 per cent were primary educated, 9.5 per cent had completed their matriculation, and 2.5 per cent were graduates. Among those not remanded in custody, the highest numbers were from the secondary education group (31.4 per cent), followed by middle schoolers (27.5 per cent) and the illiterate (20.6 per cent).

---

[18] C.C. Cottle et al., 'The Prediction of Criminal Recidivism in Juveniles: A Meta-Analysis,' *Criminal Justice and Behaviour*, Vol. 17 (2001): 367–94.

[19] Cottle et al., 'The Prediction of Criminal Recidivism.'

Juveniles were sent to police/judicial custody 65.6 per cent of the time the family was present during proceedings, and 75 per cent of the time when family members were absent. In both cases, confinement was dominant.

Authority before Which Claim of Juvenility Was Made

In an overwhelming majority (75.5 per cent) of the cases, the claim for juvenility was made before the police, while only in 24.5 per cent instances was the claim made before the court.

Claims for juvenility before a judge was most prevalent in Punjab (29 per cent), followed by Delhi (24.2 per cent) and Haryana (19.6 per cent). For all the states, the claim for minority was made before police by the maximum number of respondents.

It was found that 81.1 per cent of the illiterate made their claims before the police, while 80 per cent of graduates made their claims before a judge. There is an observable direct relationship between the level of education and claims before a judge, that is the higher the level of education, the higher the number of claims made before a judge. About 20.9 per cent primary educated respondents, 24.1 per cent of middle schoolers, 24.2 per cent of those educated up to the tenth grade, and 40.9 per cent of senior secondary level respondents chose to make their claims of minority before the court instead of the police.

Behaviour of Police Officials

In 53 per cent of the cases, the attitude of the police towards the juveniles was hostile and the majority of them reported being subjected to torture. In 27.5 per cent of the cases, police officials were indifferent to the plight of the juvenile; only in 19.5 per cent of the cases were they supportive and kind to the juvenile.

Researchers found an inverse relationship between the age of inmates and a supportive attitude from the police. While 50 per cent juveniles aged 11–13 years reported that the police were supportive of them throughout their experience, only 20 per cent of 14–15-year-olds, 19.6 per cent of those aged 16–17 years, and 15.7 per cent of respondents who were 18 years and above reported the same attitude. Nearly 59.6

per cent of those aged 18 years and above, 43.1 per cent of 16–17-year-olds, 55 per cent of 14–15-year-olds and 50 per cent of those 11–13 years old reported abuse and torture by the police, and an overall attitude of hostility.

In all three states, the maximum percentage of respondents suggested the police were hostile, followed by indifferent and in the least, supportive. Of the supportive officers, the most were in Haryana (52.5 per cent), followed by Punjab (27.1 per cent) and then Delhi (20.3 per cent). Nearly 60.6 per cent of Delhi's inmates reported hostile treatment by the police, while the figures from Haryana and Punjab stand at 42 per cent and 58.9 per cent respectively. Overall, of those who reported hostile treatment, 45.6 per cent were from Punjab, 29.4 per cent from Haryana and 25 per cent from Delhi.

The maximum percentage of respondents at all education levels, except senior secondary, suggested police hostility. Of those stating that police were hostile, 46.9 per cent were primary-level educated or lower. None of the graduates said the police was supportive. Most of the illiterate said the police were hostile. Thus, on both ends of the education spectrum, police hostility was predominant. Of those who faced torture and abuse, 20 per cent were illiterate, 26.9 per cent were educated up to the primary level, and 27.5 per cent had been in middle school. Of those towards whom the police had been supportive, 27.1 per cent were secondary educated, 32.2 per cent were middle schoolers, and 15.3 per cent were illiterate.

Within those who reported hostile treatment at the hands of the police, the providers of 28.8 per cent were daily wage labourers and for 48.1 per cent, skilled labourers. Among all occupations of the providers, hostile treatment was dominant, ranging from 43.3 per cent to 59.1 per cent.

In their study, Irving Piliavin and Scott Briar[20] found that decisions made by police officers with respect to juveniles were strongly affected by juveniles' behaviour. This, in turn, impacts the identity of the juvenile as an 'official delinquent,' which is based on the social judgement made by officers, derived from how the delinquent presents himself.

---

[20] Irving Piliavin and Scott Briar, 'Police Encounters with Juveniles,' *American Journal of Sociology*, Vol. 70, no. 2 (1964): 206–14.

R.A. Brown et al.[21] noted that based on their beliefs, officers may perceive juvenile offenders as causing more trouble than adults.

Approach by Police Officials in Uniform

An overwhelming majority (88.4 per cent) of juveniles had been approached by police officials in uniform, while only 11.6 per cent stated this wasn't the case. It was found that 90 per cent of those aged 11–13 years, 91.7 per cent of those 14–15 years old, 87.4 per cent of 16–17-year-olds and 87.6 per cent of those aged 18 years and above were approached by police officials in uniform.

About 87.9 per cent of juveniles from Delhi, 85.7 per cent from Haryana and 91.1 per cent from Punjab had been approached by policemen in uniform. Of those who weren't approached such, 22.9 per cent were from Delhi, 45.7 per cent from Haryana and 31.4 per cent from Punjab. Punjab reported the majority (42.3 per cent) of respondents approached by uniformed police.

Provision of Legal Aid

It can be seen that the inmates received legal aid from the state in only 18.9 per cent of the cases; for the vast majority (81.1 per cent), no such aid was provided. No juvenile aged 11–13 years received legal aid; 40.4 per cent and 38.6 per cent of those who received aid were in the 16–17 and 14–15 age groups respectively. Only 13.5 per cent of those 18 and above received any kind of legal aid.

A majority (54.4 per cent) of inmates who received legal aid were from Delhi, while 17.5 per cent and 28.1 per cent were from Haryana and Punjab. Of those who did not receive legal aid, 44.1 per cent (highest) were from Punjab, 41.6 per cent from Haryana and 14.3 per cent from Delhi.

In 74.4 per cent of the cases where the provider for the juvenile was a daily wage labourer, no legal aid was provided, while 40.4 per cent of all who received aid were dependent upon daily wage labourers. About 29.8 per cent of aid beneficiaries were dependent on skilled labourers,

---

[21] R.A. Brown et al., 'Identifying Variation in Police Officer Behaviour between Juveniles and Adults,' *Journal of Criminal Justice*, Vol. 37 (2009): 200–08.

while such juveniles formed the majority (50.6 per cent) of those who didn't receive legal aid.

It was found that 84.7 per cent of all juveniles who were studying, 80.8 per cent of those employed and 76.3 per cent doing neither received no legal aid. Of those who received aid, 38.6 per cent were neither employed nor studying, 26.3 per cent were gainfully employed and 35.1 per cent of the juveniles were studying.

Presence of Family Members during Proceedings

In 93.4 per cent of the cases, the family of the juvenile was present during the proceedings while in remaining 6.6 per cent, the juvenile received no such support. For all respondents between 11 and 13 years old, the parents were present at the proceedings. In cases where the parents were absent, 20 per cent were 14–15 years, 45 per cent were 16–17 years, 35 per cent were 18 years and above. Across the age groups, in more than 90 per cent cases, the family members was present. The figure was lowest for 18 and above age group, at 92.1 per cent.

For all the three states, in more than 90 per cent cases, the family was present. About 15 per cent of instances where the family members were absent were in Delhi, 40 per cent in Haryana and 45 per cent in Punjab. Family members of juveniles were absent for proceedings in only 4.5 per cent of the cases in Delhi, while the figures from Haryana and Punjab stand at 7.1 per cent and 7.3 per cent respectively.

Across all the preoccupation categories, the maximum percentage of respondents had their family members present, with the lowest number clocking in for the employed (87.2 per cent). In 30 per cent of cases where the family of the juvenile was absent, the juvenile was studying; in 50 per cent cases, the juvenile was employed, and in 20 per cent cases, the juvenile was neither studying nor employed. In 12.8 per cent of all cases where the juvenile was employed, the family of the accused was not present for the proceedings.

For all categories of offences, the maximum number of respondents had their family present, with the least (84.2 per cent) showing up for petty offence charges. In 95.5 per cent cases, where the juvenile was charged with a heinous offence, the family was present, whereas in all cases where the family of the juvenile was absent, 55 per cent had been charged with heinous offences.

Use of Stigmatising Semantics

All respondents replied in affirmative when asked if any accusatory and stigmatising terms were used for or around them during proceedings. In all instances from Delhi, Haryana and Punjab, accusatory/stigmatising terms such as arrest, warrant, accused, charge-sheet, remand, trial and prosecution, etc. were used. Irrespective of whether the offence was petty, serious or heinous, accusatory terms/stigmatising terms were used.

Brown et al., in their study, stated that stigmatisation resulting from police procedures can reinforce antisocial behaviour.[22] Attitudes of juveniles towards the police are affected by their encounters with the police.[23]

Observations

1) The majority of respondents, irrespective of their age, had committed heinous offences.
2) The majority of respondents committed the offence alone, irrespective of age. This was followed by those who committed the offence with adults.
3) The majority of respondents were non-recidivists.
4) The majority of respondents were in confinement before being sent to the home.
5) More respondents were confined with an increase in age.
6) The majority of respondents were sent to confinement irrespective of education.
7) In the majority of cases, the claim of juvenility was made before the police.
8) In the majority of cases, the police was found to be hostile.
9) In the majority of cases, the police approached the juveniles in uniforms.
10) In the majority of cases, legal aid was not provided.
11) In the majority of cases, family members were present during the proceedings.
12) All respondents said that accusatory and stigmatising terms were used.

---

[22] Piliavin and Briar, 'Police Encounters.'

[23] Brown et al., 'Identifying Variation in Police Officer Behaviour.'

Juvenile: Inside the Home

Type of Home

About 75.8 per cent of the interviewees were lodged in observation homes, while 24.2 per cent were from special homes. All children aged 11–13 years were in observation homes irrespective of the nature of offence; 52.8 per cent of those housed in observation homes were 16–17 years, and only 17 per cent were 18 years and above. About 56.2 per cent of all aged 18 years and above were in special homes. More respondents aged 11–17 years were in observation homes, and those aged 18 years and above were in special homes.

About 72.4 per cent of those charged with heinous offences were in observation homes, as were the maximum number of respondents irrespective of the nature of offence, as compared to special homes. While 91.8 per cent of those in special homes had been charged with heinous offences, this number stood at 76.9 per cent for those in observation homes.

Of the juveniles interviewed in Delhi, 24.2 per cent were kept in special homes and 75.8 per cent in observation homes. In Haryana, 27.7 per cent were from special homes, while 72.3 per cent lived in observation homes. In Punjab, 21 per cent were lodged in special homes and 79 per cent in observation homes.

Likeability of Environment Inside the Home

About 31.8 per cent of the children straightaway answered that they disliked the overall environment of the home; 68.2 per cent replied they liked the environment inside the home, prima facie.

It was observed that 72.7 per cent of juveniles from Delhi, 61.6 per cent from Haryana and 71.8 per cent from Punjab liked the prima facie environment of the home. Of those who disliked the environment of the juvenile home, 44.8 per cent were from Haryana, 36.5 per cent from Punjab and 18.8 per cent from Delhi.

Segregation

No observation home or special home segregated the children on the basis of the age, that is, all children aged 11–18 and above were housed together without any consideration of age differences. Neither in Delhi, Punjab or Haryana was any segregation done in residential facilities on the basis of the age of juveniles.

Requirement of Better Infrastructure

About 96 per cent of inmates answered that there was need for better infrastructure. Only 4 per cent replied in a straightforward manner that there was no such need. About 86.2 per cent of juveniles from Delhi, 98.2 per cent from Haryana and 99.2 per cent from Punjab felt a requirement for better infrastructure within their respective homes.

Quality Inside the Home

Of Pest/Insect Control

About 4.3 per cent of inmates replied that the quality was poor, 58.6 per cent said it was below average, 35.1 per cent said quality was average, while just 2 per cent answered that the quality was good.

About 53.8 per cent of juveniles from Delhi reported that the state of pest/insect control inside the home was poor; 45.3 per cent and 44.3 per cent juveniles from Haryana and Punjab respectively found the quality of pest/insect control to be average. About 34.5 per cent and 39 per cent of juveniles from Haryana and Punjab respectively stated that the quality of pest/insect control inside the home was below average. A comparative analysis of the respondents from different states who said that the quality was below average or poor showed that Delhi had the maximum percentage of those who said quality was poor or below average (81.8 per cent), followed by Punjab (58.1 per cent) and Haryana (57.1 per cent). It can be noted that the maximum percentage of the respondents in all three states mentioned that the quality was poor or below average.

Of Bedding/Clothing

A large majority (80.1 per cent) of the juveniles answered that the quality of the clothing and bedding provided was average; 17.5 per cent replied that the quality was below average, 1.3 per cent reported the quality to be poor and only 1 per cent stated that the quality was good.

About 62.1 per cent juveniles from Delhi, 85.7 per cent from Haryana and 84.7 per cent from Punjab reported the quality of clothing/bedding to be average. Thus, the maximum percentage of the respondents for all the states suggested that the quality was average. This was followed by those who said that quality was below average or poor. None of the respondents from Delhi and Haryana suggested that the quality was good; 43.4 per cent of juveniles from Delhi, 26.4 per cent from Haryana and 30.2 per cent from Punjab stated that the clothing/bedding provided to them was below average in quality.

Of Water for Drinking and Sanitation

A majority of the inmates (79.1 per cent) responded that the quality of water was average, while 17.2 per cent stated that the quality of water was below average. Only 0.7 per cent stated that quality was poor, while 3 per cent stated it was good.

About 56.1 per cent of juveniles from Delhi, 78.6 per cent from Haryana and 91.9 per cent from Punjab reported that the quality of water inside the home was average. Thus, across the three states, the majority of respondents suggested that the quality was average. A comparative analysis suggested that Punjab had the highest percentage of juveniles stating the quality of the water as average. Of those who reported that the quality of water was below average, 50 per cent were from Delhi while 42.3 per cent from Haryana.

Of Bathrooms (Including Sufficiency)

About 51 per cent (highest) of the interviewees stated that the quality of bathrooms and their sufficiency was below average; 37.4 per cent felt the quality of bathrooms was average, 9.6 per cent said it was poor, and only 2 per cent responded that quality was good.

About 60.6 per cent of juveniles from Delhi, 49.1 per cent from Haryana and 47.6 per cent from Punjab reported that the quality and quantity of bathrooms were below average. Thus, the majority of respondents across the states suggested that quality was below average. Around 22.3 per cent of juveniles from Haryana stated that the quality and quantity of bathrooms were poor, while 47.6 per cent from Punjab reported the quality to be average. Only 4.8 per cent of juveniles from Punjab reported the quality and quantity of bathrooms to be good, while none from Delhi or Haryana reported so.

Of Kitchen Hygiene

About 68.2 per cent (highest) of juveniles answered that the quality of the kitchen cleanliness was average, while 29.5 per cent stated that it was good; 2.3 per cent reported quality as below average, while none of the respondents said that hygiene in the kitchens was poor.

From Delhi, 68.2 per cent of juveniles, 75.9 per cent juveniles from Haryana and 61.3 per cent from Punjab reported that the quality of cleanliness inside the kitchens was average. Thus, the majority of respondents for all three state reported average kitchen hygiene quality. About 28.8 per cent of juveniles from Delhi, 19.6 per cent from Haryana and 38.7 per cent from Punjab stated that the quality of hygiene inside the kitchens was good. As compared to responses to other services previously discussed, kitchens have had higher percentages of good responses.

Of Meals

About 47 per cent (highest) responded that the quality of food was average, while a sizeable segment (38.1 per cent) stated it was below average; 10.7 per cent replied that the quality of the food was poor and deplorable. Only 4.3 per cent stated that the quality of food was good.

Where states go, 53 per cent of juveniles from Delhi and 49.1 per cent from Haryana found the quality of meals to be below average; 68.5 per cent of juveniles from Punjab reported the food to be average while 21.5 per cent from Haryana reported the quality of meals to be poor.

Routine

All inmates had to follow a routine; however where they did not attend vocational training or formal education, the routine tended to revolve around the timings of meals.

Existence of and/or Awareness about Children's Committee

Only 24.5 per cent of the respondents were aware of a children's committee in their home and 32.5 per cent were unaware. In a majority of the cases (43 per cent), there was no children's committee in the home.

About 43.9 per cent of juveniles in Delhi and 36.3 per cent in Punjab were aware of the children's committee; 56.1 per cent from Delhi and 49.2 per cent from Punjab were not. No observation home or special home in Haryana had any children's committee.

Extension of Cooperation from Staff to Children's Committee

Around 64.9 per cent of respondents who were aware of the existence of children's committees replied that it received no cooperation from the staff, while 35.1 per cent reported the committee as receiving cooperation.

Of the juveniles in Delhi who knew of children's committees, 41.4 per cent reported that the staff extended cooperation, while 58.6 per cent stated otherwise. In Punjab, 31.1 per cent of juveniles stated that the committee received staff cooperation, while 68.9 per cent believed that the staff extended no cooperation to the committee whatsoever.

Monthly Medical Check-ups

A whopping 91.4 per cent of juveniles stated that no medical check-ups were conducted on a monthly basis. Only 8.6 per cent put on record that such monthly check-ups were done.

The rate of monthly medical check-ups was the highest in Delhi, with 37.9 per cent juveniles confirming them, while only 0.9 per cent juveniles from Haryana stated the same. No juvenile from Punjab reported monthly medical check-ups.

Availability of First-Aid Kits

All respondents stated that first aid kits were available in the home for immediate treatment of minor wounds and general ailments.

Availability of Recreational Facilities

It was found that recreational facilities in one form or the other were present in every observation and special home.

Grant of Leave/Parole

In a majority of the cases (98.3 per cent), irrespective of their nature of offence, no leave/parole was granted to the juveniles. In only 1.7 per cent of the cases had the juveniles been let out on leave/parole.

About 6.1 per cent of juveniles in Delhi, 0.8 per cent in Punjab and none in Haryana had been granted any leave or parole.

Availability of Suggestion Box

None of the respondents were aware of the existence of any such box within the premises of the homes.

Permission to Meet Family/Parents

It was found that all interviewees were allowed to meet their family/parents on designated days as per the rules of the juvenile homes.

Quality and Quantity of Staff

About 44 per cent (highest) of the juveniles found that the quality and quantity of the staff within the home to be average; 33.4 per cent stated quality and quantity as below average while 12.9 per cent replied poor. Only 9.6 per cent (lowest) respondents stated that quality was good.

About 51.5 per cent inmates from Delhi found the quality of staff to be below average while 13.3 per cent deemed it poor; 41.1 per cent juveniles from Haryana found quality to be below average, while 20.5 per cent reported poorly. A significant 57.3 per cent juveniles from Punjab stated that quality of staff was average at best, while 20.2 per cent found it to be good.

Presence of House Father/House Mother

In 57 per cent of the cases, a house mother or house father was present while in 43 per cent of cases the positions of house father and house mother were vacant.

In all homes in Delhi, house fathers and house mothers were present to take care of the children. There were no house fathers/house mothers present in any observation or special homes in Haryana, while 85.5 per cent of juveniles from Punjab reported that house fathers/house mothers were present in their respective homes.

Observations

1) The majority of juveniles were in observation homes.
2) The majority of juveniles said that they liked the home environment.
3) There was no segregation on the basis of age in any of the homes.
4) The majority of juveniles said there was need for better infrastructure.
5) The majority of juveniles said there was need to improve the quality of services.
6) In most of the cases, the medical check-ups were not done on a monthly basis. First-aid kits were available.
7) Recreational facilities were present in all the homes.
8) No suggestion box was present.
9) A need to improve the quantity and quality of staff was felt.

Juvenile: Post-Release Prospects

Individual's Plan Post Release and Individual Care Plans

About 47 per cent of the inmates (highest) intended to pursue and complete their education post their release, while 18.5 per cent sought to continue the jobs they had held; 20.9 per cent of inmates wanted to look for other employment while 13.6 per cent were undecided on their future course of action.

All respondents unanimously answered that they were unaware about any post release/individual care plans being drawn up for them.

Around 22.7 per cent of juveniles from Delhi planned on finding new jobs, 37.9 per cent wanted to continue studying and 24.2 per cent were unsure of what to do. In Haryana, 60.7 per cent of juveniles wanted to continue studying. In Punjab, 39.5 per cent wanted to continue studying while 28.2 per cent wanted to find new jobs. For all the states, the maximum percentage of respondents wanted to continue their schooling.

Awareness about Date of Release and/or Appearance

In 90.4 per cent of the cases, the juveniles were aware of their date of release/next appearance, but in 9.6 per cent they weren't. However, in several instances, even when the juveniles were aware of a date for the next appearance, lack of manpower in the police force/staff to accompany them to the hearing rendered the knowledge futile.

About 93.1 per cent of juveniles unaware of the date of release or next hearing were from Punjab, while only 0.9 per cent were from Haryana and 3.4 per cent from Delhi; 21.8 per cent of all inmates interviewed from Punjab were unaware about their date of release/next hearing.

Vocational Training

In a majority of the cases (69.5 per cent), there was no provision of any kind of vocational training for the inmates. Of the 30.5 per cent cases where such training was available, only 16.6 per cent inmates attended it, while 13.9 per cent did not.

A majority of the respondents from Punjab and Haryana mentioned there was no provision of vocational training, while none of the respondents from Delhi said so. Of those who suggested there was provision and attended training, 80 per cent were from Delhi and 20 per cent from Punjab. No vocational training was being provided in any observation or special home in Haryana, while 79 per cent of juveniles from Punjab reported that there was no provision. About 60.6 per cent of juveniles from Delhi attended such vocational training, while 39.6 per cent did not.

The data suggested that irrespective of age, the majority of the respondents fell in the category of 'no provision'. About 70 per cent of those at 11–13 years, 48.3 per cent of between 14–15-year-olds, 78.3 per cent of 16–17-year-olds and 69.7 per cent of those aged 18 and above were housed in homes where there was no provision of vocational training. Around 30 per cent of those aged 14–15 years, 4.2 per cent of those aged 16–17 years, and 20.2 per cent of those aged 18 years and above were lodged in homes where vocational training was provided, but not attended. Only 30 per cent of those aged 11–13 years, 21.7 per cent of those aged 14–15 years, 17.5 per cent of those aged 16–17 years, and 10.1 per cent of those aged 18 years and above were housed in homes where vocational training was provided and they attended it regularly as well. Of those who did attend vocational training, the majority of respondents were 16–17 years old. Of those who did not attend the vocational training, the maximum percentage of respondents were 14–15 years old.

Only 27.4 per cent of those lodged in special homes and 13.1 per cent of those in observation homes received vocational training and attended it; 30.1 per cent of those in observation homes and 8.7 per cent of those in special homes were provided with vocational training but did not attend it. A total of 42.5 per cent of juveniles were lodged in special homes with no provision of vocational training while the figure stands at 78.2 per cent for those in observation homes. The maximum percentage of respondents from either kind of home did not have the provision of vocational training. Comparatively, more respondents from observation homes did not have such provision.

A total of 47.1 per cent (highest) respondents who attended the training felt there was need to introduce new vocations in addition to the existing ones. About 37.3 per cent were indifferent to such a need, while 15.7 per cent (lowest) didn't feel so.

Around 41.5 per cent of juveniles from Delhi and 70 per cent from Punjab who attended vocational training agreed that there was need to introduce new vocations; 39 per cent of children from Delhi and 30 per cent from Punjab were indifferent to any such need, while 19.5 per cent of juveniles from Delhi didn't feel such need.

Meanwhile, 41.2 per cent (highest) of juveniles who attended vocational training disagreed that such training would help them post release, while 33.3 per cent agreed; 23.5 per cent were neutral or undecided on the effectiveness of the vocational training, while 2 per cent strongly disagreed. About 41.5 per cent inmates from Delhi and 40 per cent from Punjab who attended training disagreed that it was an effective post-release aid. Only 31.5 per cent of juveniles from Delhi and 40 per cent from Punjab agreed that the vocational training they received would aid them post their release.

At least 47 per cent of the children found the attitude of the trainers to be indifferent, while 39.4 per cent found them to be helpful; 12.3 per cent stated that the trainers were incompetent while 0.3 per cent found them to be caring. A meagre 1 per cent of the sample did not respond to the query.

For the state of New Delhi, the maximum percentage of respondents suggested that the trainers were helpful (68.3 per cent) while 28.6 per cent stated that their attitude was indifferent. In Haryana, the maximum percentage of respondents suggested they were indifferent (50 per cent) and 26.8 per cent suggested they were indifferent. For the state of Punjab, 23.2 per cent stated that they were incompetent, maximum percentage of the respondents suggested that they were indifferent (54.8 per cent) while 37.1 per cent found their trainers to be helpful. A comparative analysis of the states indicated that more respondents in Delhi said that the trainers were helpful than in the other states.

E.J. Ameen and D.L. Lee[24] suggested that juvenile centres can be more effective if career opportunities are created through the vocational training. Vacca, in his study, found that youths who successfully completed academic and vocational programmes in residential facilities were at a lower rate of recidivism and had better employment opportunities.[25] According to a study conducted by Select Committee on Narcotics Abuse and Control (1993), in the US, inmates who participated in vocational and employment programmes were more likely to sustain employment and earn slightly more than inmates who did not participate in them.[26]

Formal Education

About 53.6 per cent were continuing their formal education while in the institution, whereas 46.4 per cent were not enrolled in any formal education courses.

In Delhi, 65.2 per cent of juveniles attended formal education, while the numbers stand at 54.5 per cent for children from Haryana. Here, 45.2 per cent did not have formal education. In Punjab, 46.8 per cent were attending formal education. Thus, in Delhi and Haryana, a majority of

---

[24] E.J. Ameen and D.L. Lee, 'Vocational Training in Juvenile Detention: A Call for Action,' *Career Development Quarterly*, Vol. 60, no. 2 (2012): 98.

[25] Vacca, 'Crime Can be Prevented.'

[26] Vacca, 'Crime Can be Prevented.'

the respondents were enrolled formal education whereas in Punjab, this was not the case.

Around 64.1 per cent of children who were studying prior to their confinement were pursuing formal education from the home, while 43.6 per cent juveniles who were employed prior to confinement had started formal education after coming to the home; 47.3 per cent of those who were neither studying nor employed prior to confinement had started formal education from the home. Overall, while 131 children were studying prior to confinement, a total of 162 children were availing formal education from the home, an increase of 23.67 per cent over pre-institutionalisation levels. Of the three categories, the majority of those who were studying before were attending formal education, the majority of the previously employed were not attending formal education, and the majority of those who were doing neither were also not engaged in formal education.

It was observed that only 1 per cent of the children received any encouragement to engage in voluntary services or open schooling, while 99 per cent received no encouragement. Only 4.5 per cent juveniles from Delhi received any encouragement to engage in voluntary services or open school while no child from Punjab or Haryana received any such encouragement.

Jurg Gerber and Eric Fritsch observed that educational programmes in prison were linked to lesser criminal behaviour and greater likelihood of the inmates to continue education after their release.[27] It was also related to lower recidivism rates.[28] In their evaluation of research on adult offenders, Jeffrey Bouffard et al. found that vocational education programmes were effective, defining them as providing classroom training for knowledge that will help them in work.[29]

---

[27] Jurg Gerber and Eric Fritsch, 'Adult Academic and Vocational Correctional Educational Programmes: A Review of Recent Research,' *Studies in the Education of Adults*, Vol. 35, Issue 2 (2003): 119–42.

[28] Vacca, 'Crime Can be Prevented.'

[29] Jeffrey A. Bouffard et al., 'Effectiveness of Vocational Education and Employment Programmes for Adult Offenders,' *Journal of Offender Rehabilitation*, Vol. 31, no. 1–2 (2000): 1–41.

Therapy Sessions/Counselling

Rhena Izzo and Robert Ross[30] discussed that programmes based on providing therapy to address the psychopathological condition of criminality among inmates did not demonstrate their effectiveness by way of evidence. They noted, 'Effective programmes included as a target of their intervention not only the offender's behaviour, feelings, and vocational or interpersonal skills but also his or her cognition, self-evaluation, expectations, understanding and appraisal of the world, and values.'[31] Historically, it was observed that 'psychiatric treatment to prevent delinquency was a failure'.[32]

Therapy sessions on a regular basis were provided to only 11.3 per cent of juveniles while a majority (71.2 per cent) received no such therapy at all; 17.5 per cent of juveniles had only attended one therapy session during their stay in the home.

Of those who had attended therapy, 58.6 per cent had individual sessions, while 39.1 per cent went to group sessions. Only in 2.3 per cent of cases were the juveniles called for both types of sessions. It is necessary to reiterate here that 71.2 per cent of the juveniles did not attend any therapy.

Of those who had attended therapy sessions, only 18.4 per cent (lowest) felt they were helpful while 29.9 per cent felt the sessions were helpful to some extent. A majority of the juveniles (51.7 per cent) found that the sessions did not benefit them in any way whatsoever.

About 55.3 per cent (highest) of children stated that positive reinforcement mechanisms were indeed used by the staff, trainers and counsellors in the form of rewards for good behaviour; 16.2 per cent replied that no such reinforcement was used, and 28.5 per cent were unaware of such measures.

A majority of the juveniles (56.3 per cent) found the performance of the counsellor to be average at best, while 16.1 per cent found the

---

[30] Rhena L. Izzo and Robert R. Ross, 'Meta-Analysis of Rehabilitation Programmes for Juvenile Delinquents: A Brief Report,' *Criminal Justice and Behaviour* 17, no.1 (1990): 134.

[31] Izzo and Ross, 'Meta-Analysis of Rehabilitation Programmes,' 139.

[32] C.M. Peters, 'Social Work and Juvenile Probation: Historical Tensions and Contemporary Convergences,' *Social Work*, Vol. 56 (2011): 359.

attitude towards children and the counsellor's performance good. About 26.4 per cent stated that said performance was below average, and 1.1 per cent found it to be poor.

About 65.8 per cent of those charged with petty offences, 71.4 per cent of those charged with serious offences and 72 per cent of those charged with heinous offences received no therapy sessions or counselling. Thus, for all the offences, the maximum percentage of respondents did not receive any therapy. Those attending regular sessions only formed 9.9 per cent of all charged with heinous offences; 18.1 per cent of such juveniles had only attended a therapy session once since their confinement.

In Delhi, the maximum percentage were attending sessions regularly (47 per cent) whereas in Haryana and Punjab, the majority were not attending sessions (88.4 per cent and 78.2 per cent respectively). Of those who were regularly attending, the maximum percentage were from Delhi (91.2 per cent); of those who had attended the session once, the majority were from Punjab (47.2 per cent). About 47 per cent inmates from Delhi attended regular therapy sessions while the figure stands at 0.9 per cent for Haryana and 1.6 per cent for Punjab. Around 88.4 per cent juveniles from Haryana and 78.2 per cent from Punjab had never attended therapy sessions; 24.2 per cent of children from Delhi, 10.7 per cent juveniles Haryana and 20.2 per cent from Punjab had attended therapy sessions only once.

The maximum percentage from those who responded for Delhi had group sessions (59.6 per cent) and 36.2 per cent had individual sessions. In Haryana and Punjab, the maximum percentage of the respondents had individual sessions—84.6 per cent and 85.2 per cent respectively. This data only includes respondents who had attended the sessions; 15.4 per cent in Haryana and 14.8 per cent in Punjab were given group sessions.

About 44.7 per cent of juveniles from Delhi, 61.5 per cent from Haryana and 59.3 per cent from Punjab reported that they did not find the therapy to be helpful. Only 25 per cent of juveniles from Delhi and 14.8 per cent from Punjab found the sessions useful. Thus, the maximum percentage from all the three states did not find the therapy sessions to be helpful. This data is calculated for the respondents who were had attended them (87 respondents).

Data collected from the respondents who had therapy indicated that the maximum percentage in each state reported attitude and performance to be average. This was followed by those who said that the performance and attitude of counsellors were below average. About 51 per cent of juveniles from Delhi, 76.9 per cent from Haryana and 51.9 per cent from Punjab who received regular therapy found the attitude and performance of the therapist to be average; 31.9 per cent of juveniles from Delhi, 23.1 per cent from Haryana and 18.5 per cent from Punjab found the attitude and performance of counsellors to be below average.

A higher percentage of respondents among the addicts and non-addicts (except those addicted to cannabinoids) did not attend any sessions. It was found that 90.9 per cent of those addicted to tobacco, 87.5 per cent of alcoholics, 28.6 per cent of cannabinoid addicts and 52.1 per cent of narcotics addicts had not attended therapy even once. About 57.1 per cent of those dependent on cannabinoids had attended therapy only once. Only 17.4 per cent of those addicted to narcotics and 14.3 per cent of those addicted to cannabinoids regularly attended therapy sessions.

Data suggested that irrespective of the ability to socialise, the maximum percentage of respondents were non-attendees. About 79.6 per cent of the asocial did not receive any therapy and only 7.3 per cent did. Of those found to be social, 64.2 per cent did not receive any therapy. Of those who received regular therapy, 70.6 per cent were social while 29.4 per cent were asocial. Similarly, of those who received therapy sessions only once, 66 per cent were sociable while 34 per cent were not.

According to data on special homes and observation homes, the maximum percentage of respondents did not attend any sessions. About 8.2 per cent of those in special homes and 12.2 per cent of those in observations home received regular therapy sessions; 60.3 per cent of those in special homes and 74.7 per cent of those in observation homes never received any therapy. Around 31.5 per cent of juveniles in special homes and 13.1 per cent in observation homes received therapy sessions only once.

Observations

1) The majority of respondents wanted to complete their education post release.

2) Respondents were unaware of any individual care plans.
3) The majority of respondents were aware of their date of release.
4) In the majority of cases, there was no vocational training.
5) The majority of respondents were continuing formal education within institutions.
6) The majority of respondents did not attend therapy sessions.
7) The majority of respondents said that positive reinforcement was used by the staff.
8) The majority of respondents found the performance of counsellors average.

Chapter X

Juvenile Justice (Care and Protection of Children) Act, 2015: Opening Pandora's Box

Even though the Act of 2000 made no distinction between the nature of offences, the Rules of 2007 defined heinous offences as those entailing punishment of more than seven years of imprisonment, while petty and serious offences were left undefined. However, neither the Act nor the Rules made serious distinctions in the procedure for the prosecution and trial of juveniles charged on the basis of the nature of offence. In the Act of 2015, petty offences have been defined as those entailing a punishment of less than three years of imprisonment, serious offences as those punishable with three to seven years of imprisonment and heinous offences as those punishable with more than seven years of imprisonment. The Act of 2015 allows for the possibility of the trial of a child aged 16–18 years as an adult along with several other disqualifications. It is pertinent to examine researchers' findings in the light of this.

While the circumstances surrounding the enactment of the Act of 2015 have been mentioned in earlier chapters, it is important to weigh the criticism against the substance of the provisions to verify if the controversies are merely brouhaha or based on a sound logic. For such examination, the intention of legislators should be given primacy. As informed by Secretary, Ministry of Women and Child Development, in a deposition before the Standing Committee on Human Resource Development,[1] the following concerns with respect to the working of the Act of 2000 necessitated the enactment of the Act of 2015.

1) Delays in various processes under the Act of 2000 with regard to pendency of cases due to delayed decisions by committees and boards.
2) Delay in enquiry of cases leading to children languishing in homes for years even for petty offences.
3) Increase in reported incidents of abuse of children in institutions.
4) Inadequate facilities, quality of care and rehabilitation measures in homes.
5) Disruption of adoption, delays in adoption due to faulty and incomplete process.
6) Lack of clarity regarding roles, functions and responsibilities of boards and committees.
7) Limited participation of the child in the trial process, delays in rehabilitation plans and social investigation report of every child.
8) Lack of any substantive provisions for orders to be passed in case the child is found to be innocent.
9) No specific provisions for reporting of abandoned or lost children to appropriate authority.
10) Non-registration of institutions and inability of states to enforce registration due to lack of any penal provisions for non-compliance.
11) Inadequate provisions to counter offences against children such as corporal punishment, ragging or sale of children for adoption purposes.
12) Increase in heinous offences committed by children and lack of any specific provisions to deal with such children.

As per research findings, only 12.6 per cent of juveniles had been charged with petty offences and 7 per cent had been charged with serious offences. An overwhelming majority (80.5 per cent) of inmates had been

---

[1] Parliamentary Standing Committee on Human Resource Development, *264th Report on Juvenile Justice (Care and Protection of Children) Bill, 2014*, presented on 25 February 2015.

charged under sections, which constituted heinous offences. Of these, 81.5 per cent were liable to be tried as adults under the provisions of the Act of 2015, while 83.2 per cent and 88.8 per cent respectively aged 16–17 years and 18+ had been charged with heinous offences. It should be mentioned, however, that the findings are based on interviews conducted within observation and special homes and do not reflect the number of juveniles who are not institutionalised.

For the sake of argument, let us momentarily assume the contention of those in favour of the provisions to be true—that adolescents at 16–18 years could be treated as adults given they have the maturity to differentiate between right and wrong, and that there has been a significant increase in the number of heinous offences committed by those aged 16 and above. This argument largely coloured the perceptions of lawmakers in drafting the Act of 2015, although even they didn't feel that all juveniles aged 16–18 years should be painted with the same brush, meaning that not all juveniles at that age have the mental and physical capacity to commit an offence. The same can be deduced from the fact that the Act of 2015 sets up a procedure through which the board may determine, via a preliminary assessment, the mental and physical capacity of the juvenile to commit the offence. As an added safeguard, even after the juvenile is forwarded to the children's court to be tried as an adult, the Act of 2015 requires for the court to conduct another assessment with regard to the juvenile's mental and physical capacity before proceeding with the trial or enquiry.

In light of such a large number of juveniles liable to be tried as adults, the established procedure under the Act of 2015 would not only need to be simple to ensure speedy justice, but also be watertight, so that no adolescent who didn't have the capacity to commit the offence is tried as an adult. On both accounts, success would lie with the efficacy of the implementation of the provisions, the prospects of which, going by the findings of the researchers, are bleak.

That the higher judiciary had to direct the administration to set up boards, committees and other organs of the juvenile justice system in *Sheela Barse* v. *Union of India*[2] in 1986, and reiterate the same in

[2] 1986 SCALE (2) 230.

Sampurna Behura v. *Union of India*[3] in 2011, speak volumes about the status of implementation of the Acts of 1986 and 2000. The judgement for the Sampurna Behura case[4] was rendered on 9 February 2018; seven years after the 2011 order, the court was still bemoaning the 'virtual non-implementation and tardy implementation' of the provisions of the Acts of 2000 and 2015. It went on to mandate the steps required to be taken by the state governments and ordered the High Courts to initiate *suo motu* proceedings for the implementation of the Act.

Moreover, that the budget allocated to the establishment of these institutions is measly doesn't give much hope about any improvement in the near future. Total estimated budgetary allocation to the Ministry of Women and Child Development, which spearheads the Integrated Child Protection Scheme (ICPS), was ₹ 18,584 crore in 2012–13,[5] ₹ 20,440 crore in 2013–14,[6] ₹ 19,818.1 crore in 2014–15, and ₹ 17,167 crore in 2015–16. In these years, as per the ministry's data,[7] the ICPS was allocated a budgetary estimate[8] of ₹ 400 crore in 2012–13, while only ₹ 253.84 crore were sanctioned. In 2013–14, ₹ 300 crore was allocated and ₹ 265.78 crore sanctioned. In 2014–15, ₹ 400 crore were allocated; this was revised to ₹ 450 crore of which ₹ 448.43 crore were sanctioned. In 2015–16, ₹ 402.23 crore were allocated and ₹ 362.12 crore sanctioned. On an average, the ministry allocated only 2.04 per cent of its BE to ICPS, and the amount sanctioned is bound to be lesser.

---

[3] (2011) 9 SCC 801.

[4] W.P. (Civil) No. 473 of 2005.

[5] 'Expenditure Budget Vol. 1, 2013–2014,' accessed 21 March 2019, http://indiabudget.gov.in/budget2013-2014/ub2013-14/eb/stat02.pdf.

[6] 'Expenditure Budget Vol. 1, 2014–2015,' accessed 21 March 2019, http://indiabudget.gov.in/budget2014-2015/ub2014-15/eb/stat02.pdf.

[7] *Annual Report: 2015–16*, Ministry of Women and Child Development, accessed 21 March 2019, http://wcd.nic.in/sites/default/files/annual-report-2015-16.pdf.

[8] Hereafter referred to as BE.

In 2016, under ICPS, Delhi was sanctioned ₹ 97,864,000[9] while the Punjab government was sanctioned ₹ 10 crore.[10] During the same period, Haryana was not sanctioned any amount under ICPS.[11] Even states do not fare any better in such allocations; in 2013–14, the Department of Women and Child Development, Govt. of NCT of Delhi, allocated a mere ₹ 3.5 crore towards the implementation of the Act of 2000.[12]

Given that the delay in the proceedings of the boards and committees, as well as lack of adequate infrastructure in childcare institutions were one of the major concerns highlighted by the ministry while bringing about the Act of 2015, its budgetary allocations are a pittance and completely disproportionate to the magnitude of the problem. It can be stated that the reasons, which motivated the enactment of the Act of 2015 are at odds with the priority accorded to them by the government.

As pointed out by the Secretary in his deposition, delay in proceedings is indeed an issue with respect to the implementation of the Act, leading to deferred justice. As per National Crime Records Bureau (NCRB) statistics for 2015,[13] 56,501 cases of juvenile apprehension, including 15,116 cases from the previous year, were pending disposal by the boards. At the end of 2015, the number of pending cases had increased to 21,562. However, whether the process under the Act of 2015 is simpler and, ergo, faster than under the Act of 2000, or if it provides safeguards to ensure speedy trials, remains to be seen. Provided in Figures 10.1 and 10.2 are the procedures under the two Acts.

---

[9] 'Central Share of Grant in Aid under ICPS,' Ministry of Women and Child Development, accessed 12 September 2017, http://icds-wcd.nic.in/icpsmon/pdf/sanctions/dtd04082016/Delhi%20sanction%20201617.pdf.

[10] 'Central Share of Grant in Aid to States under ICPS,' Ministry of Women and Child Development, accessed 12 September 2017, http://icds-wcd.nic.in/icpsmon/pdf/sanctions/dtd04082016/ATOZ04082016.pdf.

[11] ICDS, 'Central Share of Grant in Aid to States Under ICPS.'

[12] 'Allotment of Budget Estimates with Respect to Plan Schemes,' Department of Social Welfare, Govt. of NCT of Delhi, accessed 21 March 2019, http://www.wcddel.in/pdf/WCDBuget_2013_14.pdf.

[13] Table 10.5, 'Final Order in the Matter of Juveniles Apprehended under Various Crime Heads of IPC and SLL Crimes during 2015,' *Crime in India Statistics, 2015*, National Crime Records Bureau.

Figure 10.1: Procedure under Act of 2000

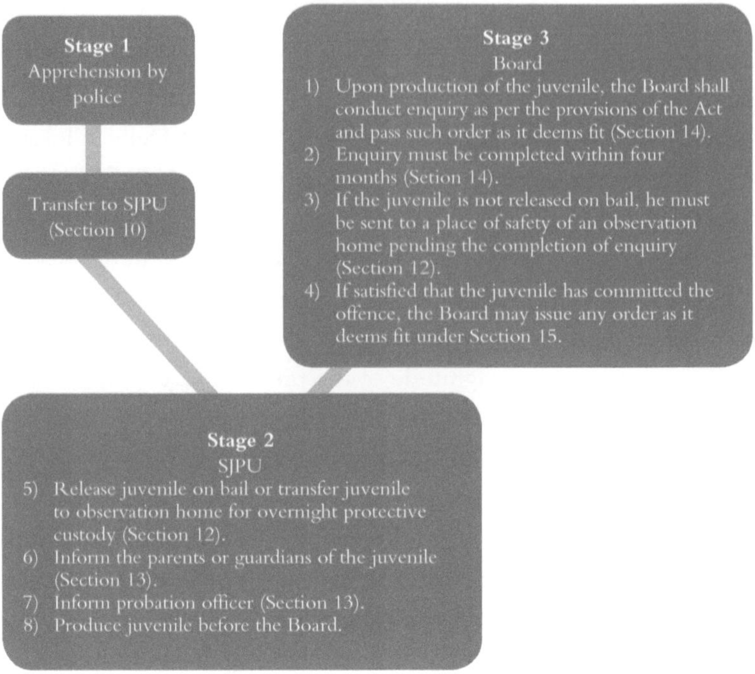

In the instance where without proper implementation, the cases kept piling up under the Act of 2000, leading to a delay in decisions and children languishing in homes for years, it is only reasonable to conclude that without better implementation than what was theoretically envisioned under the Act of 2000, the situation under the Act of 2015 will likely be worse.

As can be observed from Figures 10.1 and 10.2, the procedure under the Act of 2015 is lengthier than the procedure under the Act of 2000, in cases where the child is aged 16–18. The mechanism created under the Act of 2015 to prevent a pile-up of cases and ensure speedy trials entails the setting of a time limit of four months, plus two months for disposal of cases.[14] At the end of the six months, in case the offence the juvenile has been charged with is petty, the proceedings shall stand terminated. However, if the juvenile has been charged with a serious or heinous offence, permission can be obtained from the Chief Judicial Magistrate

[14] Section 14 (2), Act of 2015.

Figure 10.2: Procedure under Act of 2015

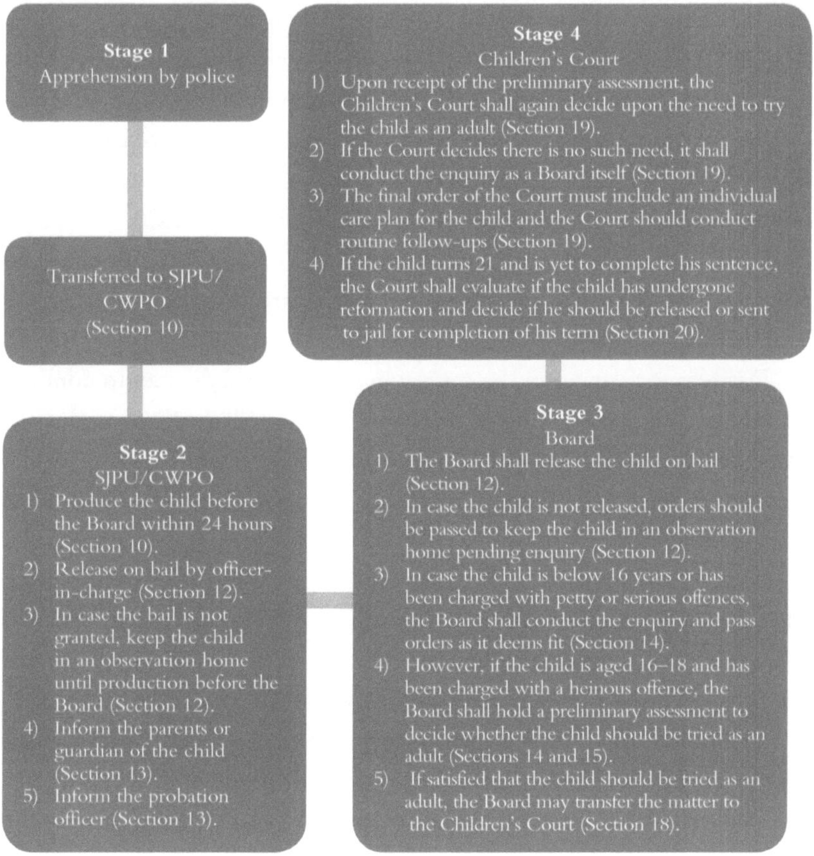

(CJM) or the Chief Metropolitan Magistrate (CMM) for an extension. No time limit is provided for in the Act in case such an extension is granted, so it can even be indefinite.

Section 14 of the Act of 2000, however, already provided for the completion of the enquiry by the Board within four months. The period could be extended at the discretion of the Board, which was bound to record the reasons with regard to the circumstances, and in special cases. No such guidelines have been provided in the Act of 2015 for the CJM or CMM to keep in mind while giving the extension.

The Children's Courts in point under the Act of 2015 were established under the Commissions for Protection of Child Rights Act,

2005[15] for speedy trial of offences against children, and were designated vide Section 28 of the Protection of Children from Sexual Offences Act, 2012 as special courts for the latter's enactment. In the event the Children's Court, after the preliminary assessment, decides not to try the juvenile as an adult, it shall, instead of remitting the case back to the Board, hold an enquiry as if it were a Board under this Act. This would indeed defeat the purpose the legislators of the Act of 2000 and Act of 2015 had in mind while putting two social workers on the Board. The purpose was to ensure that the proceedings are not mere mechanical application of the law.

Furthermore, even in the cases where the Board decides to conduct an enquiry itself, it is bound by Section 15 (2) to follow the procedure of a trial by summons under the Code of Criminal Procedure, 1973. While the chairperson of the board is a metropolitan magistrate, the two other members are social workers who may or may not have the necessary legal knowledge and acumen to conduct such proceedings under said Code. This would increase the delays. Either way, the legislative intent to do away with delays caused in the implementation of the Act of 2000 have not been addressed or remedied by the Act of 2015.

If the process cannot be simplified, another way of reducing such delays would require the government to strengthen the infrastructure that deals with the procedure. This requires financial backing. As per the annual report[16] of the Ministry of Women and Child Development, the ICPS was launched to provide financial support to state governments and union territory administrations for effective implementation of the Juvenile Justice Act. The budgetary allocation for the development of infrastructure called for under the Act is covered under ICPS, and the outcome budget[17] states its quantifiable deliverables as: the setting up of Juvenile Justice Boards/Child Welfare Committees and State Child Protection Units/District Child Protection Units throughout the country. The declared outcome is progress towards a healthy and

---

[15] Section 25.

[16] *Annual Report: 2015–16*, Ministry of Women and Child Development.

[17] 'Executive Summary,' Ministry of Women and Child Development, accessed 21 March 2019, http://wcd.nic.in/sites/default/files/OUTCOME%20BUDGET%20 2015-16Eng.pdf.

protective environment for children in need of care and protection as well as children in conflict with law.[18] However, as has been demonstrated, financial backing to the Act of 2000 and the Act of 2015 through ICPS is an abomination and in no way commensurate with the amount required for a smooth functioning of the institutions created by the Acts.

This, however, was not the focal disputation between legislators. At the time of its enactment, a major debate raged with respect to contending legislators calling for provisions of differential treatment of children aged 16–18 and charged with heinous offences. This was based on the logic that there was an increase in the incidence of crimes committed by children of this age group, and that the provisions and system under the Act of 2000 were ill-equipped to handle such a surge. Specifically, the government relied on data collected by NCRB, which showed an increase in the number of crimes committed by children aged 16–18, especially heinous offences.

The provisions have since been heavily criticised by various stakeholders involved in the field of juvenile justice chiefly on the ground that the Act of 2000 was a progressive piece of legislation completely in sync with India's international obligations. The former Act applied the principles of reformation and rehabilitation, which form the cornerstones of the juvenile justice system as differentiated from the principles of retribution and deterrence upon which the traditional criminal justice system operates. However, in their zeal to comply with populist demands largely cultured by the media in the wake of the 2012 Delhi gang rape case, Shakti Mills rape case and Guwahati rape case, legislators tampered with the foundations of the justice system governing the law applicable to juveniles. The Act of 2015, in its turn, dilutes the principles of reformation and rehabilitation, thereby allowing deterrence and retribution to take the steering wheel.

In light of the above, the impugned provisions of the Act of 2015 are in violation of several principles the act expressly seeks to adhere to. These are presumption of innocence; best interest; non-stigmatising semantics, Actions and Decisions; Equality or non-discrimination; privacy and confidentiality; and, fresh start. The provisions violate several key stipulations of various international treaties and instruments to which India was a signatory, such as the United Nations Convention on the Rights of the Child, International

[18] 'Executive Summary.'

Covenant on Civil and Political Rights, Universal Declaration of Human Rights, Beijing Rules, etc., in that it resorts to deterrence and retribution rather than the reformation and rehabilitation. They are also ignorant of several landmark judgements by the Supreme Court, which accepts reformation and rehabilitation as sine qua non in a juvenile justice system.

Moreover, the contention of the government that there has been a significant increase in the number of offences by children aged 16–18 years can also been refuted on the basis of NCRB data upon which the government had itself relied. The Standing Committee noted in its report[19] that the NCRB data was based on the registration of FIRs and not the final acquittal or conviction of the offenders. Even so, the proportion of cases of juveniles in conflict with the law to the total cognisable offences recorded by the NCRB has remained constant (Table 10.1). Between 2011 and 2015, the percentage of cases against juveniles in conflict with law has been 1.1 per cent to 1.2 per cent of the total cases registered under cognisable crimes. The number of offenders charged with heinous offences is bound to be even less, and as such could have been handled by the juvenile justice system created under the Act of 2000. The figures enumerated below assume miniscule proportions when one factors in that the total number of juveniles in India was 422 million as per the census of 2000–01.

Table 10.1: Cases Registered against Juveniles in Conflict with Law and Crime Rate in 2015

Year	*Cases against juveniles in conflict*	*Cases under total cognisable crimes*	*Percentage of cases against juveniles in conflict*
2011	25,125	2,325,575	1.1
2012	27,936	2,387,188	1.2
2013	31,725	2,647,722	1.2
2014	33,526	2,851,563	1.2
2015	31,396	2,949,400	1.1

Furthermore, the procedure for determining a child's mental and physical capacity to commit the offence has two steps. Firstly, the Board shall

[19] *264th Report on Juvenile Justice.*

conduct a preliminary assessment and for the purpose, can rely on the assistance of psychologists, psycho-social workers or other experts. Secondly, if the Board decides the child should be tried as an adult, it shall forward the case to a Children's Court, which, in turn, will decide if there is a need to try the child as an adult, and pass appropriate orders subject to provisions of the Act. For this purpose, the Court may rely on the assistance of psychologists, psycho-social workers or other experts different from those relied on by the Board.

The quality and quantity of counsellors and psychologists in this field are not nearly good enough to pay individual attention to every child as called for by the legislation, let alone shoulder the additional duties of assisting the Board. Researchers' findings point clearly at an absence of infrastructure and manpower when it comes to counsellors, psychologists and other experts who are duly qualified to provide the minimum requirement of individual therapy to each child, let alone judge their mental and physical capacity, which is a more complex task.

Therapy sessions on a regular basis were provided to only 11.3 per cent juveniles, while a majority (71.2 per cent) received no therapy at all; 17.5 per cent of juveniles had only attended one therapy session during their stay in the home. Then, 65.8 per cent of those charged with petty offences, 71.4 per cent of those charged with serious offences and 72 per cent of those charged with heinous offences received no therapy sessions or counselling. Those receiving regular therapy only formed 9.9 per cent of all charged with commission of heinous offences while 18.2 per cent of such juveniles had only attended a session once since their confinement.

That counsellors, therapists and psychologists are unable to pay individual attention to all children inside the institution can be ipso facto deduced from these points. It would be absurd to divert whatever little resources and manpower establishments have in the form of counsellors and psychologists from their primary duty of rehabilitating and reintegrating the juveniles towards court work.

These findings can be further corroborated by an official reply to a question raised in the parliament regarding shortage of mental healthcare professionals in India. The parliament was informed in 2017 by the Ministry of Health and Family Welfare that as against the requirement of 13,500 psychiatrists, only 3,827 were available; of the 20,250 clinical psychologists required, only 898 were available; of the required 37,000 psychiatric social workers required, only 850 were available.[20] With official figures pointing towards such an abysmal state of affairs, a fair implementation of the provisions is impossible.

Lastly, the principle of fresh start has been largely undermined by Section 24 (1) of the Act of 2015. The principle states[21] that the juvenile should get a new beginning and all records with relation to his conflict with law should be erased. Moreover, the state shall endeavour to promote ways for dealing with juveniles who break penal law without resorting to judicial proceedings. Section 24 (2) calls for the destruction of all records pertaining to proceedings within a reasonable period of time. However, it goes on to dilute the principle in cases of juveniles aged 16–18 who were charged with a heinous offence, as the records shall be saved by the Children's Court in case of conviction. In addition, while the principle also seeks to ensure that the child is not subjected to any disqualification emerging from a conviction, the same is not applicable to those 16–18 years old and convicted of heinous offences.

Constitutionality of the Impugned Provisions

On the constitutionality of impugned provisions, the Act of 2015 fares no better. Article 14 of the Constitution states that all persons are entitled to equality before the law and equal protection of the law. However, consequent to several Supreme Court decisions, the fundamental right to equality is not wholly unqualified. It is subject to test of reasonable classification as well as the test of arbitrariness. The former entails that the classification must be based on an intelligible differentia; latterly, there must be a nexus between the intelligible differentia and the object sought to be achieved by the Act.[22] In the application of the test, the presumption stands in favour of the constitutionality of the statute rather than against it.[23]

---

[20] 'Unstarred Question No. 2709 to be answered on 17th March, 2017,' Ministry of Health and Family Welfare, Lok Sabha, accessed 21 March 2019, http://164.100.47.194/Loksabha/Questions/QResult15.aspx?qref=48992&lsno=16.

[21] As per the Rules of 2007.

[22] *State of West Bengal* v. *Anwar Ali Sarkar*, 1952 SCR 284.

[23] *Chiranjit Lal Sahu* v. *Union of India*, 1950 SCR 869.

Bearing this in mind, it becomes necessary to examine the impugned provisions for constitutionality. Section 2 (12) of the Act of 2015 defines children as persons who have not completed 18 years. Under the Children Act of 1960 and the Act of 1986, the age classification lay between those under 16 years, and those over 16 but below 18 years. The decision to raise the age of juvenility to 18 years was taken consciously while enacting the Act of 2000 and as such, the classification was removed. The Act of 2015, however, creates two classes of people; firstly, those under 16 years, and those over 16 but below 18 years, charged with petty and serious offences; secondly, those over 16 years but below 18 years and charged with heinous offences. On the basis of this classification, a different procedure for their trial in the adult criminal justice system is then called for through Sections 15, 18 (3) and 19.

The considerations of legislators that precipitate such treatment have two prongs, which are, upon a deeper examination, different sides of the same coin; first, that the children aged 16–18 have the mental capacity to gauge the consequences of their actions and recognise them as an offence against society, and second, that there has been a significant increase in the number of children aged 16–18 committing heinous offences and therefore should be subject to deterrence and retribution.

However, the classification only seeks to try those charged with the commission of heinous offences in an adult criminal justice system. If, for the sake of argument, the reasoning of legislators that the children are, in fact, mentally capable to commit the offence, was assumed to be valid, it remains just as valid for those aged 16–18 and charged with petty and serious offences. There seems to be no intelligible differentia in the classification wherein only those charged with heinous offences, being mentally capable, are subject to the principles of retribution and deterrence, as opposed to those charged with petty and serious offences.

Primarily, therefore, the consideration of legislators for differential treatment seems to be founded on the belief that there has been a rise in the number of heinous offences committed by those over 16 years. Given that most petty and serious offences by juveniles are committed out of necessity and socioeconomic considerations, any increase in heinous offences would reflect in the total number of crimes committed by juveniles, which would jump significantly.

However, a closer look at the NCRB data as shown in Figure 10.1 suggests that there has been no significant increase in the total number of offences registered against juveniles. The increase in crimes by juveniles has been in line with the increase in the total number of crimes, that is, the rate of increase remained constant in the years preceding the enactment. The spike in the number of crimes being proportional to the number of total crimes—a situation where the heinous offences were increasing but petty and serious offences were declining—as an explanation for such proportionality is unimaginable. Even this increase is doubtful given that the data is based on the filing of FIRs and not outcome of the cases. Thus, the differentia becomes imposed or artificial rather than apparent.

The final orders of the Board in cases of juvenile apprehension can better help us understand the prevailing situation on the ground with respect to such an increase. It is obvious that the punishment awarded by the Board will be commensurate with the nature of offence. Of the 56,501 cases of juvenile apprehension,[24] pending and fresh, in 2015, 21,562 were still pending at the end of the year. Of the 34,939 cases disposed of in 2015, 13.12 per cent had been acquitted, 27.62 per cent had been sent to special homes, 7.38 per cent had been fined, 5.49 per cent had been sent to fit institutions, 25.3 per cent had been released on probation of good conduct, and 21.05 per cent had been sent back home after advice or admonishment.

Overall, in the opinion of the Boards, in 72.34 per cent of the cases, the apprehended child could be sent back into society without detention in the system to be reformed and rehabilitated. In this scenario, where there has been no serious increase in the incidence of offences committed by juveniles, and where a majority of juveniles have been deemed not to need detention or institutionalisation, the intelligibility of the differentia is certainly suspect.

The next step is to examine if there is a nexus between the objective sought to be achieved by the Act and intelligible differentia. The objective of the Act is reiterated: 'An Act to consolidate and amend the law relating to children alleged and found to be in conflict with law and children in need of care and protection by catering to their basic needs through proper care, protection, development, treatment, social reintegration,

[24] 'Final Order in the Matter of Juveniles,' NCRB.

by adopting a child-friendly approach in the adjudication and disposal of matters in the best interest of children and for their rehabilitation through processes provided, and institutions and bodies established, herein under and for matters connected therewith or incidental thereto.'

Plain reading suggests that the Act has to look out for the best interests of the child, whether he is in need of care and protection or in conflict with law. It seeks to cater to their basic needs through care, protection, development, treatment and social reintegration, while adopting a child-friendly approach in the adjudication and disposal of matters, in the best interests of children. Its last objective is to rehabilitate them through processes and institutions provided for in the Act.

In catering to basic needs, the Act works well in favour of those under the age of 16 and who have not been charged with heinous offences. However, the Act is silent as to how the procedure for those over the age of 16 and charged with heinous offences (which would subsequently lead to incarceration of the child in adult prisons upon attaining the age of 21) will cater to the needs of these children, in case of failure of rehabilitation or reformation processes during their stay in special and observation homes.

As pointed out earlier, 72 per cent of those charged with heinous offences received no therapy or counselling; those attending regular sessions only formed 9.9 per cent of all who were charged with heinous offences. In 69.5 per cent of all cases, there was no provision of any kind of vocational training for inmates; only 27.4 per cent of those lodged in special homes and 13.1 per cent of those lodged in observation homes received vocational training. All respondents unanimously answered that they were unaware of any post-release/individual care plans drawn up for them, even though such plans have to be formulated in consultation with the individual.

Given the sad state of affairs, where the correctional facilities are decrepit and completely lack the infrastructure to reform, rehabilitate and reintegrate children into society, it is atrocious to incarcerate in adult prisons those children whom we, in the first place, fail to reform, rehabilitate and reintegrate. The trial of children as adults is certainly not in the best interest of the child, and it is incomprehensible that a system which tries a child as an adult can be ever be deemed as child-friendly adjudication. It can be concluded that the procedure in its classification, supposedly based on an intelligible differentia, has no nexus with the object sought to be achieved by the impugned Act of 2015.

That the procedure is also arbitrary in nature is prima facie determinable from a plain reading of the impugned provisions. There is lack of scientific consensus with respect to the mental capacity of adolescents to commit crimes. Adolescence is a fascinating period of human development: the struggle for identity, choice of friends and first sexual partners, academic routes and vocations are but a few examples of complex behaviours the brain must implement at the brink of adulthood.[25] The study of the development of executive function and social cognition beyond childhood is a new but rapidly evolving field with applications for medical diagnoses, education and social policy.[26] The finding that changes in brain structure continue into adolescence and early adulthood challenged accepted views and has given rise to a recent spate of investigations into the way cognition might change as a consequence.[27]

The Act of 2015 expects the Board, which comprises of a principle magistrate and two social workers, to answer questions as yet indeterminable because these are unsettled and under scrutiny as a result of a vigorous debate in the scientific community. The process raises several concerns primarily with regard to the ability of the Board to judge the capacity of a child to commit the offence when, in reality, such subjective judgement of mental capacity is non-quantifiable and as such, nearly impossible. A reliance is placed on assistance from psychologists, psycho-social workers and other experts, as an inbuilt safeguard against any arbitrariness flowing into the system. Even so, as research findings show, the infrastructure for collaboration with psychologists, psycho-social workers and other experts such as counsellors is non-existent in some places and deplorable state in others. The psychologists and psycho social workers cannot even

---

[25] Tomas Paus, 'Mapping Brain Maturation and Cognitive Development during Adolescence,' *Trends in Cognitive Sciences*, Vol. 9, no. 2 (February 2005): 60.

[26] Sarah Jayne Blakemore and Suparna Choudhury, 'Development of the Adolescent Brain: Implications for Executive Function and Social Cognition,' *The Journal of Child Psychology and Psychiatry*, Vol. 47, no. 3–4 (March/April 2006): 296.

[27] Blakemore and Choudhury, 'Development of the Adolescent Brain.'

provide individual attention to juveniles already in observation homes and special homes. As such, a diversion of these resources towards court work requiring them to answer indeterminable questions is ludicrous. It can easily be deduced that in the present scenario, any determination of the child's mental capacity being on a par with an adult's would be arbitrary from the start, and by the enactment of these provisions, the odds have been stacked heavily against juveniles aged 16 or above and charged with heinous offences.

The Act of 2015 recognises that the Constitution confers powers and imposes duties under Clause (3) of Article 15, Clauses (e) and (f) of Article 39, Article 45 and Article 47 on the state to ensure that all the needs of children are met and their basic human rights fully protected. However, the impugned provisions infringe upon the spirit with which Article 15 (3) was inserted in the Constitution.

In the case of *Bai Tahira* v. *AHF Chothia*,[28] the Supreme Court stated that 'welfare laws must be so read as to be effective delivery systems of the salutary objects sought to be served by the Legislature and when the beneficiaries are the weaker sections, like destitute women, this spirit of Article 15 (3) of the Constitution must be light the meaning of the Section. The Constitution is a pervasive omnipresence brooding over the meaning and transforming the values of every measure.'

In the sense of Article 15 (3), special provision for women means that no less favourable treatment is to be given to them on gender-based criterion, which would favour the opposite sex and that women will not deliberately be selected for less favourable treatment because of their sex.[29] As the apex court in *Salil Bali* v. *Union of India*[30] recognised: 'It cannot be questioned that children are amongst the most vulnerable sections in any society. They represent almost one-third of the world's population, and unless they are provided with proper opportunities, the opportunity of making them grow into responsible citizens of tomorrow will slip out of the hands of the present generation.'

While the Act of 2015 recognises its obligation to ensure that the needs of children are met and their basic human rights are protected, the

[28] (1979) 2 SCC 316.

[29] *Air India Cabin Crew Assn.* v. *Yashaswinee Merchant*, (2003) 6 SCC 277.

[30] (2013) 7 SCC 705.

impugned provisions run contrary. In the same manner that by virtue of Article 15 (3) women cannot be treated in a less favourable manner than the opposite sex, children (as defined by the Act of 2015, anyone under the age of 18) cannot be treated in a manner less favourable to them on the whole. Every child should be given a fair chance, with all rights accruing to him from the Act of 2015, including that of the implementation of the Act for his benefit, reformation and rehabilitation. In light of Article 15 (3) he should not be discriminated against on the basis of his age and consequent trial in an adult criminal justice system.

The impugned provisions of law are also violative of Article 21 of the Constitution, which states that no person shall be deprived of his life and personal liberty except according to a procedure established by law. This right to life has been given a very wide interpretation through a plethora of judgements by the Supreme Court.[31] Though it can be deprived through a procedure established by law, the same is subject to the test of arbitrariness and reasonableness.[32] As such, the argument that the impugned procedure is arbitrary and unreasonable is also valid when such argument is tested on the touchstone of Article 21 as much as on the touchstone of Article 14.

In *Court on its Own Motion* v. *Department of Women and Child Development, Govt. of N.C.T. of Delhi*,[33] the Delhi High Court proclaimed the lodging of juveniles in adult prisons to be in violation of their right to life guaranteed under Article 21. It stated that 'there can be no cavil in saying that lodging juveniles in adult prisons amounts to deprivation of their personal liberty on multiple aspects.' The reasons were that at the time of arrest of such persons, there is no proper age verification and had that been so, the juveniles would not have been subjected to the hardship of adult criminal justice system. In other words, due to a lack of implementation of the provisions of the Act of 2000, the consequent

---

[31] See *Maneka Gandhi* v. *Union of India*, 1978 SCR (2) 621; *Rajendra Prasad* v. *State of U.P.*, (1979) 3 SCC 646; *Rudal Shah* v. *State of Bihar*, (1983) 4 SCC 141; *Olga Tellis* v. *Bombay Municipal Corporation*, 1985 SCC (3) 545; *People's Union for Democratic Rights* v. *Union of India*, 1983 SCR (1) 456.

[32] *Maneka Gandhi* v. *Union of India*, 1978.

[33] (2013) 2 RCR (Criminal) 362.

lodging of juveniles in the adult criminal justice system amounted to a violation of their right to life and personal liberty.

It can be safe to say that the same logic can be extended to the impugned provisions of the Act of 2015. Through the non-implementation of measures with respect to rehabilitation and reintegration provided for within the Act of 2015, if any child is sent to jail on account of his non-reformation upon the attainment of the age of 21, such incarceration would be against his fundamental right to life and personal liberty and in violation of Article 21.

As a parting remark it should be mentioned here that the Supreme Court, through its dismissal of the challenge to the constitutionality of the Act vide *Tehseen Poonawala* v. *Union of India*,[34] has not closed the door on any future challenges. In that case, the locus standi of the petitioner was questioned and writ petition dismissed on that ground. Future challenges to its validity can certainly be mounted on all of the aforementioned grounds by an aggrieved person.

The Act of 2015 is in itself a social piece of legislation, which, to some extent, remedies certain faults in the previous enactments. These faults are in respect to the streamlining of the procedure for adoption, lack of clarification with respect to inter-country adoption, lack of penal provisions on corporal punishment, addition of the principles to the Act of 2015 as opposed to their earlier presence in the Rules of 2007, and a clarification of the functions of various authorities and institutions created therein. To such extent, the constitutionality of the entire Act shouldn't be called into question; merely those provisions that are unconstitutional should be challenged and the severability or reading down of those provisions should be prayed for while mounting such a challenge.

---

[34] W.P. 94 of 2016.

Conclusion

In the conclusion, the major findings of researchers have been correlated with the provisions of the Act of 2000 and the Act of 2015 to identify lacunae and problems in their implementation as well as the impact of the legislations. It is structured in a manner that analyses, issue-wise, the experiences of children who enter the juvenile justice system, established by the Acts at all stages—pre-institutionalisation, in conflict with law, inside the home as well as post-release prospects.

An analysis of pre-institutionalised life is necessary to create a socioeconomic profile of the juveniles most likely to enter the system. This empowers us in the examination of how best to deal with such juveniles so as to rehabilitate and reintegrate them as contributing members of the society. The second segment, on impact and implementation, takes into account findings with regard to Chapters VI, VII and VIII.

The findings from the chapter on juvenile in conflict with law allow us to inspect their experiences when they first come in conflict and the treatment meted out to them by the various institutions in light of the provisions of the Act. The data from the chapter on juveniles inside the home shed light on the prevailing conditions and whether the environment, which is most conducive to their rehabilitation and reintegration, has been provided. Stress has been laid on the quality of the service rather than quantity, as determined by the Rules of 2007 and 2016. Lastly, the data analyses from Chapter VIII allows us to examine how well the system rehabilitates juveniles and prepares them for reintegration after their term of stay is over. The same has been correlated with findings in Chapters II, III and IV in order to provide a comprehensive outlook in the examination of the successes and failures of the legislation.

Throughout the conclusion, the hypotheses set out in the beginning of the book have been referred to and tested for their strength. These are: the institutional setup required under the JJ Act has not been established fully in many places; district-level institutions are generally deficient of infrastructure and staff to effectively implement the JJ Act; the performance of the staff is far from effective; the attitude and aptitude required to enforce the JJ Act is missing on the part of concerned personnel; the lack of implementation of the provisions hinders the rehabilitative and reformative aspects of the juvenile justice system; the lack of monitoring and supervision is also a factor in the dismal state of implementation of JJ Act; and, the abysmal state of implementation of the Act of 2000 has led to a failure in the stated aims of rehabilitation and reintegration. In the process, efforts have also been made to analyse if the provisions of the Act of 2015 provide for any drastic changes that may lead to the realisation of the goals of the Act of 2000 and cure the defects therein, or if the Act of 2015 is indeed a step back as many sections seem to portray.

Profile of Juveniles

The statistics in Chapter V and the first segment of Chapter IX are res ipsa loquitur, and such don't need elaboration except while creating a criminological profile based on socioeconomic, psychological and familial factors. As iterated in Chapter V, an understanding of this profile is crucial if we are to put into context the findings of the three subsequent chapters by way of cross-tabulations. All observations made, analyses conducted and conclusions drawn keep in mind the profile of juveniles. The following points elaborate the most significant findings in order to further our understanding of the particular demographics the juvenile justice system deals with in practicality.

1) A total of 76.8 per cent inmates were aged 16 and above, while a majority (47.4 per cent) were 16–17 years old. A vast section of children in conflict with law were adolescents.
2) A simple majority of the inmates (27.5 per cent) were educated up to middle school (sixth to ninth grade) while only 1.7 per cent had graduated college. About 22.2 per cent were educated only up to fifth grade, 21.9 per cent had completed their matriculation and only

7.3 per cent had completed senior secondary school. Even though approximately three quarters of the children in conflict with law were above the age of 16, most were only educated up to primary level.

3) A majority (44.1 per cent) of those who were illiterate fell within the age group of 16–17.
4) About 40 per cent of all inmates 11–13 years old were illiterate, while the same figure for 14–15-year-olds stands at 31.3 per cent.
5) A majority of the illiterate (55.9 per cent) and those educated only up to the primary level (43.3 per cent) were from Punjab.
6) About 57.6 per cent (highest) and 63.6 per cent (highest) of the inmates who had completed their matriculation and schooling respectively were from Haryana.
7) In a vast majority of cases (75.8 per cent), the father of the juvenile was the primary income earner, while in 8.9 per cent cases the juvenile fended for himself.
8) In most cases (46.7 per cent), the provider for the juvenile was engaged in skill labour as a factory worker, carpenter, car mechanic, farmer, plumber, etc. In 29.8 per cent (second-highest) of cases, the provider was a daily wage labourer. These statistics shed light on the socioeconomic demographic to which majority of the inmates belong, given that the providers of only 6.3 per cent inmates were salaried workers forming part of the supposedly upward mobile middle class.
9) In a majority of the cases (54.1 per cent) where the juvenile was providing for himself, he was engaged as a daily wage labourer; in 37 per cent cases, he was employed as a skilled labourer.
10) In a majority (37.5 per cent) of cases where the mother of the juvenile was the primary breadwinner, she was a daily wage labourer.
11) In a majority of the cases where the father or brother was the primary provider, they were engaged as skilled labourer (52.4 per cent and 50 per cent respectively).
12) About 43.4 per cent (highest) juveniles were studying/schooling while 25.8 per cent were employed for the purpose of remuneration; 30.8 per cent were doing neither.

13) About 40 per cent of those in the age group of 11–13 were employed for the purpose of remuneration.
14) About 43.4 per cent of those within the age group of 16–17 were studying.
15) A staggering 32.9 per cent were neither studying nor employed.
16) About 34.8 per cent of inmates interviewed in Delhi were pursuing studies prior to their institutionalisation, while 40.8 per cent were neither studying nor employed.
17) About 45.8 per cent (highest) of all inmates who were pursuing schooling and 30.8 per cent of all inmates who were employed were from Haryana.
18) In Punjab, a majority (48.7 per cent) of inmates were employed while 36.6 per cent were pursuing their education.
19) Of those who were illiterate, 57.6 per cent were employed gainfully while 42.4 per cent were neither employed nor studying.
20) Of those educated up to the primary level, 6 per cent were still pursuing their education, 44.8 per cent were employed in the service of others while 49.3 per cent were neither studying nor employed.
21) Of those educated up till middle school, 51.8 per cent were still studying, 13.3 per cent were employed while 34.9 per cent were neither studying nor employed.
22) About 95.5 per cent of those who had matriculated were still studying while the figure stands at 72.2 per cent for those educated till senior secondary level.
23) A majority of the juveniles (54.6 per cent) were social, and 45.4 per cent had difficulty making friends easily.
24) More than quarter juveniles had developed an addiction to intoxicants.
25) Almost 7.3 per cent of the juveniles were addicted to tobacco, 7.9 per cent to alcohol, 2.3 per cent to cannabinoids and 7.6 per cent to narcotics.
26) Nearly 69.6 per cent of the inmates addicted to narcotics such as heroin and smack as well as 42.9 per cent addicted to cannabinoids, 58.3 per cent addicted to alcohol and 59.1 per cent addicted to tobacco, were from Punjab.

27) While 86.4 per cent of inmates from Delhi and 81.3 per cent of inmates from Haryana reported not being addicted to any substance, the figure for the same in Punjab stands at 62.9 per cent, indicating a more serious drug abuse problem and associated crimes.
28) Nearly 8.7 per cent of the inmates addicted to narcotics were 11–13 years old.
29) About 58.3 per cent of those were addicted to alcohol were aged 18 and above.
30) Those who were illiterate or educated up to primary level formed 40.9 per cent each (highest) of those addicted to tobacco.
31) Of those who were addicted to narcotics, 56.5 per cent were illiterate while 26.1 per cent had been educated up to middle school.
32) Those educated till primary level, along with the illiterate formed 50 per cent of those who consumed alcohol. Overall, it was found that the incidence of addiction was higher among those less educated or illiterate.
33) About 56.5 per cent of narcotic addicts were neither studying nor employed, 34.8 per cent were employed gainfully and only 8.7 per cent were studying.

The demographic profile indicates that those 16 years old and above were vulnerable to delinquency. Most juveniles were literate, however, they lacked higher education. Thus the dropout rates may be checked as a prevention strategy, as well as opportunities to continue education for those released from the homes should be provided. In this study, a majority of the juveniles were from low socioeconomic backgrounds, deduced from the fact most providers were skilled labourers or daily wage labourers. In the majority of cases, the juveniles were dependent on their fathers, indicating the presence of fathers. However, one does not know the quality of relationship they shared. Also, a majority of the juveniles were studying or working before coming to the institution. This provides a platform to rehabilitate them as they can engage with schools or work post their release. Those who were doing nothing may be provided opportunities to enhance their skills while they are in the homes, so that once they are out, they can look for jobs or self-employment opportunities. Similarly, they may be provided with opportunities to continue studying when they are in the home so that there aren't long gaps in their education, which would make it easier for them to continue once they are released. Addiction was also found among juveniles, suggesting a need to prevent addiction formation. Measures should also be taken so that addicts don't go back the same way once they are released. However, studies have linked addiction with delinquency, making it possible for juveniles to become more vulnerable to delinquent acts because of addiction and peer influences. A need to involve the family is felt in exercising control over their interactions with individuals who may be a negative influence and expose children to addictions.

Impact and Implementation

Nature of Offence and Trial in Case of Heinous Offence

The majority of respondents had committed heinous offences, although all types of offences were present among the youth. The following correlations have been drawn in addition to the findings of the impugned provisions of the Act of 2015 in Chapters III and X.

1) The time limit of four plus two months for the disposal of enquiries under the Act of 2015 was already present under the Act of 2000.
2) The procedure under the Act of 2015 for extension of time for disposal of enquiries by the Chief Judicial Magistrate or Chief Metropolitan Magistrate only elongates and complicates the procedure. The Act of 2015 doesn't specify any time limit of such extension or the number of times such extension can be granted. Further, in the absence of guidelines while allowing the extension, the procedure itself becomes superfluous compared to the Act of 2000, wherein the Board could extend the enquiry provided that it recorded its reasons in special cases with regard to the circumstances of the case.
3) Provisions allowing for the possibility of the Children's Court not to try the child as an adult require the court not to remit the matter back to the Board, but to hold an enquiry as if it were the Board. Given that the Children's Court will not have two social

workers on its bench while conducting the enquiry, the provision defeats the purpose that the legislators of the Act of 2000 and the Act of 2015 had in mind while putting them on the Board—that the enquiry shouldn't be a mere mechanical application of the law.

4) Even if the Board decides to conduct an enquiry, it is bound to follow the procedure of a trial by summons as per the Code of Criminal Procedure, 1973. This would vitiate the environment of the proceedings, which are not supposed to look like trials but enquiries requiring special procedure and approach. Furthermore, in such case, only the principle magistrate has the required legal acumen to regulate the proceedings and not the other two members who are laymen in the field of law. The same wasn't recognised as a cause of inordinate delay by the drafters of the Act of 2015, who would have done well to remove the requirements of a trial by summons and instead create a new procedure under the juvenile justice system, which equips it to handle such cases efficiently.
5) The budgetary allocations to the Integrated Child Protection Scheme are a pittance, completely disproportionate to the magnitude of the problem. In light of this, the reasons, which provided impetus to the enactment of the Act of 2015, are at odds with the priority accorded to those reasons by the government.
6) While the Act of 2000 applied the principles of reformation and rehabilitation, the cornerstones of the juvenile justice system, as differentiated from the principles of retribution and deterrence upon which the traditional criminal justice system operates, the Act of 2015 dilutes said principles, thereby allowing deterrence and retribution to take the steering wheel.
7) The impugned provisions of the Act of 2015 are in violation of several principles it expressly seeks to adhere to—presumption of innocence; best interest; non-stigmatising semantics, actions and decisions; equality or non-discrimination; privacy and confidentiality; and fresh start.

8) The provisions are also ignorant of several landmark judgements of the Supreme Court, which accept reformation and rehabilitation as sine qua non in a juvenile justice system.
9) The contention of the legislators that there has been a significant increase in the number of offences in the age group of 16–18 is also misguided, and the proportion of cases of juveniles in conflict with law to the totality of cognisable offences recorded by the National Crime Records Bureau has remained constantly between 1.1 per cent and 1.2 per cent between 2011 and 2015.
10) The impugned provisions dilute the principle of fresh start in cases of juveniles aged 16–18 who were charged with the commission of a heinous offence as the records shall be saved by the Children's Court in case of conviction. In addition, while the principle also seeks to ensure that the child is not subjected to any disqualification emerging from a conviction, the same is not applicable to those aged 16–18 and convicted of heinous offences.
11) The impugned provisions are in violation of Article 14, Article 15 (3) and Article 21 of the Constitution.

Confinement in Judicial/Police Custody

The Act of 2000 provides for several safeguards to ensure that a child is not sent to judicial or police custody for any duration of time. Section 9 of the Act as amended in 2006 requires that under no condition should the juvenile be kept in police lockup or sent to prison. Section 12 requires for bail to be granted by the police as well as the Board in case of juvenility of the offender irrespective of whether the offence is bailable or non-bailable. Section 7 states that any magistrate not empowered by the Act should forward the juvenile to a competent authority after recording his findings, in case he is of the opinion that the child brought before him is a juvenile.

However, the state of affairs have been found to be appalling. A vast majority (66.2 per cent) of juveniles in this study had been confined in police or judicial custody before being sent to the home, making it clear that the aforementioned provisions have not been followed.

Further analysing the trend, the researchers observed that when inmates had been confined to police/judicial custody, they had made their claims of juvenility before the police in 70.5 per cent of cases and before the courts in 29.5 per cent of cases. Moreover, the juveniles were sent to judicial/police custody in 79.7 per cent cases where the claims were made before a judge, as compared to 61.8 per cent cases where the claims were made before the police.

Researchers observed a direct relationship between the variables of confinement and age, that is an increased trend of confinement to custody with an increase in age. About 50 per cent of juveniles (lowest) aged 11–13 reported being sent to judicial/police custody, while 58.3 per cent respondents aged 14–15 were sent to custody. The figures stand at 63.6 per cent for those aged 16–17 and 77.5 per cent (highest) for those 18 years old and above. Those aged 16–17 years, and 18 and above, were more likely to be sent to jail or police lockup primarily on the basis of their facial features and physical stature.

At this stage, it is important to reiterate the observations of the Supreme Court in the Sheela Barse case: 'There can be no doubt that incarceration in jail would have the effect of dwarfing the development of the child, exposing him to baneful influences, coarsening his conscience and alienating him from the society'. Even if one child was sent to judicial or police custody, it was in violation of the principles of presumption of innocence, dignity and worth, and most importantly, safety. The same should require disciplining and admonishment of errant officials. However, the violation of the principles and provisions of the Act of 2000 and the Act of 2015 on such a large scale requires urgent action after deep introspection on the part of law and policymakers to ensure their strict implementation.

Behaviour of Police Officials

The Act of 2000 and the Act of 2015 provide for the transfer of the child to the Special Juvenile Police Unit or Child Welfare Police Officer soon after apprehension. Officers who frequently or exclusively deal with juveniles are required to be specially trained and instructed in order to perform their functions more effectively. In this light, the findings are not encouraging.

In 53 per cent cases, the behaviour and attitude of the police towards the juveniles were hostile and the majority of them reported being tortured, while in 27.5 per cent of the cases, police officials were indifferent to the plight of the juvenile. Only in 19.5 per cent cases were the officials supportive and kind. The researchers found an inverse relationship between the age of the inmates and a supportive attitude of police officials. While 50 per cent of the juveniles aged 11–13 reported police supportiveness throughout their experience, only 20 per cent of 14–15-year-olds reported the same. About 19.6 per cent of those aged 16–17 and 15.7 per cent of those aged 18 and above reported that the police were supportive in their attitude and behaviour.

In line with trends, the researchers found a direct relationship between the age of the juveniles and the hostile attitude of police officials towards them. Nearly 59.6 per cent of those aged 18 and above, 43.1 per cent of those aged 16–17, 55 per cent of those aged 14–15, and 50 per cent of those aged 11–13 reported being abused or tortured by the police, with the overall attitude being hostile to them.

Among those who reported hostile treatment at the hands of the police, the providers of 28.8 per cent were daily wage labourers, and providers for 48.1 per cent were skilled labourers. No matter the provider's occupation, though, hostile treatment at the hands of the police was the dominant, ranging from 43.3 per cent to 59.1 per cent. About 54.2 per cent of all illiterate, 64.2 per cent of all primary educated, 53 per cent of middle schoolers, and 47.3 per cent of secondary educated have faced police hostility.

It is quite plain that with the police being the first point of contact with the system, a majority of juveniles face an adverse and hostile environment from the word go. The same is not only in violation of their human rights, but also the principles of dignity and self-worth, best interest, safety, and presumption of innocence as affirmed by the Acts.

Moreover, Section 75 of the Rules of 2007 require police officials to be in plain clothes and not uniforms while dealing with juveniles. In contravention though, our research indicates that an overwhelming majority (88.4 per cent) of juveniles were approached by officials in uniform while only 11.6 per cent stated they weren't approached by police in uniform.

Provision of Legal Aid

The principle of presumption of innocence under the Rules of 2007 called for the provision of legal aid, guardian ad litem and other such assistance for juveniles at the expense of the state. Section 8 and Section 30 of the Act of 2015 casts responsibility on the Board and the committee respectively, to ensure that juveniles are provided with legal aid through legal services institutions. However, researchers observed that in practice, the provisions have failed to secure such legal aid for juveniles.

Inmates received legal aid from the state in only 18.9 per cent cases, while in a vast majority (81.1 per cent), no such aid was provided. No juvenile aged 11–13 received legal aid; 40.4 per cent of those who received aid were 16–17 years old, while 38.6 per cent were 14–15. Only 13.5 per cent of those aged 18 and above received any kind of legal aid. Of those who did not received aid, 44.1 per cent (highest) were from Punjab, 41.6 per cent from Haryana and 14.3 per cent from Delhi. A majority (54.4 per cent) of the inmates who received legal aid were from Delhi, while 17.5 per cent and 28.1 per cent were from Haryana and Punjab respectively. In 74.4 per cent of cases, where the provider for the juvenile was a daily wage labourer, no legal aid was provided.

Use of Stigmatising Semantics

The language of the Act of 2000, Rules of 2007, Act of 2015 and the Rules of 2016 largely avoid the usage of stigmatising semantics and terms. The Rules of 2007 state this in the form of the principle of non-stigmatising semantics, decisions and action. The use of adversarial or accusatory words, such as arrest, remand, accused, charge sheet, trial, prosecution, warrant, summons, conviction, inmate, delinquent, neglected, custody or jail is prohibited in the processes pertaining to the child or juvenile in conflict with law under the Act. The principle is enshrined in the Act of 2015 as well, though the language of the provision has been diluted to state that adversarial or accusatory words are not to be used in the processes pertaining to a child.

However, the findings show that all respondents, irrespective of state, age or nature of offence were subject to accusatory and stigmatising terms, used for or around them during proceedings.

Likeability of the Environment

The Rules of 2007 cast a responsibility upon the institutions under the Act to create an environment inside the home that is conducive to the growth and development of the child. It states that homes should be child-friendly and in no way look like jail or lockup. About 31.8 per cent of children answered straightaway that they disliked the overall environment of the home, while 68.2 per cent replied that they liked it, prima facie. About 72.7 per cent of juveniles from Delhi, 61.6 per cent from Haryana and 71.8 per cent from Punjab liked the prima facie environment of the home.

It is important at this juncture to refer to the profiles of juveniles lodged in the homes. A large majority came from underprivileged backgrounds, where the primary breadwinner was either a skilled labourer or a daily wage labourer. Both vocations rarely afford beyond minimum wages. It is not surprising, therefore, that a majority of the juveniles would prima facie like the environment inside the home as compared to the harsh realities they had to face on the outside. As we go on, we'll see that the quality of infrastructure and life inside the institutions is well below expected standards.

Segregation

Section 40 of the Rules of 2007, Section 47 of the Act of 2015 and Section 29 of the Rules of 2016 emphasise the need to segregate children in observation and special homes on the basis of age, sex, mental capacity and nature of offence. While different homes for boys and girls have been established in all states, there has been no effort at segregation of the children on the basis of age, mental capacity and degree of offence. All of them are housed together in dormitories in violation of provisions. The situation was the same in all homes in Delhi, Punjab and Haryana.

Requirement of Better Infrastructure

Section 40 of the Rules of 2007 and Section 29 of the Rules of 2016 lay down a meticulous set of minimum requirements that must be adhered to in the homes. Dormitories, classrooms, sickrooms, kitchens, dining halls, stores, recreation rooms, libraries, bathrooms, toilets, office rooms, counselling and guidance rooms, workshops, residences for persons in charge, and rooms for Boards and committees be set up inside the institutions, along with minimum area requirements for the same. While the researchers were unable to measure if the area rules were being followed, they did find critical infrastructure to either be missing or dilapidated in condition.

Overall, 96 per cent inmates answered that there was need for better infrastructure—86.2 per cent from Delhi, 98.2 per cent from Haryana and 99.2 per cent from Punjab. This goes to show, in sync with research findings, that the homes in Delhi performed only marginally better than the homes in Haryana and Punjab in terms of infrastructure.

Quality of Pest Control

Under Section 42 of the Rules of 2007 and Section 31 of the Rules of 2016, annual pest control is listed under sanitation and hygiene regulations. First, for an institution of the size and number of residents such as a juvenile home, only one annual pest control is an understatement. Second, findings show that the status of pest and insect control inside the homes is well below even these standards—4.3 per cent inmates replied that the quality was poor while a majority of the inmates (58.6 per cent) answered that the quality was at best below average. About 35.1 per cent felt quality was average while only 2 per cent answered that quality was good. Nearly 53.8 per cent of juveniles from Delhi reported that the state of pest/insect control was poor; 34.5 per cent and 39 per cent of juveniles from Haryana and Punjab respectively stated that the quality of pest/insect control was below average.

Quality of Bedding/Clothing

Section 41 of the Rules of 2007 and Section 31 of the Rules of 2016 require providing clothing and bedding for juveniles as per scale and the climactic conditions of the state where the home is located. However, while the rules quantify the requirements, they don't stress upon the quality of the clothing/bedding. A large majority (80.1 per cent) of juveniles found the quality average, 17.5 per cent found quality below average, 1.3 per cent reported quality to be poor and only

1 per cent stated that the quality was good. About 62.1 per cent juveniles from Delhi, 85.7 per cent from Haryana and 84.7 per cent from Punjab stated that the quality of clothing/bedding provided was average.

Quality of Water for Drinking and Sanitation

A majority of inmates (79.1 per cent) responded that the quality of water was average, 17.2 per cent found it below average, 0.7 per cent deemed it poor while 3 per cent stated that the quality of water provided to them was good. About 56.1 per cent of juveniles from Delhi, 78.6 per cent from Haryana and 91.9 per cent from Punjab reported that the quality of water inside the home was average. Of those who reported that quality of water was below average, 50 per cent were from Delhi and 42.3 per cent from Haryana.

Quality and Sufficiency of Bathrooms

The Rules of 2007 and the Rules of 2016 require the homes to have at least one toilet for every seven children and one bathroom for every 10 children, and they should be well-lit and airy. However, 51 per cent (highest) of the interviewees said that the quality of bathrooms and their sufficiency was below average. About 37.4 per cent felt that the quality of bathroom was average, 9.6 per cent felt that quality was poor while 2 per cent felt quality was good. Around 60.6 per cent of juveniles from Delhi, 49.1 per cent from Haryana and 47.6 per cent from Punjab reported that the quality and quantity of bathrooms was below average; 22.3 per cent juveniles from Haryana stated that the quality and quantity of bathrooms was poor, while 47.6 per cent of juveniles from Punjab reported quality to be average. Only 4.8 per cent of juveniles reported that the quality and quantity of bathrooms was good—none were from Delhi or Haryana.

Quality of Kitchen Hygiene

The Rules of 2000 requires the kitchen to be clean and fly-proof with a segregated area for washing utensils. The Rules of 2015 go further and specify that vegetables should be washed, food should be prepared in a hygienic manner and that the slabs, floor and gas (burner) should be cleaned after every meal. About 68.2 per cent (highest) of juveniles answered that the quality of the kitchen cleanliness was average while 29.5 per cent found quality was good; 2.3 per cent found quality was below average, but none of the respondents said that hygiene in the kitchens was poor. About 68.2 per cent of juveniles from Delhi, 75.9 per cent from Haryana and 61.3 per cent from Punjab reported that quality of cleanliness inside the kitchens was average; 28.8 per cent of juveniles from Delhi, 19.6 per cent from Haryana and 38.7 per cent from Punjab stated that the quality of hygiene inside the kitchens was good.

Quality and Quantity of Meals

Both the Rules of 2000 and Rules of 2016 provide an elaborate diet chart to be followed by the institution. However, these charts focus on quantity rather than quality. About 47 per cent (highest) children responded that the quality of food was average. A sizeable segment (38.1 per cent) stated quality was below average, while 10.7 per cent said quality of the food was poor and deplorable. Only 4.3 per cent (lowest) stated that the quality of food was good. About 53 per cent of juveniles from Delhi and 49.1 per cent from Haryana found the quality of meals to be below average; 68.5 per cent juveniles from Punjab reported the food to be average while 21.5 per cent juveniles from Haryana found the quality to be poor.

The Rules also state that a minimum four meals are to be given to children per day. However all respondents, irrespective of the state or type of home said they were provided only three meals a day.

Children's Committee

The first mention of a children's committee comes in Section 43 of the Rules of 2007, which states that a routine shall be developed in consultation with the children's committee. The Rules provide that a representative of the children's committee must be given membership in the management committee of the institution. The committees have to be set up by the officer-in-charge of the institution with three different age groups—6–10, 11–15 and 16–18—having their own committees.

The children's committee should be encouraged to participate in the improvement of the institution; review the standards of care; prepare daily routines and diet scales; develop educational, recreational and vocational plans; report abuse and exploitation by peers; allow creative expression of views; and manage the institution through a management committee. Therefore, the role of the children's committees is essential to the implementation of the provisions of the Act and forward the best interests of the children.

However, only 24.5 per cent of respondents were aware about a children's committee while 32.5 per cent were unaware. In a majority of cases (43 per cent) there was no children's committee in the home. Only 43.9 per cent of juveniles in Delhi and 36.3 per cent of juveniles in Punjab were aware of the existence of the children's committee; 56.1 per cent juveniles in Delhi and 49.2 per cent from Punjab were not. No observation home or special home in Haryana had any children's committee.

Furthermore, 64.9 per cent of respondents who were aware of children's committee replied that it received no cooperation from the staff while only 35.1 per cent stated that the committee received cooperation. About 41.4 per cent juveniles from Delhi and 31.1 per cent from Punjab who were aware of the committee reported that the staff extended cooperation.

Monthly Medical Check-ups and First Aid

Both the Rules of 2007 and the Rules of 2015 call for the maintenance of first-aid kits and more importantly, for a monthly medical check-up of the children vide Sections 45 and 34 respectively. All respondents stated that first-aid kits were available in the home for immediate treatment of minor wounds and general ailments.

However, 91.4 per cent of the juveniles stated that no medical check-ups were done monthly. Only 8.6 per cent put on record that such check-ups were conducted. The rate of monthly medical check-ups was the highest in Delhi (37.9 per cent), while only 0.9 per cent juveniles from Haryana stated the same. No juvenile from Punjab reported monthly medical check-ups.

Suggestion Boxes

Section 55 (7) of the Rules of 2007 and Section 39 (5) of the Rules of 2016 cast a responsibility upon the management committee to install suggestion boxes at places accessible to children; suggestions should be reviewed at a meeting by the management committee, and once a month by the Board or a Committee. The installation of these boxes is to help children report their problems or any kind of abuse, anonymously or otherwise, and give suggestions with regard to improving conditions inside the home. However, the researchers found that none of the children were aware of the existence of such suggestion boxes.

Quality and Quantity of Staff

Most juveniles found the quality of staff to be average (44 per cent) or below average (33.4 per cent) while 12.9 per cent replied that it was poor. Only 9.6 per cent respondents stated that quality was good. State-wise, 51.5 per cent inmates from Delhi found staff quality to be below average while 13.3 per cent deemed it poor; 41.1 per cent inmates from Haryana staff quality to be below average, while 20.5 per cent deemed it poor; and 57.3 per cent of juveniles from Punjab stated that staff quality was average at best, while 20.2 per cent found it to be good.

The importance of the role of the housefather/housemother has been emphasised in Chapter III. However, only in 57 per cent of the cases was a house mother or house father present while in 43 per cent of the cases, the positions were vacant. In all homes in Delhi, house fathers and house mothers were present to take care of the children, while 85.5 per cent of juveniles from Punjab reported the same. There were no house fathers/house mothers in Haryana's homes.

Individual Care Plan and the Juvenile's Plan Post-Release

The Individual Care Plan is the fulcrum on which rides the efficacy of the aims of rehabilitation and reintegration as envisaged in the Acts of 2000 and 2015. The plan has to be made in consultation with the juvenile in order to restore his self-esteem and self-worth and nurture him into a responsible citizen, keeping in mind his emotional, health and psychological needs, leisurely activities, attachments, protection from abuse and social mainstreaming.

The researchers found that 47 per cent of inmates (highest) intended to complete their education post release while 18.5 per cent sought to continue in the jobs they held. About 20.9 per cent inmates wanted to look for other employment opportunities, while 13.6 per cent were undecided on their future course of action. However, all respondents unanimously answered that they were unaware of any post release/individual care plans being drawn up for them. If that is indeed the case, then either of the following conclusions can be drawn. First, that the individual care plans weren't made in consultation with the children or secondly, the plans weren't made at all. Both conclusions would result in a failure of the Acts.

Vocational Training

Vocational training was made mandatory by various provisions of the Act of 2000 and the Act of 2015 to ensure that children have the requisite skills to sustain themselves upon release. It is an integral part of the reformation, rehabilitation and reintegration objectives, but the status of implementation of provisions pertaining to vocational training was found to be abysmal.

In a large majority of the cases (69.5 per cent), there was no provision of any kind of vocational training. Of the 30.5 per cent of the cases where such training was available, only 16.6 per cent attended it while 13.9 per cent did not. It was found that 80 per cent of all children who attended training were in Delhi while 20 per cent were in Punjab, although 79 per cent of juveniles from Punjab reported that there was no provision of vocational training. No training was provided in any observation or special home in Haryana either.

The situation becomes even more appalling when it is observed that irrespective of the interests of the children, which are bound to be varied, in most of the homes with vocational training, rarely more than one or two vocations were addressed. A total of 47.1 per cent (highest) respondents who attended the training felt there was need to introduce new vocations. As a result, 41.2 per cent (highest) of the juveniles who attended vocational training did not believe it would help them post release. About 41.5 per cent inmates from Delhi and 40 per cent inmates from Punjab who attended said training thought it an effective post-release aid.

To make matters worse, the attitude of the trainers was also found to be lax; 47 per cent of the children found that their attitude indifferent, while 39.4 per cent found them helpful. In total, 59.3 per cent of the respondents found the attitude of the trainers to be indifferent or found the trainers to be incompetent.

Formal Education

The provision of formal education is a sure way to empower children and instil some form of confidence in them to life on the outside after their release. On this account, while we see that institutions have performed better than they have on other parameters, they are still nowhere close to the envisioned target and objective.

About 64.1 per cent of the children who were studying prior to their confinement were pursuing formal education within the home, and 43.6 per cent who were employed prior to their confinement, and 47.3 per cent of those who were doing neither had started formal education after coming to the home. Overall while 131 children were studying prior to their confinement, a total of 162 children were availing formal education from inside the home, an increase of 23.67 per cent over pre-institutionalisation levels.

However, only 53.6 per cent were continuing their formal education while inside the institution while the rest were not. State-wise, 65.2 per cent juveniles in Delhi, 54.5 per cent in Haryana and 46.8 per cent in Punjab received formal education, leaving vast numbers not pursuing this course of action.

Moreover, only 1 per cent of the children received any kind of encouragement to engage in voluntary services or open schooling; this number extends to only 4.5 per cent juveniles from Delhi who were thus encouraged. No child from Punjab or Haryana received encouragement.

Therapy / Counselling

Provision of therapy and counselling to the children with each child getting individual attention, not only for the purpose of assessing his mental health but also for his reformation, rehabilitation and reintegration, is one of the pillars upon which the success of the Act is based. In the context of trial in cases of heinous offences, the collaboration of institutions and counsellors, therapists and psychologists is virtually non-existent in many places, and wherever available, nearly not enough to handle all the children entering the system.

Therapy sessions on a regular basis were provided to only 11.3 per cent of juveniles while a majority (71.2 per cent) received no therapy at all; 17.5 per cent of juveniles had only attended one session during their stay in the home. Of those who had attended therapy, 58.6 per cent attended individual sessions, while 39.1 per cent attended group sessions. Only in 2.3 per cent of the cases were the juveniles called for both types of sessions. About 44.7 per cent of juveniles from Delhi, 61.5 per cent juveniles from Haryana and 59.3 per cent of juveniles from Punjab reported that they did not find the therapy sessions to be helpful. Only 25 per cent of juveniles from Delhi, 14.8 per cent of juveniles from Punjab and none of the juveniles from Haryana found the sessions helpful.

State-wise, the situation seems to be better in Delhi with 47 per cent of inmates attended regular therapy while similar figures are 0.9 per cent from Haryana and 1.6 per cent from Punjab. About 88.4 per cent of juveniles from Haryana and 78.2 per cent inmates from Punjab had never attended therapy; 24.2 per cent of children from Delhi, 10.7 per cent from Haryana and 20.2 per cent children from Punjab had attended therapy only once.

However, 36.2 per cent of juveniles who attended therapy sessions even once in Delhi were given individual therapy sessions while 59.2 per cent were given group sessions. In Haryana, 84.6 per cent were given individual sessions while 15.4 per cent stated that they were given group sessions. In Punjab, 85.2 per cent of juveniles reported being given individual sessions while 14.8 per cent stated that they were given group sessions.

About 65.8 per cent of those charged with petty offences, 71.4 per cent of those charged with serious offences and 72 per cent of those charged with heinous offences received no counselling. Those receiving regular therapy sessions only formed 9.9 per cent of all who were charged with heinous offences, while 18.2 per cent of such juveniles had only attended a therapy session once since their confinement.

Even out of those who had attended therapy sessions, only a miniscule portion (18.4 per cent) of juveniles felt that the sessions were helpful, while 29.9 per cent felt that they were helpful to some extent. A majority of the juveniles (51.7 per cent) found the sessions unbeneficial.

With regard to the performance of counsellors, a majority of the juveniles (56.3 per cent) found it to be average at best. About 16.1 per cent found their attitude towards children and performance to be good, 26.4 per cent stated that the performance of the therapist/counsellor was below average, while 1.1 per cent found it to be poor.

It was found that 90.9 per cent of those addicted to tobacco, 87.5 per cent of those addicted to alcohol, 28.6 per cent of those addicted to cannabinoids and 52.1 per cent of the those addicted to narcotics had not attended a therapy session even once. About 57.1 per cent of those dependent on cannabinoids had attended a session only once. Only 17.4 per cent of those addicted to narcotics and 14.3 per cent of those addicted to cannabinoids regularly attended therapy.

About 79.6 per cent of asocial respondents did not receive any therapy while only 7.3 per cent did. Of those found to be social, 64.2 per cent did not receive any therapy. Of those who received regular therapy, 70.6 per cent were social while 29.4 per cent were asocial. Similarly, of those who received therapy sessions only once, 66 per cent were sociable while 34 per cent were not.

Nearly 8.2 per cent of those lodged in special homes and 12.2 per cent of those in observation home received regular therapy, while 60.3 per cent of those in special homes and 74.7 per cent of respondents in observation homes never received any therapy at all. About 31.5 per cent of juveniles in special homes and 13.1 per cent of those in observation homes received therapy only once.

However, on the count of rewards for good behaviour and work, the institutions fared slightly better—55.3 per cent (highest) of the children stated that positive reinforcement mechanisms were indeed used by the staff, trainers and counsellors in the form of rewards for good behaviour. About 16.2 per cent replied said no such positive reinforcement was used, and 28.5 per cent were unaware of any such measures.

Annexure I

Sample of Interview Schedule

NATIONAL LAW UNIVERSITY, DELHI

Project on

IMPACT AND IMPLEMENTATION OF JUVENILE JUSTICE ACT, 2000

Survey and Questionnaire Form for Inmates

General

1. Name:
2. Age:
3. Place of residence:
4. Family members:
5. Education level:
   i. None
   ii. Primary
   iii. Middle
   iv. Secondary
   v. Senior Secondary
   vi. Dropout
   vii. Graduate
6. Education level of parents:
   i. Primary
   ii. Middle
   iii. Secondary
   iv. Higher
   v. None

7. Source of income (occupation):
    i. Self-dependent
    ii. Mother
    iii. Father
    iv. Brother
    v. Others
8. Life prior to institutionalisation:
    i. Studying
    ii. Working
    iii. Neither
9. Hobbies and Interests:
10. Days spent in the institution:
11. Nature of offence:
    i. Petty
    ii. Serious
    iii. Heinous (Rape)
12. How was the offence committed?
    i. Alone
    ii. With other juveniles
    iii. With other adults
13. Is it your first offence?
14. Who do you think is responsible for the crime?
    i. Parent/Guardian
    ii. Relatives
    iii. Friends
    iv. Self
    v. Other reason
15. Do you have friends?
    i. Yes
    ii. No
16. Have you made friends here?
    i. Yes
    ii. No
    iii. Uncertain

17. Intoxicating addiction status:
    i. Tobacco
    ii. Alcohol
    iii. Narcotics
    iv. Cannabis
18. What do you want to do after being released?
    i. Study
    ii. Continue previous job
    iii. Move to a new job
    iv. Vacation
19. During the proceedings, were you ever sent to jail or a police station lockup?
    i. Yes (three days)
    ii. No
20. To who did you make your claim for minority?
    i. Police
    ii. Court
    iii. Others
21. Behaviour and treatment of officials during your interaction with police:
    i. Supportive
    ii. Hostile (torture)
    iii. Indifferent
22. Any legal aid provided?
    i. Yes
    ii. No
23. Was there any involvement from your family in the decision-making? Were your parents or family members present during the proceedings?
    i. Yes
    ii. No
24. Were any stigmatising or accusatory words used by the officials, such as remand, arrest, warrant, charge sheet, trial, prosecution, etc.?
    i. Yes
    ii. No

25. Did you feel any kind of discrimination based on your gender, age, religion, caste or socioeconomic status?
    i. Yes
    ii. No
26. Do you like the environment of your observation/special home?
    i. Yes
    ii. No
27. Are there separate residential facilities based on age groups in your juvenile home?
    i. Yes
    ii. No
28. Do you attend the vocational training being provided here?
    i. Yes
    ii. No
29. Do you think this training will help you with your life outside the institution?
    i. Agree
    ii. Neutral
    iii. Disagree
    iv. Strongly disagree
30. What are the reasons for not attending?
    i. Not interested
    ii. Do not find it beneficial
    iii. Any other reason
31. Do you feel the need of other options in vocational training?
    i. Agree
    ii. Indifferent
    iii. Disagree
    iv. Strongly disagree
32. How would you describe your trainers?
    i. Caring
    ii. Helpful
    iii. Indifferent
    iv. Incompetent

33. Do you think this institution requires better infrastructure?
    i. Yes
    ii. No
    iii. Indifferent
34. Are you aware of post release plan/individual care plan?
    i. Yes
    ii. No
35. Are you aware of your date of release from this institution or next appearance in JJB?
    i. Yes
    ii. No

Facilities, hygiene and sanitation

36. Clothing and bedding:
    i. Poor
    ii. Below average
    iii. Average
    iv. Good
37. Drinking water, cleaning water and sanitation—availability and quality:
    i. Poor
    ii. Below average
    iii. Average
    iv. Good
38. Pest control and protection from mosquitoes:
    i. Poor
    ii. Below average
    iii. Average
    iv. Good
39. Availability of bathrooms and toilets in proportion to the number of inmates[1] and cleanliness:
    i. Poor
    ii. Below average
    iii. Average
    iv. Good

[1] Ideal number: one bathroom for 10 children, and one toilet for seven children.

40. Have you been to the kitchen? If yes, then describe the state:
    i. Poor
    ii. Below average
    iii. Average
    iv. Good
41. Are you aware of any children's committee in your institution? Have you ever been consulted or asked to give your opinion on a matter related to the institution?
    i. Yes
    ii. No

    If yes, do you think that such committee has encouraged the participation of children and increased their confidence?
    i. Yes
    ii. No
    iii. Indifferent

    Does such committee get full cooperation from the staff?
    i. Yes
    ii. No
    iii. Indifferent
42. Do you follow a particular routine or any routine prescribed by the institution?[2]
    i. Yes
    ii. No
43. How many meals are provided in a day?
44. How do you feel about the quality of the meals?
    i. Poor
    ii. Below average
    iii. Average
    iv. Good

    Are you provided with a special diet as needed in sickness?
    i. Yes
    ii. No

---

[2] Not many activities are planned for the day for inmates who do not attend any of the vocational or formal educational classes. The daily routine usually revolves around the timings of breakfast, lunch and dinner.

45. Do you get a medical check-up every month?
    i. Yes
    ii. No
46. Is there a first-aid kit available in your institution?
    i. Yes
    ii. No
47. Are there any recreational facilities available such as indoor games, music, television, etc.?
    i. Yes
    ii. No
48. Do you attend any kind of school or teachings or formal education?
    i. Yes
    ii. No
49. Have you been encouraged to take up voluntary service or open schooling?
    i. Yes
    ii. No
50. Do you attend regular therapy sessions?
    i. Yes
    ii. No
    iii. Once

    What kinds of sessions are taken?
    i. Group
    ii. Individual
    iii. Both

    Do you find such sessions helpful?
    i. Yes
    ii. To some extent
    iii. No
51. Is there a practice of rewarding children for their steady work and good behaviour?
    i. Yes
    ii. No
    iii. Don't know

52. How do you find the attitude and performance of counsellors/ therapists towards children?
    i. Poor
    ii. Below average
    iii. Average
    iv. Good
53. Have you ever gone out on leave or parole?
    i. Yes
    ii. No
54. Is there any children's suggestion box in your institution?
    i. Yes
    ii. No
    iii. Not aware
55. Are you allowed to meet your family and parents?
    i. Yes
    ii. No
56. What is the level of satisfaction with the available staff quality and quantity of staff?
    i. Poor
    ii. Below average
    iii. Average
    iv. Good
57. Is there a house mother or house father in your institution?
    i. Yes
    ii. No

    If any other programme ______________________________
58. Have you ever been approached by the police in their official uniform?
    i. Yes
    ii. No

Annexure II

List of Heinous Offences

Indian Penal Code, 1860

1) Section 121: Waging or attempting or abetting to wage war against the Government of India.
2) Section 195: Giving or fabricating false evidence with intent to procure conviction of offense with imprisonment for life or imprisonment.
3) Section 195A: Threatening any person to give false evidence—if any innocent person is convicted and sentenced in consequence of such false evidence with death or imprisonment for more than seven years.
4) Section 302: Punishment for murder.
5) Section 304B: Dowry death.
6) Section 311: Punishment for thugs.
7) Section 326A: Acid attack causing permanent or partial damage/ deformity.
8) Section 370 (2): Trafficking
9) Section 370 (3): Trafficking of more than one person.
10) Section 370 (4): Trafficking of minor.
11) Section 370 (5): Trafficking of more than one minor.
12) Section 370 (6): Trafficking of minor on more than one occasion.
13) Section 370 (7): Trafficking by public servant or police officer.
14) Section 376 (1): Punishment for rape.

15) Section 376 (2): Custodial rape, rape on minor or pregnant women, etc.
16) Section 376A: Rape resulting in death or permanent vegetative state of women.
17) Section 376D: Gang rape
18) Section 376E: Repeat of S.376, 376A or 376D.
19) Section 397: Robbery, or dacoity, with attempt to cause death or grievous hurt.
20) Section 398: Attempt to commit robbery or dacoity when armed with deadly weapon.

Commission of Sati (Prevention) Act, 1987

1) Section 4 (i): Abetment of sati when sati committed.
2) Section 4 (ii): Abetment of sati when sati attempted.

Narcotic Drugs and Psychotropic Substances Act, 1985

1) Section 15(c): Punishment for contravention in relation to poppy straw involving commercial quantity
2) Section 17(c): Punishment for contravention in relation to prepared opium involving commercial quantity.
3) Section 18(b): Punishment for contravention in relation to opium poppy and opium involving commercial quantity.
4) Section 19: Punishment for embezzlement of opium by cultivator.
5) Section 20C: Punishment for contravention in relation to cannabis plant and cannabis involving commercial quantity.
6) Section 21C: Punishment for contravention in relation to manufactured drugs and preparations involving commercial quantity.
7) Section 22C: Punishment for contravention in relation to psychotropic substances involving commercial quantity.
8) Section 23C: Punishment for illegal import into India, export from India or transhipment of narcotic drugs and psychotropic substances involving commercial quantity.

9) Section 24: Punishment for external dealings in narcotic drugs and psychotropic substances.
10) Section 25: Punishment for allowing premises, etc., to be used for commission of an offence.
11) Section 27A: Punishment for financing illicit traffic and harbouring offenders.
12) Section 29: Punishment for abetment and criminal conspiracy.
13) Section 31A: Repetition by persons convicted of commission, attempt, abetment, conspiracy of offenses under S.19, 24, and 27A and for offences involving commercial quantity of any narcotic drug or psychotropic substance who are subsequently convicted of the commission, attempt, abetment, criminal conspiracy of an offence in relation to certain ND&PS above a specified quantity.

Arms Act, 1959

1) Section 27 (2): Use of any prohibited arms or prohibited ammunition in contravention of Section 7 (relating to 'Prohibition of acquisition or possession, or of manufacture or sale, of prohibited arms or prohibited ammunition').
2) Section 27 (3): Use of any prohibited arms or prohibited ammunition or does any act in contravention of Section 7 that results in death.

Unlawful Activities (Prevention) Act, 1967

1) Section 10(b)(i): Penalty for being member of an unlawful association, etc. who does any act that results in death of any person.
2) Section 16(1)(a): Punishment for terrorist act if such act has resulted in the death of any person.

The Food Safety and Standards Act, 2006

1) Section 59 (iv): Punishment for unsafe food where a contravention or failure results in death of a person.

The Scheduled Castes and Scheduled Tribes (Prevention of Atrocities) Act, 1989

1) Section 3(2)(i): Giving or fabricates false evidence intending to lead to a conviction of any member of a Scheduled Caste or a Scheduled Tribe to be convicted of a capital offence.
2) Section 3(2)(iv): Commission of mischief by fire or explosive substance intending to cause destruction of a building used by a member of SC/ST.
3) Section 3(2)(v): Commission of any IPC offense with imprisonment of more than 10 years against the person or property of a member of SC/ST.

Maharashtra Control of Organised Crime Act, 1999

1) Section 3(1)(i): Punishment for organised crime, which has resulted in death of a person.

Protection of Children from Sexual Offences Act, 2012

1) Section 4: Punishment for penetrative sexual assault
2) Section 6: Punishment for aggravated penetrative sexual assault

Annexure III

Cross-Tabulation Tables

Table 5.4: Cross-Tabulation of 'Age' and 'Level of Education'

Cross-Tabulation			Level of Education: Illiterate	Primary	Middle	Secon-dary	Senior Secondary	Graduate	Total
Age	11–13	Count	4	1	5	0	0	0	**10**
		% within Age	40	10	50	0	0	0	**100**
		% within Level of Education	6.8	1.5	6	0	0	0	**3.3**
	14–15	Count	19	10	24	7	0	0	**60**
		% within Age	31.7	16.7	40	11.7	0	0	**100**
		% within Level of Education	32.2	14.9	28.9	10.6	0	0	**19.9**
	16–17	Count	26	36	35	39	7	0	**143**
		% within Age	18.2	25.2	24.5	27.3	4.9	0	**100**
		% within Level of Education	44.1	53.7	42.2	59.1	31.8	0	**47.4**
	18>	Count	10	20	19	20	15	5	**89**
		% within Age	11.2	22.5	21.3	22.5	16.9	5.6	**100**
		% within Level of Education	16.9	29.9	22.9	30.3	68.2	100	**29.5**
Total		Count	**59**	**67**	**83**	**66**	**22**	**5**	**302**
		% of Total	**19.5**	**22.2**	**27.5**	**21.9**	**7.3**	**1.7**	**100**

Table 5.5: Cross-Tabulation of 'State' and 'Level of Education'

Cross-Tabulation			Level of Education						Total
			Illiterate	Primary	Middle	Secon-dary	Senior Secondary	Graduate	
State	Delhi	Count	17	19	22	5	0	3	**66**
		% within State	25.8	28.8	33.3	7.6	0	4.5	**100**
		% within Level of Education	28.8	28.4	26.5	7.6	0	60	**21.9**
	Haryana	Count	9	19	30	38	14	2	**112**
		% within State	8	17	26.8	33.9	12.5	1.8	**100**
		% within Level of Education	15.3	28.4	36.1	57.6	63.6	40	**37.1**
	Punjab	Count	33	29	31	23	8	0	**124**
		% within State	26.6	23.4	25	18.5	6.5	0	**100**
		% within Level of Education	55.9	43.3	37.3	34.8	36.4	0	**41.1**
Total		Count	**59**	**67**	**83**	**66**	**22**	**5**	**302**
		% of Total	**19.5**	**22.2**	**27.5**	**21.9**	**7.3**	**1.7**	**100**

Table 5.6: Cross-Tabulation of 'Age of the Inmate' and 'Preoccupation Prior to Institutionalisation'

Cross-Tabulation			Pre-occupation Prior to Institutionalisation			Total
			Studying	Employed	Neither	
Age	11–13	Count	5	4	1	**10**
		% within Age	50	40	10	**100**
		% within Preoccupation Prior to Institutionalisation	3.8	5.1	1.1	**3.3**
	14–15	Count	28	12	20	**60**
		% within Age	46.7	20	33.3	**100**
		% within Preoccupation Prior to Institutionalisation	21.4	15.4	21.5	**19.9**
	16–17	Count	62	34	47	**143**
		% within Age	43.4	23.8	32.9	**100**
		% within Preoccupation Prior to Institutionalisation	47.3	43.6	50.5	**47.4**
	18>	Count	36	28	25	**89**
		% within Age	40.4	31.5	28.1	**100**
		% within Preoccupation Prior to Institutionalisation	27.5	35.9	26.9	**29.5**
Total		Count	**131**	**78**	**93**	**302**
		% of Total	**43.4**	**25.8**	**30.8**	**100**

Table 5.7: Cross-Tabulation of 'Level of Education' and 'Preoccupation Prior to Institutionalisation'

Cross-Tabulation			Preoccupation Prior to Institutionalisation			Total
			Studying	Employed	Neither	
Level of Education	Illiterate	Count	0	34	25	**59**
		% within Education	0	57.6	42.4	**100**
		% within Preoccupation	0	43.6	26.9	**19.5**
	Primary	Count	4	30	33	**67**
		% within Education	6	44.8	49.3	**100**
		% within Preoccupation	3.1	38.5	35.5	**22.2**
	Middle	Count	43	11	29	**83**
		% within Education	51.8	13.3	34.9	**100**
		% within Preoccupation	32.8	14.1	31.2	**27.5**
	Secondary	Count	63	1	2	**66**
		% within Education	95.5	1.5	3	**100**
		% within Preoccupation	48.1	1.3	2.2	**21.9**
	Senior Secondary	Count	16	2	4	**22**
		% within Education	72.7	9.1	18.2	**100**
		% within Preoccupation	12.2	2.6	4.3	**7.3**
	Graduate	Count	5	0	0	**5**
		% within Education	100	0	0	**100**
		% within Preoccupation	3.8	0	0	**1.7**
Total		Count	**131**	**78**	**93**	**302**
		% of Total	**43.4**	**25.8**	**30.8**	**100**

Table 5.8: Cross-Tabulation of 'State' and 'Preoccupation Prior to Institutionalisation'

Cross-Tabulation			Preoccupation Prior to Institutionalisation			Total
			Studying	Employed	Neither	
State	Delhi	Count	23	16	27	**66**
		% within State	34.8	24.2	40.9	**100**
		% within Preoccupation Prior to Institutionalisation	17.6	20.5	29	**21.9**
	Haryana	Count	60	24	28	**112**
		% within State	53.6	21.4	25	**100**
		% within Preoccupation Prior to Institutionalisation	45.8	30.8	30.1	**37.1**
	Punjab	Count	48	38	38	**124**
		% within State	38.7	30.6	30.6	**100**
		% within Preoccupation Prior to Institutionalisation	36.6	48.7	40.9	**41.1**
Total		Count	**131**	**78**	**93**	**302**
		% of Total	**43.4**	**25.8**	**30.8**	**100**

Table 5.9: Cross-Tabulation of 'Age of the Inmate' and 'Provider for Inmate'

Cross-Tabulation			Provider					Total
			Self	Mother	Father	Brother	Others	
Age	11–13	Count	0	1	9	0	0	**10**
		% within Age	0	10	90	0	0	**100**
		% within Provider	0	4.2	3.9	0	0	**3.3**
	14–15	Count	4	6	47	1	2	**60**
		% within Age	6.7	10	78.3	1.7	3.3	**100**
		% within Provider	14.8	25	20.5	6.3	33.3	**19.9**
	16–17	Count	13	13	99	14	4	**143**
		% within Age	9.1	9.1	69.2	9.8	2.8	**100**
		% within Provider	48.1	54.2	43.2	87.5	66.7	**47.4**
	18>	Count	10	4	74	1	0	**89**
		% within Age	11.2	4.5	83.1	1.1	0	**100**
		% within Provider	37	16.7	32.3	6.3	0	**29.5**
Total		Count	**27**	**24**	**229**	**16**	**6**	**302**
		% of Total	**8.9**	**7.9**	**75.8**	**5.3**	**2**	**100**

Table 5.10: Cross-Tabulation between 'Provider for Inmate' and 'Occupation of Provider'

Cross-Tabulation			Occupation of Provider					Total
			Daily Wage Labourer	Skilled Labourer	Business	Salaried Worker	Not Specified	
Provider	Self	Count	14	10	0	0	3	**27**
		% within Provider	51.9	37	0	0	11	**100**
		% within Occupation of Provider	15.6	7.1	0	0	13.6	**8.9**
	Mother	Count	9	3	1	5	6	**24**
		% within Provider	37.5	12.5	4.2	20.8	25	**100**
		% within Occupation of Provider	10	2.1	3.3	26.3	27.3	**7.9**
	Father	Count	64	120	26	14	5	**229**
		% within Provider	27.9	52.4	11.4	6.1	2.2	**100**
		% within Occupation of Provider	71.1	85.1	86.7	73.7	22.7	**75.8**
	Brother	Count	2	8	3	0	3	**16**
		% within Provider	12.5	50	18.8	0	18.8	**100**
		% within Occupation of Provider	2.2	5.7	10	0	13.6	**5.3**
	Others	Count	1	0	0	0	5	**6**
		% within Provider	16.7	0	0	0	83.3	**100**
		% within Occupation of Provider	1.1	0	0	0	22.7	**2**
Total		Count	**90**	**141**	**30**	**19**	**22**	**302**
		% of Total	**29.8**	**46.7**	**9.9**	**6.3**	**7.3**	**100**

Table 5.11: Cross-Tabulation of 'Age of Inmates' and 'Addiction to Intoxicants'

Cross-Tabulation			Addiction to Intoxicants					Total
			Tobacco	Alcohol	Cannabi-noids	Narcotics	None	
Age	11–13	Count	0	0	0	2	8	**10**
		% within Age	0	0	0	20	80	**100**
		% within Addiction	0	0	0	8.7	3.5	**3.3**
	14–15	Count	1	0	2	6	51	**60**
		% within Age	1.7	0	3.3	10	85	**100**
		% within Addiction	4.5	0	28.6	26.1	22.6	**19.9**
	16–17	Count	14	10	3	7	109	**143**
		% within Age	9.8	7	2.1	4.9	76.2	**100**
		% within Addiction	63.6	41.7	42.9	30.4	48.2	**47.4**
	18>	Count	7	14	2	8	58	**89**
		% within Age	7.9	15.7	2.2	9	65.2	**100**
		% within Addiction	31.8	58.3	28.6	34.8	25.7	**29.5**
Total		Count	**22**	**24**	**7**	**23**	**226**	**302**
		% of Total	**7.3**	**7.9**	**2.3**	**7.6**	**74.8**	**100**

Table 5.12: Cross-Tabulation of 'State' and 'Addiction to Intoxicants'

Cross-Tabulation			Addiction to Intoxicants					Total
			Tobacco	Alcohol	Cannabinoids	Narcotics	None	
State	Delhi	Count	1	2	3	3	57	**66**
		% within State	1.5	3	4.5	4.5	86.4	**100**
		% within Addiction to Intoxicants	4.5	8.3	42.9	13	25.2	**21.9**
	Haryana	Count	8	8	1	4	91	**112**
		% within State	7.1	7.1	0.9	3.6	81.3	**100**
		% within Addiction to Intoxicants	36.4	33.3	14.3	17.4	40.3	**37.1**
	Punjab	Count	13	14	3	16	78	**124**
		% within State	10.5	11.3	2.4	12.9	62.9	**100**
		% within Addiction to Intoxicants	59.1	58.3	42.9	69.6	34.5	**41.1**
Total		Count	**22**	**24**	**7**	**23**	**226**	**302**
		% of Total	**7.3**	**7.9**	**2.3**	**7.6**	**74.8**	**100**

Table 5.13: Cross-Tabulation of 'Level of Education' and 'Ability to Socialise'

Cross-Tabulation			Ability to Socialise: Yes	Ability to Socialise: No	Total
Level of Education	Illiterate	Count	35	24	**59**
		% within Education	59.3	40.7	**100.0**
		% within Sociability	21.2	17.5	**19.5**
	Primary	Count	37	30	**67**
		% within Education	55.2	44.8	**100**
		% within Sociability	22.4	21.9	**22.2**
	Middle	Count	47	36	**83**
		% within Education	56.6	43.4	**100**
		% within Sociability	28.5	26.3	**27.5**
	Secondary	Count	34	32	**66**
		% within Education	51.5	48.5	**100**
		% within Sociability	20.6	23.4	**21.9**
	Senior Secondary	Count	9	13	**22**
		% within Education	40.9	59.1	**100**
		% within Sociability	5.5	9.5	**7.3**
	Graduate	Count	3	2	**5**
		% within Education	60	40	**100**
		% within Sociability	1.8	1.5	**1.7**
Total		Count	**165**	**137**	**302**
		% of Total	**54.6**	**45.4**	**100**

Table 5.14: Cross-Tabulation of 'Level of education' and 'Addiction'

Cross-Tabulation			Addiction to Intoxicants					Total
			Tobacco	Alcohol	Cannabi-noids	Narcotics	None	
Level of Education	Illiterate	Count	9	5	2	13	30	**59**
		% within Education	15.3	8.5	3.4	22	50.8	**100**
		% within Intoxicants	40.9	20.8	28.6	56.5	13.3	**19.5**
	Primary	Count	9	7	2	3	46	**67**
		% within Education	13.4	10.4	3	4.5	68.7	**100**
		% within Intoxicants	40.9	29.2	28.6	13	20.4	**22.2**
	Middle	Count	4	4	1	6	68	**83**
		% within Education	4.8	4.8	1.2	7.2	81.9	**100**
		% within Intoxicants	18.2	16.7	14.3	26.1	30.1	**27.5**
	Secondary	Count	0	3	1	1	61	**66**
		% within Education	0	4.5	1.5	1.5	92.4	**100**
		% within Intoxicants	0	12.5	14.3	4.3	27	**21.9**
	Senior Secondary	Count	0	4	1	0	17	22
		% within Education	0	18.2	4.5	0	77.3	**100**
		% within Intoxicants	0	16.7	14.3	0	7.5	**7.3**
	Graduate	Count	0	1	0	0	4	**5**
		% within Education	0	20	0	0	80	**100**
		% within Intoxicants	0	4.2	0	0	1.8	**1.7**
Total		Count	**22**	**24**	**7**	**23**	**226**	**302**
		% of Total	**7.3**	**7.9**	**2.3**	**7.6**	**74.8**	**100**

Table 5.15: Cross-Tabulation of 'Addiction to Intoxicants' and 'Ability to Socialise'

Cross-Tabulation			Ability to Socialise		Total
			Yes	No	
Addiction to Intoxicants	Tobacco	Count	14	8	**22**
		% within Addiction	63.6	36.4	**100**
		% within Sociability	8.5	5.8	**7.3**
	Alcohol	Count	12	12	**24**
		% within Addiction	50.	50	**100**
		% within Sociability	7.3	8.8	**7.9**
	Cannabinoids	Count	3	4	**7**
		% within Addiction	42.9	57.1	**100**
		% within Sociability	1.8	2.9	**2.3**
	Narcotics	Count	10	13	**23**
		% within Addiction	43.5	56.5	**100**
		% within Sociability	6.1	9.5	**7.6**
	None	Count	126	100	**226**
		% within Addiction	55.8	44.2	**100**
		% within Sociability	76.4	73	**74.8**
Total		Count	**165**	**137**	**302**
		% of Total	**54.6**	**45.4**	**100**

Table 5.16: Cross-Tabulation of 'Addiction to Intoxicants' and 'Preoccupation Prior to Institutionalisation'

Cross-Tabulation			Preoccupation Prior to Institutionalisation			Total
			Studying	Employed	Neither	
Addiction to Intoxicants	Tobacco	Count	0	13	9	**22**
		% within Addiction	0	59.1	40.9	**100**
		% within Preoccupation	0	16.7	9.7	**7.3**
	Alcohol	Count	11	6	7	**24**
		% within Addiction	45.8	25	29.2	**100**
		% within Preoccupation	8.4	7.7	7.5	**7.9**
	Cannabinoids	Count	2	4	1	**7**
		% within Addiction	28.6	57.1	14.3	**100**
		% within Preoccupation	1.5	5.1	1.1	**2.3**
	Narcotics	Count	2	8	13	**23**
		% within Addiction	8.7	34.8	56.5	**100**
		% within Preoccupation	1.5	10.3	14	**7.6**
	None	Count	116	47	63	**226**
		% within Addiction	51.3	20.8	27.9	**100**
		% within Preoccupation	88.5	60.3	67.7	**74.8**
Total		Count	**131**	**78**	**93**	**302**
		% of Total	**43.4**	**25.8**	**30.8**	**100**

Table 6.3: Cross-Tabulation of 'Age of the Inmate' and 'Nature of Offence

Cross-Tabulation			Nature of Offence			Total
			Petty	Serious	Heinous	
Age	11–13	Count	3	0	7	**10**
		% within Age	30	0	70	**100**
		% within Nature of Offence	7.9	0	2.9	**3.3**
	14–15	Count	14	8	38	**60**
		% within Age	23.3	13.3	63.3	**100**
		% within Nature of Offence	36.8	38.1	15.6	**19.9**
	16–17	Count	18	6	119	**143**
		% within Age	12.6	4.2	83.2	**100**
		% within Nature of Offence	47.4	28.6	49	**47.4**
	18>	Count	3	7	79	**89**
		% within Age	3.4	7.9	88.8	**100**
		% within Nature of Offence	7.9	33.3	32.5	**29.5**
Total		Count	**38**	**21**	**243**	**302**
		% of Total	**12.6**	**7**	**80.5**	**100**

Table 6.4: Cross-Tabulation of 'Age of Inmates' and 'Company at the Time of Offence'

Cross-Tabulation			Company at the Time of Offence				Total
			None	Other Juveniles	Adults	Juveniles at the Behest of Adults	
Age	11–13	Count	5	4	1	0	**10**
		% within Age	50	40	10	0	**100**
		% within Company	4.1	6.8	1	0	**3.3**
	14–15	Count	25	11	21	3	**60**
		% within Age	41.7	18.3	35	5	**100**
		% within Company	20.7	18.6	21	13.6	**19.9**
	16–17	Count	57	25	50	11	**143**
		% within Age	39.9	17.5	35	7.7	**100**
		% within Company	47.1	42.4	50	50	**47.4**
	18>	Count	34	19	28	8	**89**
		% within Age	38.2	21.3	31.5	9	**100**
		% within Company	28.1	32.2	28	36.4	**29.5**
Total		Count	**121**	**59**	**100**	**22**	**302**
		% of Total	**40.1**	**19.5**	**33.1**	**7.3**	**100**

Table 6.5: Cross-Tabulation between 'Age of the Inmate' and 'Recidivism'

Cross-Tabulation			Recidivist		Total
			Yes	No	
Age	11–13	Count	1	9	**10**
		% within Age	10	90	**100**
		% within Recidivist	3	3.3	**3.3**
	14–15	Count	4	56	**60**
		% within Age	6.7	93.3	**100**
		% within Recidivist	12.1	20.8	**19.9**
	16–17	Count	14	129	**143**
		% within Age	9.8	90.2	**100**
		% within Recidivist	42.4	48	**47.4**
	18>	Count	14	75	**89**
		% within Age	15.7	84.3	**100**
		% within Recidivist	42.4	27.9	**29.5**
Total		Count	**33**	**269**	**302**
		% of Total	**10.9**	**89.1**	**100**

Table 6.6: Cross-Tabulation of 'State' and 'Recidivism'

Cross-Tabulation			Recidivist		Total
			Yes	No	
State	Delhi	Count	11	55	**66**
		% within State	16.7	83.3	**100**
		% within Recidivist	33.3	20.4	**21.9**
	Haryana	Count	10	102	**112**
		% within State	8.9	91.1	**100**
		% within Recidivist	30.3	37.9	**37.1**
	Punjab	Count	12	112	**124**
		% within State	9.7	90.3	**100**
		% within Recidivist	36.4	41.6	**41.1**
Total		Count	**33**	**269**	**302**
		% of Total	**10.9**	**89.1**	**100**

Table 6.7: Cross-Tabulation of 'Level of Education' and 'Nature of Offence'

Cross-Tabulation			Nature of Offence			Total
			Petty	Serious	Heinous	
Level of Education	Illiterate	Count	17	10	32	**59**
		% within Education	28.8	16.9	54.2	**100**
		% within Offence	44.7	47.6	13.2	**19.5**
	Primary	Count	15	2	50	**67**
		% within Education	22.4	3	74.6	**100**
		% within Offence	39.5	9.5	20.6	**22.2**
	Middle	Count	6	1	76	**83**
		% within Education	7.2	1.2	91.6	**100**
		% within Offence	15.8	4.8	31.3	**27.5**
	Secondary	Count	0	5	61	**66**
		% within Education	0	7.6	92.4	**100**
		% within Offence	0	23.8	25.1	**21.9**
	Senior Secondary	Count	0	3	19	**22**
		% within Education	0	13.6	86.4	**100**
		% within Offence	0	14.3	7.8	**7.3**
	Graduate	Count	0	0	5	**5**
		% within Education	0	0	100	**100**
		% within Offence	0	0	2.1	**1.7**
Total		Count	**38**	**21**	**243**	**302**
		% of Total	**12.6**	**7**	**80.5**	**100**

Table 6.8: Cross-Tabulation of 'Level of Education' and 'Recidivism'

Cross-Tabulation			Recidivist		Total
			Yes	No	
Level of Education	Illiterate	Count	7	52	**59**
		% within Education	11.9	88.1	**100**
		% within Recidivist	21.2	19.3	**19.5**
	Primary	Count	8	59	**67**
		% within Education	11.9	88.1	**100**
		% within Recidivist	24.2	21.9	**22.2**
	Middle	Count	11	72	**83**
		% within Education	13.3	86.7	**100**
		% within Recidivist	33.3	26.8	**27.5**
	Secondary	Count	4	62	**66**
		% within Education	6.1	93.9	**100**
		% within Recidivist	12.1	23	**21.9**
	Senior Secondary	Count	3	19	**22**
		% within Education	13.6	86.4	**100**
		% within Recidivist	9.1	7.1	**7.3**
	Graduate	Count	0	5	**5**
		% within Education	0	100	**100**
		% within Recidivist	0	1.9	**1.7**
Total		Count	**33**	**269**	**302**
		% of Total	**10.9**	**89.1**	**100**

Table 6.9: Cross-Tabulation of 'Ability to Socialise' and 'Nature of Offence'

Cross-Tabulation			Nature of Offence			Total
			Petty	Serious	Heinous	
Ability to Socialise	Yes	Count	23	8	134	**165**
		% within Sociability	13.9	4.8	81.2	**100**
		% within Offence	60.5	38.1	55.1	**54.6**
	No	Count	15	13	109	**137**
		% within Sociability	10.9	9.5	79.6	**100**
		% within Offence	39.5	61.9	44.9	**45.4**
Total		Count	**38**	**21**	**243**	**302**
		% of Total	**12.6**	**7**	**80.5**	**100**

Table 6.10: Cross-Tabulation of 'Ability to Socialise' and 'Recidivism'

Cross-Tabulation			Recidivist		Total
			Yes	No	
Ability to Socialise	Yes	Count	17	148	**165**
		% within Sociability	10.3	89.7	**100**
		% within Recidivist	51.5	55	**54.6**
	No	Count	16	121	**137**
		% within Sociability	11.7	88.3	**100**
		% within Recidivist	48.5	45	**45.4**
Total		Count	**33**	**269**	**302**
		% of Total	**10.9**	**89.1**	**100**

Table 6.11: Cross-Tabulation of 'Nature of Offence' and 'Addiction to Intoxicants'

Cross-Tabulation			Addiction to Intoxicants					Total
			Tobacco	Alcohol	Cannabi-noids	Narcotics	None	
Nature of Offence	Petty	Count	3	2	1	6	26	**38**
		% within Offence	7.9	5.3	2.6	15.8	68.4	**100**
		% within Intoxicants	13.6	8.3	14.3	26.1	11.5	**12.6**
	Serious	Count	3	1	2	3	12	**21**
		% within Offence	14.3	4.8	9.5	14.3	57.1	**100**
		% within Intoxicants	13.6	4.2	28.6	13	5.3	**7**
	Heinous	Count	16	21	4	14	188	**243**
		% within Offence	6.6	8.6	1.6	5.8	77.4	**100**
		% within Intoxicants	72.7	87.5	57.1	60.9	83.2	**80.5**
Total		Count	**22**	**24**	**7**	**23**	**226**	**302**
		% of Total	**7.3**	**7.9**	**2.3**	**7.6**	**74.8**	**100**

Table 6.12: Cross-Tabulation of 'Age of the Inmate' and 'Confinement to Police/Judicial Custody'

Cross-Tabulation			Confinement in Judicial/Police Custody		Total
			Yes	No	
Age	11–13	Count	5	5	**10**
		% within Age	50	50	**100**
		% within Confinement	2.5	4.9	**3.3**
	14–15	Count	35	25	**60**
		% within Age	58.3	41.7	**100**
		% within Confinement	17.5	24.5	**19.9**
	16–17	Count	91	52	**143**
		% within Age	63.6	36.4	**100**
		% within Confinement	45.5	51	**47.4**
	18>	Count	69	20	**89**
		% within Age	77.5	22.5	**100**
		% within Confinement	34.5	19.6	**29.5**
Total		Count	**200**	**102**	**302**
		% of Total	**66.2**	**33.8**	**100**

Table 6.13: Cross-Tabulation of 'Age of the Inmate' and 'Behaviour of Police Officials'

Cross-Tabulation			Behaviour of Police Officials			Total
			Supportive	Hostile	Indifferent	
Age	11–13	Count	5	5	0	**10**
		% within Age	50	50	0	**100**
		% within Behaviour	8.5	3.1	0	**3.3**
	14–15	Count	12	33	15	**60**
		% within Age	20	55	25	**100**
		% of Total	4	10.9	5	**19.9**
	16–17	Count	28	69	46	**143**
		% within Age	19.6	48.3	32.2	**100**
		% within Behaviour	47.5	43.1	55.4	**47.4**
	18>	Count	14	53	22	**89**
		% within Age	15.7	59.6	24.7	**100**
		% within Behaviour	23.7	33.1	26.5	**29.5**
Total		Count	**59**	**160**	**83**	**302**
		% of Total	**19.5**	**53**	**27.5**	**100**

Table 6.14: Cross-Tabulation of 'Age of Inmate' and 'Provision of Legal Aid'

Cross-Tabulation			Provision of Legal Aid		Total
			Yes	No	
Age	11–13	Count	0	10	**10**
		% within Age	0	100	**100**
		% within Legal Aid	0	4.1	**3.3**
	14–15	Count	22	38	**60**
		% within Age	36.7	63.3	**100**
		% within Legal Aid	38.6	15.5	**19.9**
	16–17	Count	23	120	**143**
		% within Age	16.1	83.9	**100**
		% within Legal Aid	40.4	49	**47.4**
	18>	Count	12	77	**89**
		% within Age	13.5	86.5	**100**
		% within Legal Aid	21.1	31.4	**29.5**
Total		Count	**57**	**245**	**302**
		% of Total	**18.9**	**81.1**	**100**

Table 6.15: Cross-Tabulation of 'Age of the Inmate' and 'Approach by Police Officials in Uniform'

Cross-Tabulation			Approached by Policemen in Uniform		Total
			Yes	No	
Age	11–13	Count	9	1	**10**
		% within Age	90	10	**100**
		% within Uniform	3.4	2.9	**3.3**
	14–15	Count	55	5	**60**
		% within Age	91.7	8.3	**100**
		% within Uniform	20.6	14.3	**19.9**
	16–17	Count	125	18	**143**
		% within Age	87.4	12.6	**100**
		% within Uniform	46.8	51.4	**47.4**
	18>	Count	78	11	**89**
		% within Age	87.6	12.4	**100**
		% within Uniform	29.2	31.4	**29.5**
Total		Count	**267**	**35**	**302**
		% of Total	**88.4**	**11.6**	**100**

Table 6.16: Cross-Tabulation of 'State' and 'Authority before Which Claim of Minority Was Made'

Cross-Tabulation			Authority before Which Claim for Minority Was Made		Total
			Police	Judge	
State	Delhi	Count	50	16	**66**
		% within State	75.8	24.2	**100**
		% within Authority	21.9	21.6	**21.9**
	Haryana	Count	90	22	**112**
		% within State	80.4	19.6	**100**
		% within Authority	39.5	29.7	**37.1**
	Punjab	Count	88	36	**124**
		% within State	71	29	**100**
		% within Authority	38.6	48.6	**41.1**
Total		Count	**228**	**74**	**302**
		% of Total	**75.5**	**24.5**	**100**

Table 6.17: Cross-Tabulation of 'Confinement to Judicial/ Police Custody' and 'Authority before Which Claim for Minority Was Made'

Cross-Tabulation			Authority before Which Claim for Minority Was Made		Total
			Police	Judge	
Confinement in Judicial/Police Custody	Yes	Count	141	59	**200**
		% within Confinement	70.5%	29.5%	**100**
		% within Authority	61.8%	79.7%	**66.2**
	No	Count	87	15	**102**
		% within Confinement	85.3%	14.7%	**100**
		% within Authority	38.2%	20.3%	**33.8**
Total		Count	**228**	**74**	**302**
		% of Total	**75.5**	**24.5**	**100**

Table 6.18: Cross-Tabulation of 'State' and 'Behaviour of Police Officials'

Cross-Tabulation			Behaviour of Police Officials			Total
			Supportive	Hostile	Indifferent	
State	Delhi	Count	12	40	14	**66**
		% within State	18.2	60.6	21.2	**100**
		% within Behaviour	20.3	25	16.9	**21.9**
	Haryana	Count	31	47	34	**112**
		% within State	27.7	42	30.4	**100**
		% within Behaviour	52.5	29.4	41	**37.1**
	Punjab	Count	16	73	35	**124**
		% within State	12.9	58.9	28.2	**100**
		% within Behaviour	27.1	45.6	42.2	**41.1**
Total		Count	**59**	**160**	**83**	**302**
		% of Total	**19.5**	**53**	**27.5**	**100**

Table 6.19: Cross-Tabulation of 'State' and 'Provision of Legal Aid'

Cross-Tabulation			Provision of Legal Aid		Total
			Yes	No	
State	Delhi	Count	31	35	**66**
		% within State	47	53	**100**
		% within Provision	54.4	14.3	**21.9**
	Haryana	Count	10	102	**112**
		% within State	8.9	91.1	**100**
		% within Provision	17.5	41.6	**37.1**
	Punjab	Count	16	108	**124**
		% within State	12.9	87.1	**100**
		% within Provision	28.1	44.1	**41.1**
Total		Count	**57**	**245**	**302**
		% of Total	**18.9**	**81.1**	**100**

Table 6.20: Cross-Tabulation of 'Level of Education' and 'Authority before Which Claim for Minority Was Made'

Cross-Tabulation			Authority before Which Claim for Minority Was Made		Total
			Police	Judge	
Level of Education	Illiterate	Count	48	11	**59**
		% within Education	81.4	18.6	**100**
		% within Authority	21.1	14.9	**19.5**
	Primary	Count	53	14	**67**
		% within Education	79.1	20.9	**100**
		% within Authority	23.2	18.9	**22.2**
	Middle	Count	63	20	**83**
		% within Education	75.9	24.1	**100**
		% within Authority	27.6	27	**27.5**
	Secondary	Count	50	16	**66**
		% within Education	75.8	24.2	**100**
		% within Authority	21.9	21.6	**21.9**
	Senior Secondary	Count	13	9	**22**
		% within Education	59.1	40.9	**100**
		% within Authority	5.7	12.2	**7.3**
	Graduate	Count	1	4	**5**
		% within Education	20	80	**100**
		% within Authority	0.4	5.4	**1.7**
Total		Count	**228**	**74**	**302**
		% of Total	**75.5**	**24.5**	**100**

Table 6.21: Cross-Tabulation of 'Level of Education' and 'Confinement to Police/Judicial Custody'

Cross-Tabulation			Confinement in Judicial/Police Custody		Total
			Yes	No	
Level of Education	Illiterate	Count	41	18	**59**
		% within Education	69.5	30.5	**100**
		% within Confinement	20.5	17.6	**19.5**
	Primary	Count	46	21	**67**
		% within Education	68.7	31.3	**100**
		% within Confinement	23	20.6	**22.2**
	Middle	Count	55	28	**83**
		% within Education	66.3	33.7	**100**
		% within Confinement	27.5	27.5	**27.5**
	Secondary	Count	34	32	**66**
		% within Education	51.5	48.5	**100**
		% within Confinement	17	31.4	**21.9**
	Senior Secondary	Count	19	3	**22**
		% within Education	86.4	13.6	**100**
		% within Confinement	9.5	2.9	**7.3**
	Graduate	Count	5	0	**5**
		% within Education	100	0	**100**
		% within Confinement	2.5	0	**1.7**
Total		Count	**200**	**102**	**302**
		% of Total	**66.2**	**33.8**	**100**

Table 6.22: Cross-Tabulation of 'Level of Education' and 'Behaviour of Police Officials'

Cross-Tabulation			Behaviour of Police Officials			Total
			Supportive	Hostile	Indifferent	
Level of Education	Illiterate	Count	9	32	18	**59**
		% within Education	15.3	54.2	30.5	**100**
		% within Behaviour	15.3	20	21.7	**19.5**
	Primary	Count	10	43	14	**67**
		% within Education	14.9	64.2	20.9	**100**
		% within Behaviour	16.9	26.9	16.9	**22.2**
	Middle	Count	19	44	20	**83**
		% within Education	22.9	53	24.1	**100**
		% within Behaviour	32.2	27.5	24.1	**27.5**
	Secondary	Count	16	29	21	**66**
		% within Education	24.2	43.9	31.8	**100**
		% within Behaviour	27.1	18.1	25.3	**21.9**
	Senior Secondary	Count	5	8	9	**22**
		% within Education	22.7	36.4	40.9	**100**
		% within Behaviour	8.5	5	10.8	**7.3**
	Graduate	Count	0	4	1	**5**
		% within Education	0	80	20	**100**
		% within Behaviour	0	2.5	1.2	**1.7**
Total		Count	**59**	**160**	**83**	**302**
		% of Total	**19.5**	**53**	**27.5**	**100**

Table 6.23: Cross-Tabulation of 'Occupation of Provider' and 'Behaviour of Police Officials'

Cross-Tabulation			Behaviour of Police Officials			Total
			Supportive	Hostile	Indifferent	
Occupation of Provider	Daily Wage Labourer	Count	17	46	27	**90**
		% within Occupation	18.9	51.1	30	**100**
		% within Behaviour	28.8	28.8	32.5	**29.8**
	Skilled Labourer	Count	26	77	38	**141**
		% within Occupation	18.4	54.6	27	**100**
		% within Behaviour	44.1	48.1	45.8	**46.7**
	Business	Count	8	13	9	**30**
		% within Occupation	26.7	43.3	30	**100**
		% within Behaviour	13.6	8.1	10.8	**9.9**
	Salaried Worker	Count	1	11	7	**19**
		% within Occupation	5.3	57.9	36.8	**100**
		% within Behaviour	1.7	6.9	8.4	**6.3**
	Not Specified	Count	7	13	2	**22**
		% within Occupation	31.8	59.1	9.1	**100**
		% within Behaviour	11.9	8.1	2.4	**7.3**
Total		Count	**59**	**160**	**83**	**302**
		% of Total	**19.5**	**53**	**27.5**	**100**

Table 6.24: Cross-Tabulation of 'Occupation of Provider' and 'Provision of Legal Aid'

Cross-Tabulation			Provision of Legal Aid		Total
			Yes	No	
Occupation of Provider	Daily Wage Labourer	Count	23	67	**90**
		% within Occupation	25.6	74.4	**100**
		% within Legal Aid	40.4	27.3	**29.8**
	Skilled Labourer	Count	17	124	**141**
		% within Occupation	12.1	87.9	**100**
		% within Legal Aid	29.8	50.6	**46.7**
	Business	Count	4	26	**30**
		% within Occupation	13.3	86.7	**100**
		% within Legal Aid	7	10.6	**9.9**
	Salaried Worker	Count	2	17	**19**
		% within Occupation	10.5	89.5	**100**
		% within Legal Aid	3.5	6.9	**6.3**
	Not Specified	Count	11	11	**22**
		% within Occupation	50	50	**100**
		% within Legal Aid	19.3	4.5	**7.3**
Total		Count	**57**	**245**	**302**
		% of Total	**18.9**	**81.1**	**100**

Table 6.25: Cross-Tabulation of 'Preoccupation Prior to Institutionalisation' and 'Provision of Legal Aid'

Cross-Tabulation			Provision of Legal Aid		Total
			Yes	No	
Preoccupation Prior to Institutionalisation	Studying	Count	20	111	**131**
		% within Preoccupation	15.3	84.7	**100**
		% within Legal Aid	35.1	45.3	**43.4**
	Employed	Count	15	63	**78**
		% within Preoccupation	19.2	80.8	**100**
		% within Legal Aid	26.3	25.7	**25.8**
	Neither	Count	22	71	**93**
		% within Preoccupation	23.7	76.3	**100**
		% within Legal Aid	38.6	29	**30.8**
Total		Count	**57**	**245**	**302**
		% of Total	**18.9**	**81.1**	**100**

Table 6.26: Cross-Tabulation of 'Presence of Family Members during Proceedings' and 'Age of the Inmate'

Cross-Tabulation			Age				Total
			11–13	14–15	16–17	18>	
Presence of Family Members during Proceedings	Yes	Count	10	56	134	82	**282**
		% within Presence	3.5	19.9	47.5	29.1	**100**
		% within Age	100	93.3	93.7	92.1	**93.4**
	No	Count	0	4	9	7	**20**
		% within Presence	0	20	45	35	**10**
		% within Age	0	6.7	6.3	7.9	**6.6**
Total		Count	**10**	**60**	**143**	**89**	**302**
		% of Total	**3.3**	**19.9**	**47.4**	**29.5**	**100**

Table 6.27: Cross-Tabulation of 'Presence of Family Members during Proceedings' and 'State'

Cross-Tabulation			State			Total
			Delhi	Haryana	Punjab	
Presence of Family Members during Proceedings	Yes	Count	63	104	115	**282**
		% within Presence	22.3	36.9	40.8	**100**
		% within State	95.5	92.9	92.7	**93.4**
	No	Count	3	8	9	**20**
		% within Presence	15	40	45	**100**
		% within State	4.5	7.1	7.3	**6.6**
Total		Count	**66**	**112**	**124**	**302**
		% of Total	**21.9**	**37.1**	**41.1**	**100**

Table 6.28: Cross-Tabulation of the 'Presence of Family Members during Proceedings' and 'Preoccupation Prior to Institutionalisation'

Cross-Tabulation			Preoccupation Prior to Institutionalisation			Total
			Studying	Employed	Neither	
Presence of Family Members during Proceedings	Yes	Count	125	68	89	**282**
		% within Presence	44.3	24.1	31.6	**100**
		% within Preoccupation	95.4	87.2	95.7	**93.4**
	No	Count	6	10	4	**20**
		% within Presence	30	50	20	**100**
		% within Preoccupation	4.6	12.8	4.3	**6.6**
Total		Count	**131**	**78**	**93**	**302**
		% of Total	**43.4**	**25.8**	**30.8**	**100**

Table 6.29: Cross-Tabulation of 'Presence of Family Members' and 'Confinement to Police/Judicial Custody'

Cross-Tabulation			Confinement in Judicial/Police Custody		Total
			Yes	No	
Presence of Family Members during Proceedings	Yes	Count	185	97	**282**
		% within Presence	65.6	34.4	**100**
		% within Confinement	92.5	95.1	**93.4**
	No	Count	15	5	**20**
		% within Presence of	75	25	**100**
		% within Confinement	7.5	4.9	**6.6**
Total		Count	**200**	**102**	**302**
		% of Total	**66.2**	**33.8**	**100**

Table 6.30: Cross-Tabulation of 'Presence of Family Members during Proceedings' and 'Nature of Offence'

Cross-Tabulation			Nature of Offence			Total
			Petty	Serious	Heinous	
Presence of Family Members during Proceedings	Yes	Count	32	18	232	**282**
		% within Presence	11.3	6.4	82.3	**100**
		% within Offence	84.2	85.7	95.5	**93.4**
	No	Count	6	3	11	**20**
		% within Presence	30	15	55	**100**
		% within Offence	15.8	14.3	4.5	**6.6**
Total		Count	**38**	**21**	**243**	**302**
		% of Total	**12.6**	**7**	**80.5**	**100**

Table 6.31: Cross-Tabulation of 'State' and 'Approach by Police Officials in Uniform'

Cross-Tabulation			Approached by Policemen in Uniform		Total
			Yes	No	
State	Delhi	Count	58	8	**66**
		% within State	87.9	12.1	**100**
		% within Uniform	21.7	22.9	**21.9**
	Haryana	Count	96	16	**112**
		% within State	85.7	14.3	**100**
		% within Uniform	36	45.7	**37.1**
	Punjab	Count	113	11	**124**
		% within State	91.1	8.9	**100**
		% within Uniform	42.3	31.4	**41.1**
Total		Count	**267**	**35**	**302**
		% of Total	**88.4**	**11.6**	**100**

Table 6.32: Cross-Tabulation of 'State' and 'Use of Stigmatising Terms'

Cross-Tabulation			Use of Stigmatising Terms	Total
			Yes	
State	Delhi	Count	66	**66**
		% within State	100	**100**
		% within Stigmatising Terms	21.9	**21.9**
	Haryana	Count	112	**112**
		% within State	100	**100**
		% within Stigmatising Terms	37.1	**37.1**
	Punjab	Count	124	**124**
		% within State	100	**100**
		% within Stigmatising Terms	41.1	**41.1**
Total		Count	**302**	**302**
		% of Total	**100**	**100**

Table 6.33: Cross-Tabulation of 'Nature of Offence' and 'Use of Stigmatising Terms'

Cross-Tabulation			Use of Stigmatising Terms	Total
			Yes	
Nature of Offence	Petty	Count	38	**38**
		% within Nature of Offence	100	**100**
		% within Use of Stigmatising Terms	12.6	**12.6**
		% of Total	12.6	**12.6**
	Serious	Count	21	**21**
		% within Offence	100	**100**
		% within Use of Stigmatising Terms	7	**7**
	Heinous	Count	243	**243**
		% within Offence	100	**100**
		% within Use of Stigmatising Terms	80.5	**80.5**
Total		Count	**302**	**302**
		% of Total	**100**	**100**

Table 7.2: Cross-Tabulation of 'Age of Inmate' and 'Type of Home'

Cross-Tabulation			Type of Home		Total
			Special Home	Observation Home	
Age	11–13	Count	0	10	**10**
		% within Age	0	100	**100**
		% within Type of Home	0	4.4	**3.3**
	14–15	Count	1	59	**60**
		% within Age	1.7	98.3	**100**
		% within Type of Home	1.4	25.8	**19.9**
	16–17	Count	22	121	**143**
		% within Age	15.4	84.6	**100**
		% within Type of Home	30.1	52.8	**47.4**
	18>	Count	50	39	**89**
		% within Age	56.2	43.8	**100**
		% within Type of Home	68.5	17	**29.5**
Total		Count	**73**	**229**	**302**
		% of Total	**24.2**	**75.8**	**100**

Table 7.3: Cross-Tabulation of 'Nature of Offence' and 'Type of Home'

Cross-Tabulation			Type of Home: Special Home	Type of Home: Observation Home	Total
Nature of Offence	Petty	Count	1	37	**38**
		% within Offence	2.6	97.4	**100**
		% within Home	1.4	16.2	**12.6**
	Serious	Count	5	16	**21**
		% within Offence	23.8	76.2	**100**
		% within Home	6.8	7	**7**
	Heinous	Count	67	176	**243**
		% within Offence	27.6	72.4	**100**
		% within Home	91.8	76.9	**80.5**
Total		Count	**73**	**229**	**302**
		% of Total	**24.2**	**75.8**	**100**

Table 7.4: Cross-Tabulation of 'State' and 'Type of Home'

Cross-Tabulation			Type of Home: Special Home	Type of Home: Observation Home	Total
State	Delhi	Count	16	50	**66**
		% within State	24.2	75.8	**100**
		% within Type of Home	21.9	21.8	**21.9**
	Haryana	Count	31	81	**112**
		% within State	27.7	72.3	**100**
		% within Type of Home	42.5	35.4	**37.1**
	Punjab	Count	26	98	**124**
		% within State	21	79	**100**
		% within Type of Home	35.6	42.8	**41.1**
Total		Count	**73**	**229**	**302**
		% of Total	**24.2**	**75.8**	**100**

Table 7.5: Cross-Tabulation of 'State' and 'Likeability of Environment Inside Home'

Cross-Tabulation			Likability: Like	Likability: Dislike	Total
State	Delhi	Count	48	18	**66**
		% within State	72.7	27.3	**100**
		% within Likeability	23.3	18.8	**21.9**
	Haryana	Count	69	43	**112**
		% within State	61.6	38.4	**100**
		% within Likeability	33.5	44.8	**37.1**
	Punjab	Count	89	35	**124**
		% within State	71.8	28.2	**100**
		% within Likeability	43.2	36.5	**41.1**
Total		Count	**206**	**96**	**302**
		% of Total	**68.2**	**31.8**	**100**

Table 7.6: Cross-Tabulation of 'State' and 'Segregation of Residential Facilities on the Basis of Age'

Cross-Tabulation			Segregation of Residential Facilities on the Basis of Age	Total
			No Segregation	
State	Delhi	Count	66	**66**
		% within State	100	**100**
		% within Segregation	21.9	**21.9**
	Haryana	Count	112	**112**
		% within State	100	**100**
		% within Segregation	37.1	**37.1**
	Punjab	Count	124	**124**
		% within State	100	**100**
		% within Segregation	41.1	**41.1**
Total		Count	**302**	**302**
		% of Total	**100**	**100**

Table 7.7: Cross-Tabulation of 'State' and 'Requirement of Better Infrastructure'

Cross-Tabulation			Requirement of Better Infrastructure		Total
			Yes	No	
State	Delhi	Count	57	9	**66**
		% within State	86.4	13.6	**100**
		% within Requirement	19.7	75	**21.9**
	Haryana	Count	110	2	**112**
		% within State	98.2	1.8	**100**
		% within Requirement	37.9	16.7	**37.1**
	Punjab	Count	123	1	**124**
		% within State	99.2	0.8	**100**
		% within Requirement	42.4	8.3	**41.1**
Total		Count	**290**	**12**	**302**
		% of Total	**96**	**4**	**100**

Table 7.8: Cross-Tabulation of 'State' and 'Quality of Pest/ Insect Control in Home'

Cross-Tabulation			Pest/Insect Control in Home				Total
			Poor	Below Average	Average	Good	
State	Delhi	Count	7	47	11	1	**66**
		% within State	10.6	71.2	16.7	1.5	**100**
		% within Pest/ Insect Control	53.8	26.6	10.4	16.7	**21.9**
	Haryana	Count	3	61	48	0	**112**
		% within State	2.7	54.5	42.9	0	**100**
		% within Pest/ Insect Control	23.1	34.5	45.3	0	**37.1**
	Punjab	Count	3	69	47	5	**124**
		% within State	2.4	55.6	37.9	4	**100**
		% within Pest/ Insect Control	23.1	39	44.3	83.3	**41.1**
Total		Count	**13**	**177**	**106**	**6**	**302**
		% of Total	**4.3**	**58.6**	**35.1**	**2**	**100**

Table 7.9: Cross-Tabulation of 'State' and 'Quality of Bedding/Clothing'

Cross-Tabulation			Quality of Clothing/Bedding				Total
			Poor	Below Average	Average	Good	
State	Delhi	Count	2	23	41	0	**66**
		% within State	3	34.8	62.1	0	**100**
		% within Quality	50	43.4	16.9	0	**21.9**
	Haryana	Count	2	14	96	0	**112**
		% within State	1.8	12.5	85.7	0	**100**
		% within Quality	50	26.4	39.7	0	**37.1**
	Punjab	Count	0	16	105	3	**124**
		% within State	0	12.9	84.7	2.4	**100**
		% within Quality	0	30.2	43.4	100	**41.1**
Total		Count	**4**	**53**	**242**	**3**	**302**
		% of Total	**1.3**	**17.5**	**80.1**	**1**	**100**

Table 7.10: Cross-Tabulation of 'State' and 'Quality of Water for Drinking and Sanitation'

Cross-Tabulation			Quality of Water for Drinking and Sanitation				Total
			Poor	Below Average	Average	Good	
State	Delhi	Count	0	26	37	3	**66**
		% within State	0	39.4	56.1	4.5	**100**
		% within Quality	0	50	15.5	33.3	**21.9**
	Haryana	Count	2	22	88	0	**112**
		% within State	1.8	19.6	78.6	0	**100**
		% within Quality	100	42.3	36.8	0	**37.1**
	Punjab	Count	0	4	114	6	**124**
		% within State	0	3.2	91.9	4.8	**100**
		% within Quality	0	7.7	47.7	66.7	**41.1**
Total		Count	**2**	**52**	**239**	**9**	**302**
		% of Total	**0.7**	**17.2**	**79.1**	**3**	**100**

Table 7.11: Cross-Tabulation of 'State' and 'Quality and Quantity of Bathrooms'

Cross-Tabulation			Quality and Quantity of Bathrooms				Total
			Average	Below Average	Poor	Good	
State	Delhi	Count	22	40	4	0	**66**
		% within State	33.3	60.6	6.1	0	**100**
		% within Quality	19.5	26	13.8	0	**21.9**
	Haryana	Count	32	55	25	0	**112**
		% within State	28.6	49.1	22.3	0	**100**
		% within Quality	28.3	35.7	86.2	0	**37.1**
	Punjab	Count	59	59	0	6	**124**
		% within State	47.6	47.6	0	4.8	**100**
		% Quality	52.2	38.3	0	100	**41.1**
Total		Count	**113**	**154**	**29**	**6**	**302**
		% of Total	**37.4**	**51**	**9.6**	**2**	**100**

Table 7.12: Cross-Tabulation of 'State' and 'Quality of Kitchens (Hygiene)'

Cross-Tabulation			Quality of Kitchen (Hygiene)			Total
			Below Average	Average	Good	
State	Delhi	Count	2	45	19	**66**
		% within State	3	68.2	28.8	**100**
		% within Quality	28.6	21.8	21.3	**21.9**
	Haryana	Count	5	85	22	**112**
		% within State	4.5	75.9	19.6	**100**
		% within Quality	71.4	41.3	24.7	**37.1**
	Punjab	Count	0	76	48	**124**
		% within State	0	61.3	38.7	**100**
		% within Quality	0	36.9	53.9	**41.1**
Total		Count	**7**	**206**	**89**	**302**
		% of Total	**2.3**	**68.2**	**29.5**	**100**

Table 7.13: Cross-Tabulation of 'State' and 'Quality of Kitchen (Meals)'

Cross-Tabulation			Quality of Kitchen (Meals)				Total
			Poor	Below Average	Average	Good	
State	Delhi	Count	5	35	24	2	**66**
		% within State	7.6	53	36.4	3	**100**
		% within Quality	15.6	30.4	16.9	15.4	**21.9**
	Haryana	Count	24	55	33	0	**112**
		% within State	21.4	49.1	29.5	0	**100**
		% within Quality	75	47.8	23.2	0	**37.1**
	Punjab	Count	3	25	85	11	**124**
		% within State	2.4	20.2	68.5	8.9	**100**
		% within Quality	9.4	21.7	59.9	84.6	**41.1**
Total		Count	**32**	**115**	**142**	**13**	**302**
		% of Total	**10.6**	**38.1**	**47**	**4.3**	**100**

Table 7.14: Cross-Tabulation of 'State' and 'Existence of and/ or Awareness about Children's Committee'

Cross-Tabulation			Awareness about Children's Committee			Total
			Yes	No	No Committee Present	
State	Delhi	Count	29	37	0	**66**
		% within State	43.9	56.1	0	**100**
		% within Awareness	39.2	37.8	0	**21.9**
	Haryana	Count	0	0	112	**112**
		% within State	0	0	100	**100**
		% within Awareness	0	0	86.2	**37.1**
	Punjab	Count	45	61	18	**124**
		% within State	36.3	49.2	14.5	**100**
		% within Awareness	60.8	62.2	13.8	**41.1**
Total		Count	**74**	**98**	**130**	**302**
		% of Total	**24.5**	**32.5**	**43**	**100**

Table 7.15: Cross-Tabulation of 'State' and 'Extension of Cooperation from Staff to Children's Committee'

Cross-Tabulation			Extension of Cooperation		Total
			Yes	No	
State	Delhi	Count	12	17	**29**
		% within State	41.4	58.6	**100**
		% within Cooperation	46.2	35.4	**39.2**
	Punjab	Count	14	31	**45**
		% within State	31.1	68.9	**100**
		% within Cooperation	53.8	64.6	**60.8**
Total		Count	**26**	**48**	**74**
		% of Total	**35.1**	**64.9**	**100**

Table 7.16: Cross-Tabulation of 'State' and 'Requirement to Follow Routine'

Cross-Tabulation			Requirement to Follow Routine	Total
			Yes	
State	Delhi	Count	66	**66**
		% within State	100	**100**
		% within Requirement	21.9	**21.9**
	Haryana	Count	112	**112**
		% within State	100	**100**
		% within Requirement	37.1	**37.1**
	Punjab	Count	124	**124**
		% within State	100	**100**
		% within Requirement	41.1	**41.1**
Total		Count	**302**	**302**
		% of Total	**100**	**100**

Table 7.17: Cross-Tabulation of 'State' and 'Number of Meals Provided'

Cross-Tabulation			Number of Meals Provided	Total
			3	
State	Delhi	Count	66	**66**
		% within State	100	**100**
		% within Meals	21.9	**21.9**
	Haryana	Count	112	**112**
		% within State	100	**100**
		% within Meals	37.1	**37.1**
	Punjab	Count	124	**124**
		% within State	100	**100**
		% within Meals	41.1	**41.1**
Total		Count	**302**	**302**
		% of Total	**100**	**100**

Table 7.18: Cross-Tabulation of 'State' and 'Monthly Medical Check-ups'

Cross-Tabulation			Monthly Medical Check-ups		Total
			Yes	No	
State	Delhi	Count	25	41	**66**
		% within State	37.9	62.1	**100**
		% within Medical	96.2	14.9	**21.9**
	Haryana	Count	1	111	**112**
		% within State	0.9	99.1	**100**
		% within Medical	3.8	40.2	**37.1**
	Punjab	Count	0	124	**124**
		% within State	0	100	**100**
		% within Medical	0	44.9	**41.1**
Total		Count	**26**	**276**	**302**
		% of Total	**8.6**	**91.4**	**100**

Table 7.19: Cross-Tabulation of 'State' and 'Availability of First-Aid Kits

Cross-Tabulation			Availability of First-Aid Kits	Total
			Yes	
State	Delhi	Count	66	66
		% within State	100	100
		% within First-Aid Kits	21.9	21.9
	Haryana	Count	112	112
		% within State	100	100
		% within First-Aid Kits	37.1	37.1
	Punjab	Count	124	124
		% within State	100	100
		% within First-Aid Kits	41.1	41.1
Total		Count	302	302
		% of Total	100	100

Table 7.20: Cross-Tabulation of 'State' and 'Availability of Recreational Facilities'

Cross-Tabulation			Availability of Recreational Facilities	Total
			Yes	
State	Delhi	Count	66	66
		% within State	100	100
		% within Recreational Facilities	21.9	21.9
	Haryana	Count	112	112
		% within State	100	100
		% within Recreational Facilities	37.1	37.1
	Punjab	Count	124	124
		% within State	100	100
		% within Recreational Facilities	41.1	41.1
Total		Count	302	302
		% of Total	100	100

Table 7.21: Cross-Tabulation of 'State' and 'Grant of Leave/Parole'

Cross-Tabulation			Grant of Leave/ Parole		Total
			Yes	No	
State	Delhi	Count	4	62	**66**
		% within State	6.1	93.9	**100**
		% within Leave/Parole	80	20.9	**21.9**
	Haryana	Count	0	112	**112**
		% within State	0	100	**100**
		% within Leave/Parole	0	37.7	**37.1**
	Punjab	Count	1	123	**124**
		% within State	0.8	99.2	**100**
		% within Leave/Parole	20	41.4	**41.1**
Total		Count	**5**	**297**	**302**
		% of Total	**1.7**	**98.3**	**100**

Table 7.22: Cross-Tabulation of 'State' and 'Availability of Suggestion Box'

Cross-Tabulation			Availability of Suggestion Box	Total
			Unaware	
State	Delhi	Count	66	**66**
		% within State	100	**100**
		% within Suggestion Box	21.9	**21.9**
	Haryana	Count	112	**112**
		% within State	100	**100**
		% within Suggestion Box	37.1	**37.1**
	Punjab	Count	124	**124**
		% within State	100	**100**
		% within Suggestion Box	41.1	**41.1**
Total		Count	**302**	**302**
		% of Total	**100**	**100**

Table 7.23: Cross-Tabulation of 'State' and 'Permission to Meet Family'

Cross-Tabulation			Permission to Meet Family/Parents	Total
			Yes	
State	Delhi	Count	66	**66**
		% within State	100	**100**
		% within Permission	21.9	**21.9**
	Haryana	Count	112	**112**
		% within State	100	**100**
		% within Permission	37.1	**37.1**
	Punjab	Count	124	**124**
		% within State	100	**100**
		% within Permission	41.1	**41.1**
Total		Count	**302**	**302**
		% of Total	**100**	**100**

Table 7.24: Cross-Tabulation of 'State' and 'Quality and Quantity of Staff'

Cross-Tabulation			Quality and Quantity of Staff				Total
			Poor	Below Average	Average	Good	
State	Delhi	Count	9	34	20	3	**66**
		% within State	13.6	51.5	30.3	4.5	**100**
		% within Quality	23.1	33.7	15	10.3	**21.9**
	Haryana	Count	23	46	42	1	**112**
		% within State	20.5	41.1	37.5	0.9	**100**
		% within Quality	59	45.5	31.6	3.4	**37.1**
	Punjab	Count	7	21	71	25	**124**
		% within State	5.6	16.9	57.3	20.2	**100**
		% within Quality	17.9	20.8	53.4	86.2	**41.1**
Total		Count	**39**	**101**	**133**	**29**	**302**
		% of Total	**12.9**	**33.4**	**44**	**9.6**	**100**

Table 7.25: Cross-Tabulation of 'State' and 'Presence of House Father/House Mother'

Cross-Tabulation			Presence of House Father/House Mother		Total
			Yes	No	
State	Delhi	Count	66	0	**66**
		% within State	100	0	**100**
		% within Presence	38.4	0	**21.9**
	Haryana	Count	0	112	**112**
		% within State	0	100	**100**
		% within Presence	0	86.2	**37.1**
	Punjab	Count	106	18	**124**
		% within State	85.5	14.5	**100**
		% within Presence	61.6	13.8	**41.1**
Total		Count	**172**	**130**	**302**
		% of Total	**57**	**43**	**100**

Table 8.2: Cross-Tabulation of 'Preoccupation Prior to Institutionalisation' and 'Attendance of Formal Education'

Cross-Tabulation			Attendance of Formal Education		Total
			Yes	No	
Preoccupation Prior to Institutionalisation	Studying	Count	84	47	131
		% within Preoccupation	64.1	35.9	100
		% within Formal Education	51.9	33.6	43.4
	Employed	Count	34	44	78
		% within Preoccupation	43.6	56.4	100
		% within Formal Education	21	31.4	25.8
	Neither	Count	44	49	93
		% within Preoccupation	47.3	52.7	100
		% within Formal Education	27.2	35	30.8
Total		Count	162	140	302
		% of Total	53.6	46.4	100

Table 8.3: Cross-Tabulation of 'Nature of Offence' and 'Attendance of Therapy Sessions'

Cross-Tabulation			Attendance of Therapy Sessions			Total
			Yes	No	Once	
Nature of Offence	Petty	Count	8	25	5	**38**
		% within Offence	21.1	65.8	13.2	**100**
		% within Therapy Sessions	23.5	11.6	9.4	**12.6**
	Serious	Count	2	15	4	**21**
		% within Offence	9.5	71.4	19	**100**
		% within Therapy Sessions	5.9	7	7.5	**7**
	Heinous	Count	24	175	44	**243**
		% within Offence	9.9	72	18.1	**100**
		% within Therapy Sessions	70.6	81.4	83	**80.5**
Total		Count	**34**	**215**	**53**	**302**
		% of Total	**11.3**	**71.2**	**17.5**	**100**

Table 8.4: Cross-Tabulation of 'State' and 'Inmates Plan Post-Release'

Cross-Tabulation			Inmates Plan Post-Release				Total
			Continue Schooling	Continue Previous Job	Find New Job	Don't Know	
State	Delhi	Count	25	10	15	16	**66**
		% within State	37.9	15.2	22.7	24.2	**100**
		% within Plan	17.6	17.9	23.8	39	**21.9**
	Haryana	Count	68	17	13	14	**112**
		% within State	60.7	15.2	11.6	12.5	**100**
		% within Plan	47.9	30.4	20.6	34.1	**37.1**
	Punjab	Count	49	29	35	11	**124**
		% within State	39.5	23.4	28.2	8.9	**100**
		% within Plan	34.5	51.8	55.6	26.8	**41.1**
Total		Count	**142**	**56**	**63**	**41**	302
		% of Total	**47**	**18.5**	**20.9**	**13.6**	100

Table 8.5: Cross-Tabulation of 'State' and 'Awareness of ICP/ Post Release Plan'

Cross-Tabulation			Awareness about Post Release Plan/ Individual Care Plan	Total
			No	
State	Delhi	Count	66	**66**
		% within State	100	**100**
		% within Awareness	21.9	**21.9**
	Haryana	Count	112	**112**
		% within State	100	**100**
		% within Awareness	37.1	**37.1**
	Punjab	Count	124	**124**
		% within State	100	**100**
		% within Awareness	41.1	**41.1**
Total		Count	**302**	**302**
		% of Total	**100**	**100**

Table 8.6: Cross-Tabulation of 'State' and 'Awareness about Date of Release/Next Hearing'

Cross-Tabulation			Awareness about Date of Release/Next Appearance		Total
			Yes	No	
State	Delhi	Count	65	1	**66**
		% within State	98.5	1.5	**100**
		% within Awareness	23.8	3.4	**21.9**
	Haryana	Count	111	1	**112**
		% within State	99.1	0.9	**100**
		% within Awareness	40.7	3.4	**37.1**
	Punjab	Count	97	27	**124**
		% within State	78.2	21.8	**100**
		% within Awareness	35.5	93.1	**41.1**
Total		Count	**273**	**29**	**302**
		% of Total	**90.4**	**9.6**	**100**

Table 8.7: Cross-Tabulation of 'State' and 'Provision of Vocational Training'

Cross-Tabulation			Provision of Vocational Training			Total
			Yes	No	No Provision	
State	Delhi	Count	40	26	0	**66**
		% within State	60.6	39.4	0	**100**
		% within Vocational Training	80	61.9	0	**21.9**
	Haryana	Count	0	0	112	**112**
		% within State	0	0	100	**100**
		% within Vocational Training	0	0	53.3	**37.1**
	Punjab	Count	10	16	98	**124**
		% within State	8.1	12.9	79	**100**
		% within Vocational Training	20	38.1	46.7	**41.1**
Total		Count	**50**	**42**	**210**	**302**
		% of Total	**16.6**	**13.9**	**69.5**	**100**

Table 8.8: Cross-Tabulation of 'State' and 'Attitude and Performance of Trainers'

Cross-Tabulation			Attitude and Performance of Trainers				Total
			Caring	Helpful	Indifferent	Incompetent	
State	Delhi	Count	0	43	18	2	**63**
		% within State	0	68.3	28.6	3.2	**100**
		% within Attitude	0	36.1	12.7	5.4	**21.1**
	Haryana	Count	0	30	56	26	**112**
		% within State	0	26.8	50	23.2	**100**
		% within Attitude	0	25.2	39.4	70.3	**37.5**
	Punjab	Count	1	46	68	9	**124**
		% within State	0.8	37.1	54.8	7.3	**100**
		% within Attitude	100	38.7	47.9	24.3	**41.5**
Total		Count	**1**	**119**	**142**	**37**	**299**
		% of Total	**0.3**	**39.8**	**47.5**	**12.4**	**100**

Table 8.9: Cross-Tabulation of 'State' and 'Attendance of Formal Education'

Cross-Tabulation			Attendance of Formal Education		Total
State	Delhi	Count	43	23	**66**
		% within State	65.2	34.8	**100**
		% within Attendance	26.5	16.4	**21.9**
	Haryana	Count	61	51	**112**
		% within State	54.5	45.5	**100**
		% within Attendance	37.7	36.4	**37.1**
	Punjab	Count	58	66	**124**
		% within State	46.8	53.2	**100**
		% within Attendance	35.8	47.1	**41.1**
Total		Count	**162**	**140**	**302**
		% of Total	**53.6**	**46.4**	**100**

Table 8.10: Cross-Tabulation of 'State' and 'Encouragement to Engage in Voluntary Service or Open Schooling'

Cross-Tabulation			Encouragement to Engage in Voluntary Service or Open Schooling		Total
			Yes	No	
State	Delhi	Count	3	63	**66**
		% within State	4.5	95.5	**100**
		% within Encouragement	100	21.1	**21.9**
	Haryana	Count	0	112	**112**
		% within State	0	100	**100**
		% within Encouragement	0	37.5	**37.1**
	Punjab	Count	0	124	**124**
		% within State	0	100	**100**
		% within Encouragement	0	41.5	**41.1**
Total		Count	**3**	**299**	**302**
		% of Total	**1**	**99**	**100**

Table 8.11: Cross-Tabulation of 'State' and 'Regularity and Attendance of Therapy Sessions'

Cross-Tabulation			Regularity and Attendance of Therapy Sessions			Total
			Yes	No	Once	
State	Delhi	Count	31	19	16	**66**
		% within State	47	28.8	24.2	**100**
		% within Therapy Sessions	91.2	8.8	30.2	**21.9**
	Haryana	Count	1	99	12	**112**
		% within State	0.9	88.4	10.7	**100**
		% within Therapy Sessions	2.9	46	22.6	**37.1**
		% of Total	0.3	32.8	4	**37.1**
	Punjab	Count	2	97	25	**124**
		% within State	1.6	78.2	20.2	**100**
		% within Therapy Sessions	5.9	45.1	47.2	**41.1**
Total		Count	**34**	**215**	**53**	**302**
		% of Total	**11.3**	**71.2**	**17.5**	**100**

Table 8.12: Cross-Tabulation of 'State' and 'Type of Therapy Sessions'

Cross-Tabulation			Type of Therapy Sessions			Total
			Individual	Group	Both	
State	Delhi	Count	17	28	2	**47**
		% within State	36.2	59.6	4.3	**100**
		% within Type	33.3	82.4	100	**54**
	Haryana	Count	11	2	0	**13**
		% within State	84.6	15.4	0	**100**
		% within Type	21.6	5.9	0	**14.9**
	Punjab	Count	23	4	0	**27**
		% within State	85.2	14.8	0	**100**
		% within Type	45.1	11.8	0	**31**
Total		Count	**51**	**34**	**2**	**87**
		% of Total	**58.6**	**39.1**	**2.3**	**100**

Table 8.13: Cross-Tabulation of 'State' and 'Utility of Therapy Sessions'

Cross-Tabulation			Utility of Therapy Sessions			Total
			Yes	To Some Extent	No	
State	Delhi	Count	12	14	21	**47**
		% within State	25.5	29.8	44.7	**100**
		% within Utility	75	53.8	46.7	**54**
	Haryana	Count	0	5	8	**13**
		% within State	0	38.5	61.5	**100**
		% within Utility	0	19.2	17.8	**14.9**
	Punjab	Count	4	7	16	**27**
		% within State	14.8	25.9	59.3	**100**
		% within Utility	25	26.9	35.6	**31**
Total		Count	**16**	**26**	**45**	**87**
		% of Total	**18.4**	**29.9**	**51.7**	**100**

Table 8.14: Cross-Tabulation of 'State' and 'Attitude and Performance of Counsellor'

Cross-Tabulation			Attitude and Performance of Counsellor				Total
			Poor	Below Average	Average	Good	
State	Delhi	Count	1	15	25	6	**47**
		% within State	2.1	31.9	53.2	12.8	**100**
		% within Attitude	100	65.2	51	42.9	**50**
	Haryana	Count	0	3	10	0	**13**
		% within State	0	23.1	76.9	0	**100**
		% within Attitude	0	13	20.4	0	**14.9**
	Punjab	Count	0	5	14	8	**27**
		% within State	0	18.5	51.9	29.6	**100**
		% within Attitude	0	21.7	28.6	57.1	**31**
Total		Count	**1**	**23**	**49**	**14**	**87**
		% of Total	**1.1**	**26.4**	**56.3**	**16.1**	**100**

Table 8.15: Cross-Tabulation of 'Addiction to Intoxicants' and 'Regularity in and Attendance of Therapy Sessions'

Cross-Tabulation			Regularity in and Attendance of Therapy Sessions			Total
			Yes	No	Once	
Addiction to Intoxicants	Tobacco	Count	0	20	2	**22**
		% within Addiction	0	90.9	9.1	**100**
		% within Therapy Sessions	0	9.3	3.8	**7.3**
	Alcohol	Count	0	21	3	**24**
		% within Addiction	0	87.5	12.5	**100**
		% within Therapy Sessions	0	9.8	5.7	**7.9**
	Cannabinoids	Count	1	2	4	**7**
		% within Addiction	14.3	28.6	57.1	**100**
		% within Therapy Sessions	2.9	0.9	7.5	**2.3**
	Narcotics	Count	4	12	7	**23**
		% within Addiction	17.4	52.2	30.4	**100**
		% within Therapy Sessions	11.8	5.6	13.2	**7.6**
	None	Count	29	160	37	**226**
		% within Addiction	12.8	70.8	16.4	**100**
		% within Therapy Sessions	85.3	74.4	69.8	**74.8**
Total		Count	**34**	**215**	**53**	**302**
		% of Total	**11.3**	**71.2**	**17.5**	**100**

Table 8.16: Cross-Tabulation of 'Ability to Socialise' and 'Regularity in and Attendance of Therapy Sessions'

Cross-Tabulation			Regularity in and Attendance of Therapy Sessions			Total
			Yes	No	Once	
Ability to Socialise	Yes	Count	24	106	35	**165**
		% within Ability to Socialise	14.5	64.2	21.2	**100**
		% within Therapy Sessions	70.6	49.3	66	**54.6**
	No	Count	10	109	18	**137**
		% within Ability to Socialise	7.3	79.6	13.1	**100**
		% within Therapy Sessions	29.4	50.7	34	**45.4**
Total		Count	**34**	**215**	**53**	**302**
		% of Total	**11.3**	**71.2**	**17.5**	**100**

Table 8.17: Cross-Tabulation of 'Type of Home' and 'Regularity in and Attendance of Therapy Sessions'

Cross-Tabulation			Regularity in and Attendance of Therapy Sessions			Total
			Yes	No	Once	
Type of Home	Special Home	Count	6	44	23	**73**
		% within Type of Home	8.2	60.3	31.5	**100**
		% within Therapy Sessions	17.6	20.5	43.4	**24.2**
	Observation Home	Count	28	171	30	**229**
		% within Type of Home	12.2	74.7	13.1	**100**
		% within Therapy Sessions	82.4	79.5	56.6	**75.8**
Total		Count	**34**	**215**	**53**	**302**
		% of Total	**11.3**	**71.2**	**17.5**	**100**

Table 8.18: Cross-Tabulation of 'Age of Inmate' and 'Regularity in and Attendance of Therapy Sessions'

Cross-Tabulation			Regularity in and Attendance of Therapy Sessions			Total
			Yes	No	Once	
Age	11–13	Count	1	9	0	**10**
		% within Age	10	90	0	**100**
		% within Therapy Sessions	2.9	4.2	0	**3.3**
	14–15	Count	15	32	13	**60**
		% within Age	25	53.3	21.7	**100**
		% within Therapy Sessions	44.1	14.9	24.5	**19.9**
	16–17	Count	15	106	22	**143**
		% within Age	10.5	74.1	15.4	**100**
		% within Therapy Sessions	44.1	49.3	41.5	**47.4**
	18>	Count	3	68	18	**89**
		% within Age	3.4	76.4	20.2	**100**
		% within Therapy Sessions	8.8	31.6	34	**29.5**
Total		Count	**34**	**215**	**53**	**302**
		% of Total	**11.3**	**71.2**	**17.5**	**100**

Table 8.19: Cross-Tabulation of 'Type of Home' and 'Provision of Vocational Training'

Cross-Tabulation			Provision of Vocational Training			Total
			Yes	No	No Provision	
Type of Home	Special Home	Count	20	22	31	**73**
		% within Type of Home	27.4	30.1	42.5	**100**
		% within Provision	40	52.4	14.8	**24.2**
	Observation Home	Count	30	20	179	**229**
		% within Type of Home	13.1	8.7	78.2	**100**
		% within Provision	60	47.6	85.2	**75.8**
Total		Count	**50**	**42**	**210**	**302**
		% of Total	**16.6**	**13.9**	**69.5**	**100**

Table 8.20: Cross-Tabulation of 'Age of Inmate' and 'Provision of Vocational Training'

Cross-Tabulation			Provision of Vocational Training			Total
			Yes	No	No Provision	
Age	11–13	Count	3	0	7	**10**
		% within Age	30	0	70	**100**
		% within Provision	6	0	3.3	**3.3**
	14–15	Count	13	18	29	**60**
		% within Age	21.7	30	48.3	**100**
		% within Provision	26	42.9	13.8	**19.9**
	16–17	Count	25	6	112	**143**
		% within Age	17.5	4.2	78.3	**100**
		% within Provision	50	14.3	53.3	**47.4**
	18>	Count	9	18	62	**89**
		% within Age	10.1	20.2	69.7	**100**
		% within Provision	18	42.9	29.5	**29.5**
Total		Count	**50**	**42**	**210**	**302**
		% of Total	**16.6**	**13.9**	**69.5**	**100**

Glossary

ACP	Assistant Commissioner of Police
Act of 1986	Juvenile Justice (Care and Protection of Children) Act, 1986
Act of 2000	Juvenile Justice (Care and Protection of Children) Act, 2000
Act of 2015	Juvenile Justice (Care and Protection of Children) Act, 2015
APD	Antisocial Personality Disorder
BE	Budgetary Estimate
Beijing Rules	UN Standard Minimum Rules for Administration of Juvenile Justice, 1985
Board	Juvenile Justice Board
CCL	Centre for Child and the Law
CJM	Chief Judicial Magistrate
CMM	Chief Metropolitan Magistrate
Code/CrPC	Code of Criminal Procedure
CWC	Child Welfare Committee
CWB	Child Welfare Board
CWO	Child Welfare Officer
CWPO	Child Welfare Police Officer
DCP	Deputy Commissioner of Police
DCPU	District Child Protection Unit
DCW	Delhi Commission for Women
DGP	Director General of Police
DLSA	District Legal Services Authority
FIR	First Information Report

GPA	Grade Point Average
ICCPR	International Covenant on Civil and Political Rights
ICDS	Integrated Child Development Scheme
ICPS	Integrated Child Protection Scheme
IO	Investigating Officer
IPC	Indian Penal Code
JAPU	Juvenile Aid Police Unit
JJB	Juvenile Justice Board
NCRB	National Crime Records Bureau
NGO	Non-Governmental Organisation
NISD	National Institute of Social Defence
NLSIU	National Law School of India University
POSCO Act	Protection of Children from Sexual Offenses Act
Rules of 2007	Juvenile Justice (Care and Protection of Children) Model Rules, 2007
Rules of 2016	Juvenile Justice (Care and Protection of Children) Model Rules, 2016
SCPU	State Child Protection Unit
SES	Socioeconomic Status
SHO	Station House Officer
SJPU	Special Juvenile Police Unit
SLSA	State Legal Services Authority
Standing Committee	Parliamentary Standing Committee on Human Resource Development
UDHR	Universal Declaration of Human Rights
UNCRC	United Nations Convention on Rights of the Child
VOM	Victim Offender Mediation

Bibliography

Books, Articles and Factsheets

Adenwalla, Maharukh. *Child Protection and Juvenile Justice System for Juvenile in Conflict with Law* (Mumbai: Childline India Foundation, 2006).

Agnew, Robert. 'Foundation for a General Strain Theory for Crime and Delinquency.' *Criminology* 30, no. 1 (February 1992): 47–88.

Ameen, E.J., and D.L. Lee. 'Vocational Training in Juvenile Detention: A Call for Action.' *Career Development Quarterly* 60, no. 2 (June 2012): 98.

Barton, W.H. 'Discretionary Decision-Making in Juvenile Justice.' *Crime & Delinquency* 22, no. 4 (1976): 470–80.

Bharucha, R.N. *My God is a Juvenile Delinquent* (New Delhi: Sainathann Communication, 2008).

Bishop, Donna M. 'Juvenile Offenders in the Adult Criminal Justice System.' *Crime and Justice* 27 (2000): 81.

Blakemore, S.J., and S. Choudhary. 'Development of the Adolescent Brain: Implications for Executive Function and Social Cognition.' *Journal of Child Psychology and Psychiatry* 47, no. 3/4 (2006): 296.

Bouffard, Jeffrey A., Doris L. Mackenzie, and Laura J. Hickman. 'Effectiveness of Vocational Education and Employment Programs for Adult Offenders.' *Journal of Offender Rehabilitation* 31, no. 1-2 (2000): 1-41.

Brown, R.A., K.J. Novak, and J. Frank. 'Identifying Variation in Police Officer Behaviour between Juveniles and Adults.' *Journal of Criminal Justice* 37 (2009): 200–8.

Brownell, P., and A.R. Roberts. 'A Century of Social Work in Criminal Justice and Correctional Settings.' *Journal of Offender Rehabilitation* 35, no. 2 (2002): 1–17.

Chilton, Roland J., and Gerald E. Markle. 'Family Disruption, Delinquent Conduct and the Effect of Subclassification.' *American Sociological Review* 37, no. 1 (1972): 93–99.

Chung, H.L., and L. Steinberg. 'Relations Between Neighbourhood Factors, Parenting Behaviours, Peer Deviance, and Delinquency among Serious Juvenile Offenders.' *Developmental Psychology* 42, no. 2 (2006): 319–31.

Clarke, Stevens H. 'Getting Em' Out of Circulation: Does Incarceration of Juvenile Offenders Reduce Crime?' *The Journal of Criminal Law and Criminology* 65, no. 4 (1974): 538.

Coalition for Juvenile Justice. '16th Annual Report on Serving the Mental Health Needs of Young Offenders' (Washington, 2000).

Cottle, C.C., R.J. Lee, and K. Heilbrun. 'The Prediction of Criminal Recidivism in Juveniles: A Meta-analysis.' *Criminal Justice and Behaviour* 28, no. 3 (June 2001): 367–94.

Department of Social Welfare, Govt. of N.C.T. of Delhi. 'Allotment of Budget Estimates with Respect to Plan Schemes.' Accessed 23 March 2019. http://www.wcddel.in/pdf/WCDBuget_2013_14.pdf.

DeRosier, M.E., and S.W. Lloyd. 'The Impact of Children's Social Adjustment on Academic Outcomes.' *Reading & Writing Quarterly* 27, no. 1–2 (2011): 25–47.

Dietrich, K.N., M.D. Ris, P.A. Succop, O.G. Berger, and R.L. Bornschein. 'Early Exposure to Lead and Juvenile Delinquency.' *Neurotoxicology and Teratology* 23 (2001): 511–18.

Dirikx, Astrid, and Jan Van den Bulck. 'Media Use and the Process-Based Model for Police Cooperation: An Integrative Approach towards Explaining Adolescents' Intentions to Cooperate with the Police.' *The British Journal of Criminology* 54, no. 2 (March 2014): 344–65.

Elrod, P., and R.S. Ryder. *Juvenile Justice: A Social, Historical, and Legal Perspective, Third Edition* (Boston: Jones and Bartlett, 2011).

Farrington, D.P. 'Early Predictors of Adolescent Aggression and Adult Violence.' *Violence and Victims* 4, no. 2 (1989): 79–100.

Farrington, D.P., B. Gallagher, L. Morley, R.J. St Ledger, and D. West. 'Are There Any Successful Men from Criminogenic Backgrounds?' *Psychiatry* 51, no. 2 (1988): 116–30.

Farrington, D.P., R. Loeber, Y. Yin, and S.J. Anderson. 'Are Within-Individual Causes of Delinquency the Same as Between-Individual Causes?' *Criminal Behaviour and Mental Health* 12, no. 1 (2002): 53–68.

Grisso, T. 'Adolescent Offenders with Mental Disorders.' *The Future of Children* 18, no. 2 (2008): 143–64.

Grisso, T., G.M. Vincent, and Daniel Seagrave, eds. *Mental Health Screening and Assessment in Juvenile Justice* (Guilford Publications, 2005).

Hansaria, Vijay, and P.I. Jose. *Juvenile Justice System* (New Delhi: Universal Law Publishing, 2010).

Hansen, Mark. 'What's the Matter with Kids Today: A Revolution in Thinking about Kids Minds is Sparking Change in Juvenile Justice.' *ABA Journal* 96, no. 7 (July 2010): 50.

Heishman, S.J., K. Arasteh, and M.L. Stitzer. 'Comparative Effects of Alcohol and Marijuana on Mood, Memory, and Performance.' *Pharmacology Biochemistry and Behaviour* 58, no.1 (September 1997): 93–101.

Hirschi, Travis. *Causes of Delinquency* (New Jersey: Transaction Publisher, 2002).

Hoeve, M., J.S. Dubas, V.I. Eichelsheim, Peter H. van der Laan, W. Smeenk, and Jan R.M. Gerris. 'The Relationship between Parenting and Delinquency: A Meta-analysis.' *Journal of Abnormal Child Psychology* 37, no. 6 (August 2009): 749.

Izzo, Rhena L., and Robert R. Ross. 'Meta-Analysis of Rehabilitation Programmes for Juvenile Delinquents: A Brief Report.' *Criminal Justice and Behaviour* 17, no. 1 (1990): 134–42.

Jagota, Rupam. 'Juvenile Justice System in India: An Attempt at Reformation.' *RMLNLUJ* 2 (2010): 84.

Jeenger, K. 'Excessive Protection to Juveniles and Minors: A Plea for Legislative Amendments to Law.' 3 (2) SCC (J) 2015.

Joe, Karen A., and Meda Chesney-Lind. '"Just Every Mother's Angel": An Analysis of Gender and Ethnic Variations in Youth Gang Membership.' *Gender and Society* 9, no. 4 (August 1995): 408–31.

Johnson, R.E. 'Mother's versus Father's Role in Causing Delinquency.' *Adolescence* 22, no. 86 (1987): 305–15.

'Juvenile Delinquency and its Justice System in India: A Critical Study with Special Reference to Juvenile Justice (Care And Protection of Children) Act, 2000.' Accessed 12 December 2018. http://shodhganga.inflibnet.ac.in/bitstream/10603/188816/2/01%20summary.pdf.

Katsiyannis, Antonis, Joseph B. Ryan, Dalun Zhang, and Anastasia Spann. 'Juvenile Delinquency and Recidivism: The Impact of Academic Achievement.' *Reading & Writing Quarterly* 24, no. 2 (2008): 177–96.

Kerig, P.K., R.M. Ward, K.L. Vanderzee, and M.A. Moeddel. 'Posttraumatic Stress as a Mediator of the Relationship between Trauma and Mental Health Problems among Juvenile Delinquents.' *Journal of Youth and Adolescence* 38, no. 9 (2009): 1214.

Khan, T.H. 'Juvenile Justice System in India: An Appraisal.' *Central India Law Quarterly* VIII, no. 1 (1994): 61.

K.M., Ashok. 'Hit and Run Case: Minor to be Tried as Adult by Applying New Juvenile Justice Act.' *LiveLaw.in*, 4 June 2016. http://www.livelaw.in/hit-run-case-minor-tried-adult-applying-new-juvenile-justice-act/.

Kolivoski, Karen M., Jeffery J. Shook, Sara Goodkind and Kevin H. Kim. 'Developmental Trajectories and Predictors of Juvenile Detention, Placement and Jail among Youth with Out of Home Placement.' *Journal of the Society for Social Work and Research* 5, no. 2 (2014): 137.

Kotov, R., W. Gamez, F. Schmidt, and D. Watson. 'Linking "Big" Personality Traits to Anxiety, Depressive, and Substance Use Disorders: A Meta-analysis.' *Psychological Bulletin* 136 (2010): 768–821.

Kumari, Ved. 'Relevant Date for Applying the Juvenile Justice Act.' (2000) 6 SCC (Jour) 9.

Kumari, Ved. 'Juvenile Justice: Securing the Rights of Children during 1998–2008.' *NUJS Law Review* 2, no. 4 (2009): 557.

Kumari, Ved. *The Juvenile Justice in India: From Welfare to Rights* (New Delhi: Oxford University Press, 2010).

Kupersmidt, J.B., and M.E. DeRosier. 'How Peer Problems Lead to Negative Outcomes: An Integrative Mediational Model.' In *Children's Peer Relations: From Development to Intervention*, edited by J.B. Kupersmidt and K.A. Dodge (Washington: American Psychological Association, 2004): 119–38.

Law Library—American Law and Legal Information. 'Crime Causation: Sociological Theories—Strain Theory.' Accessed 23 March 2019. http://law.jrank.org/pages/814/Crime-Causation-Sociological-Theories-Strain-theory.html Crime Causation: Sociological Theories - Strain Theory.

Levitt, Steven D. 'Juvenile Crime and Punishment.' *Journal of Political Economy* 106, no. 6 (1998): 1156.

Lipsey, M.W. 'Can Intervention Rehabilitate Serious Delinquents?' *The ANNALS of the American Academy of Political and Social Science* 564, no. 1 (1999): 142–66.

Live Law News Network. 'SC refuses to entertain plea against new Juvenile Justice Act.' *LiveLaw.in*, 26 February 2016. http://www.livelaw.in/sc-refuses-to-entertain-plea-against-new-juvenile-justice-act-2/.

Live Laws News Network. 'DCW moves SC at 1 AM to Stall Nirbhaya Case Juvenile's Release; SC Agrees to Hear on Monday.' *LiveLaw.in*, 20 December 2015. http://www.livelaw.in/dcw-moves-sc-at-1-am-to-stall-nirbhaya-case-juveniles-release-sc-agrees-to-hear-on-monday/.

Loeber, R., J.D. Burke, B.B. Lahey, A. Winters, and M. Zera. 'Oppositional Defiant and Conduct Disorder: A Review of the Past 10 Years, Part I.' *Journal of the American Academy of Child and Adolescent Psychiatry* 39, no. 12 (December 2000): 1468–84.

Loeber, R., and M. Stouthamer-Loeber. 'Family Factors as Correlates and Predictors of Juvenile Conduct Problems and Delinquency.' *Crime and Justice* 7 (1986): 29–149.

Loeber, R., M. Stouthamer-Loeber, and H.R. White. 'Developmental Aspects of Delinquency and Internalising Problems and Their Association with Persistent Juvenile Substance Use between Ages 7 and 18.' *Journal of Clinical Child Psychology* 28, no.3 (1999): 322.

Lundman, Richard. *Prevention and Control of Juvenile Delinquency, Third Edition* (Oxford University Press, 2001): 29.

Maguin, Eugene, and Rolf Loeber. 'Academic Performance and Delinquency.' *Crime and Justice* 20 (1996): 145–264.

Mahoney, Anne Rankin. 'The Effect of Labelling upon Youths in the Juvenile Justice System: A Review of the Evidence.' *Law & Society Review* 8, no. 4 (1974): 583–614.

Masten, A., S. Miliotis, S. Graham-Bermann, M. Ramirez, and J. Neemann. 'Children in Homeless Families: Risks to Mental Health and Development.' *Journal of Consulting and Clinical Psychology* 61, no. 2 (January 1993): 335–43.

Mayer, R.E., *Educational Psychology: A Cognitive Approach* (Boston: Little, Brown & Co., 1987).

McCord, J. 'Family Relationships, Juvenile Delinquency, and Adult Criminality.' *Criminology* 29 (1991): 397–417.

Ministry of Children, Community and Social Services, Ontario. 'Review of the Roots of Youth Violence: Literature Reviews.' Accessed 23 March 2019. http://www.children.gov.on.ca/htdocs/English/professionals/oyap/roots/volume5/chapter04_social_disorganization.aspx.

Ministry of Finance. 'Statement 3a, Annual Financial Statement, Budget 2017–18.' Accessed 12 September, 2017. http://indiabudget.nic.in/ub2017-18/eb/stat3b.pdf.

Ministry of Finance. 'Statement 3b, Demand for Grants, Budget 2017–18.' Accessed 12 September 2017. http://indiabudget.nic.in/ub2017-18/eb/stat3a.pdf.

Ministry of Health and Family Welfare. 'Unstarred Question No. 2709 to be Answered on 17th March 2017.' Accessed 11 February 2018. http://164.100.47.190/loksabhaquestions/annex/11/AU2709.pdf.

Ministry of Women and Child Development. *Annual Report: 2015–16.* Accessed 23 March 2019. http://wcd.nic.in/sites/default/files/annual-report-2015-16.pdf.

Ministry of Women and Child Development. 'Central Share of Grant in Aid under ICPS.' Accessed 12 September 2017. http://icds-wcd.nic.in/icpsmon/pdf/sanctions/dtd04082016/Delhi%20sanction%20201617.pdf.

Ministry of Women and Child Development. 'Central Share of Grant in Aid to States under ICPS.' Accessed 12 September 2017. http://icds-wcd.nic.in/icpsmon/pdf/sanctions/dtd04082016/ATOZ04082016.pdf.

Ministry of Women and Child Development. 'Executive Summary.' Accessed 23 March 2019. http://wcd.nic.in/sites/default/files/OUTCOME%20BUDGET%202015-16Eng.pdf.

Mistry, R.S., E.A. Vandewater, A.C. Huston, and V.C. McLoyd. 'Economic Well-being and Children's Social Adjustment: The Role of Family Process in an Ethnically Diverse Low-income Sample.' *Child Development* 73 (2002): 935–51.

Monahan, K.C., L. Steinberg, and E. Cauffman. 'Affiliation with Antisocial Peers, Susceptibility to Peer Influence, and Antisocial Behaviour during the Transition to Adulthood.' *Developmental Psychology* 45, no. 6 (2009): 1520–30.

Morrow, W.J., L.E. Nuno, and Philip Mulvey. 'Examining the Situational and Suspect-Level Predictors of Police Use of Force Among a Juvenile Arrestee Population.' *Justice Policy Journal* 15, no. 1 (Spring 2018).

Mulder, E., E. Brand, R. Bullens, and H. van Marle. 'Risk Factors for Overall Recidivism and Severity of Recidivism in Serious Juvenile Offenders.' *International Journal of Offender Therapy and Comparative Criminology* 55 (2011): 118–35.

Mulder, E., E. Brand, R. Bullens, and H. van Marle. 'A Classification of Risk Factors in Serious Juvenile Offenders and the Relation between Patterns of Risk Factors and Recidivism.' *Criminal Behaviour and Mental Health* 20, no. 1 (2010): 23–28.

Murray, J., and D.P. Farrington. 'Risk Factors for Conduct Disorder and Delinquency: Key Findings from Longitudinal Studies.' *Canadian Journal of Psychiatry* 55 (2010): 633–42.

Narrain, A. 'A Critique of Juvenile Justice Act, 2000.' Alternative Law Forum. Accessed 11 September 2017. http://altlawforum.org/publications/a-critique-of-the-juvenile-justice-act-2002.

National Crime Records Bureau. Table 10.5, 'Final Order in the Matter of Juveniles Apprehended under Various Crime Heads of IPC and SLL Crimes during 2015.'

National Crime Records Bureau. 'Crime in India 2016 Statistics.'

Officer of the Registrar General & Census Commissioner. 'Age Structure and Marital Status.' Accessed 7 September 2017. http://censusindia.gov.in/Census_And_You/age_structure_and_marital_status.aspx.

Ollendick, T.H., and M. Hersen. 'Social Skills Training for Juvenile Delinquents.' *Behavior Research and Therapy* 17, no. 6 (1979): 547–54.

Osgood, D.W., and D.L. Haynie. 'Reconsidering Peers and Delinquency: How Do Peers Matter?' *Social Forces* 84, no. 2 (2005): 1109–30.

Pandey, B.B. 'Child Rights Law.' *Annual Survey of Indian Law* XLIX (2013): 93.

Pandey, B.B., *Rethinking Juvenile Justice: Amit Das Style* (2000) 6 SCC (Jour) 1.

Parker J.G., and S.R. Asher. 'Peer Relations and Later Personal Adjustment: Are Low Accepted Children at Risk?' *Psychological Bulletin* 102, no. 3 (1987): 357–89.

Parker J.G., K.H. Rubin, S.A. Earth, J.C. Wojslawowics, and A.A. Buskirk. 'Peer Relationships, Child Development, and Adjustment: A Developmental Psychopathology Perspective.' *Risk, Disorder, and Adaptation* 2 (1995): 96–161.

Parliamentary Standing Committee on Human Resource Development. '264th Report on Juvenile Justice (Care and Protection of Children) Bill, 2014.' Presented 25 February 2015.

Paus, Tomas. 'Mapping Brain Maturation and Cognitive Development during Adolescence.' *Trends in Cognitive Sciences* 9, no. 2 (2005): 60.

Peters, C.M. 'Social Work and Juvenile Probation: Historical Tensions and Contemporary Convergences.' *Social Work* 56, no. 4 (2011): 355–65.

Petrosino, Anthony, Carolyn Turpin-Petrosino, and Sarah Guckenburg. 'Formal System Processing of Juveniles: Effects on Delinquency.' *Crime Prevention Research Review* 9 (2013).

Piliavin, Irving, and Scott Briar. 'Police Encounters with Juveniles.' *American Journal of Sociology* 70, no. 2 (1964): 206–14.

Pillai, G., and S. Upadhyaya. 'Juvenile Maturity and Heinous Crimes: A Relook at Juvenile Justice Policy in India.' 10 *NUJS Law Review* 49 (2017).

Pitts, John. 'Youth Justice in England and Wales.' In *The New Politics of Crime and Punishment*, edited by Roger Mathews and Jock Young (Oregon: Willan Publishing, 2003): 71.

Porter, S.R., and J. Pryor. 'The Effects of Heavy Episodic Alcohol Use on Student Engagement, Academic Performance, and Time Use.' *Journal of College Student Development* 48 (2007): 455–46.

Prakash, A. 'Juvenile Justice Act, 1986: An Outline.' *CNLU Law Journal* 1, 107 (2010).

Rakshit, Shiladitya, and Bani Brar. 'Missing the "Justice" in the Juvenile Justice (Care and Protection of Children) Bill 2014.' *Law and Policy Brief* 1, no. 8 (2015).

Reiss, Albert J. Jr., and D.P. Farrington. 'Advancing Knowledge about Co-offending: Results From a Prospective Longitudinal Survey of London Males.' *Journal of Criminal Law and Criminology* 82 (1991): 360–95.

Rickard, E., and J.M. Szanyi. 'Bringing Justice to India's Children: Three Reforms to Bridge Practises with Promises in India's Juvenile Justice System.' *UC Davis Journal of Juvenile Law and Policy* 14, no. 1 (Winter 2010): 109.

Rodriguez, N. 'Restorative Justice at Work: Examining the Impact of Restorative Justice Resolutions on Juvenile Recidivism.' *Crime & Delinquency* 53, no. 3 (2007): 355–79.

Sampson, R.J., and J.H. Laub. 'Urban Poverty and the Family Context of Delinquency: A New Look at Structure and Process in a Classic Study.' *Child Development* 65 (1994): 523–40.

Santesso, D.L., L.A. Schmidt, and N.A. Fox. 'Are Shyness and Sociability Still a Dangerous Combination for Substance Use? Evidence from a US and Canadian sample.' *Personality and Individual Differences 37*, no. 1 (2004): 5-17.

Sawyer, S.M., P.S. Azzopardi, D. Wickremarathne, and G.C. Patton. 'The Age of Adolescence.' *The Lancet Child and Adolescent Health* 2, no. 3 (March 2018): 223–28.

Sen, Satadru. 'A Separate Punishment: Juvenile Offenders in Colonial India.' *Association of Asian Studies* 63, no. 1 (2004): 81–104.

Scott, E.S., and L. Steinberg. 'Adolescent Development and the Regulation of Youth Crime.' *The Future of Children* 18, no. 2 (2008): 15–33.

Shaw, Clifford R., and H.D. McKay. *Juvenile Delinquency and Urban Areas* (Chicago: University of Chicago Press, 1972).

Sher, K.J., and T.J. Trull. 'Personality and Disinhibitory Psychopathology: Alcoholism and Antisocial Personality Disorder.' *Journal of Abnormal Psychology* 103 (1994): 92–102.

Sinha R., and C. Easton. 'Substance Abuse and Criminality.' *Journal of the American Academy of Psychiatry and the Law* 27 (1999): 513–26.

Squeglia, L.M., A.D. Spadoni, M.A. Infante, M.G. Myers, and S.F. Tapert. 'Initiating Moderate to Heavy Alcohol Use Predicts Changes in Neuropsychological Functioning for Adolescent Girls and Boys.' *Journal of the Society of Psychologists in Addictive Behaviors* 23, no. 4 (2009): 715–22.

Sterling, R.W. 'Juvenile Sex Offender Registration: An Impermissible Life Sentence.' *The University of Chicago Law Review* 82, no. 1 (2015): 295.

Stolzenberg, L., and S.J. D'Alessio. 'Co-Offending and the Age-Crime Curve.' *Journal of Research in Crime and Delinquency* 45, no. 1 (2008): 65–86.

Sullivan, Mercer L. 'Youth Perspectives on the Experience of Reentry.' *Youth Violence and Juvenile Justice* 2 (2004): 56–71.

Thornberry, T.P., C.A. Smith, C. Rivera, D. Huizinga, and M. Stouthamer-Loeber. 'Family Disruption and Delinquency.' *Juvenile Justice Bulletin*. Office of Juvenile Justice and Delinquency Prevention, US Department of Justice (1999).

Tittle, Charles R., and Robert F. Meier. 'Specifying the SES-Delinquency Relationship.' *Criminology* 28 (1990): 271–99.

Tiwari, M., and M. Shakti. 'Analytical View on the Concept of Juvenile Delinquency.' *International Journal of Research in Economic and Social Sciences* 5, no. 9 (September 2015).

Tremblay, R.E., B. Mâsse, D. Perron, M. LeBlanc, A.E. Schwartzman, and J.E. Ledingham. 'Early Disruptive Behaviour, Poor School Achievement, Delinquent Behaviour and Delinquent Personality: Longitudinal Analyses.' *Journal of Consulting and Clinical Psychology* 60 (1992): 64–72.

Umbreit, M.S., R.B. Coates, and B. Vos. 'Victim Impact of Meeting with Young Offenders: Two Decades of Victim-Offender Mediation Practice and Research.' *Restorative Justice for Juveniles: Conferencing,*

Mediation and Circles, edited by Allison Morris and Gabriel Maxwell (Oxford and Oregan, Hart Publisher, 2001): 121-43

UNDP. 'Youth Strategy 2014–17: Empowered Youth, Sustainable Future.' Accessed 23 March 2019. http://www.undp.org/content/dam/undp/library/Democratic%20Governance/Youth/UNDP_Youth-Strategy-2014-17_Web.pdf.

Vacca, J.S. 'Crime Can be Prevented if Schools Teach Juvenile Offenders to Read.' *Children and Youth Services Review* 30 (2008): 1055–106.

Van Dam, C., J.M.A.M. Janssens, and E.E.J. De Bruyn. 'PEN, Big Five, Juvenile Delinquency and Criminal Recidivism.' *Personality and Individual Differences* 39, no. 1 (2005): 7–19.

Warr, Mark. 'Parents/Peers, and Delinquency.' *Social Forces* 72, no. 1 (September 1993): 247–64.

Wasserman, G.A., L.S. McReynolds, S.S. Craig, J.M. Keating, and S.A. Jones. 'Psychiatric Disorder, Comorbidity, and Suicidal Behaviour in Juvenile Justice Youth.' *Criminal Justice and Behaviour* 37, no. 12 (2010): 1361–76.

Widom, C.S., and M.G. Maxfield. 'An Update on the "Cycle of Violence".' U.S. Dept. of Justice, Office of Justice Programs (2001).

Windle, M. 'A Longitudinal Study of Antisocial Behaviours in Early Adolescence as Predictors of Late Adolescent Substance Use: Gender and Ethnic Group Differences.' *Journal of Abnormal Psychology* 99 (1990): 86–91.

Witte, A.D. 'Crime.' In *The Social Benefits of Education,* edited by J. Behrman and N. Stacey (Ann Arbor: University of Michigan Press, 1997).

Wizner, Stephen, and Mary F. Keller. 'The Penal Model of Juvenile Justice: Is Juvenile Court Delinquency Jurisdiction Obsolete?' (1977). Faculty Scholarship Series (Yale University, 1997).

Wright, Bradley R.E., A. Caspi, T.E. Moffitt, R.A. Miech, and P.A. Silva. 'Reconsidering the Relationship between SES and Delinquency: Causation But Not Correlation.' *Criminology* 37 (1999): 175–94.

Zabel, Robert, and Frank Nigro. 'Occupational Interests and Aptitudes of Juvenile Offenders: Influence of Special Education Experience and Gender.' *Journal of Correctional Education* 58, no. 4 (2007): 337.

Statutes, Policies and International Treaties

Statutes

1) Constitution of India, 1950
2) Indian Penal Code, 1860
3) Code of Criminal Procedure, 1898
4) Code of Criminal Procedure, 1973
5) Representation of People Act, 1951
6) Reformatory Schools Act, 1897
7) Bombay Borstal Act, 1920
8) Madras Borstal Schools Act, 1924
9) Bengal Children Act, 1922
10) Children Act, 1960
11) Rajasthan Children Act, 1970
12) Madras Children Act, 1920
13) Bombay Children Act, 1920
14) Haryana Children Act, 1974
15) Bihar Children Act, 1970
16) Juvenile Justice (Care and Protection of Children) Act, 1986
17) Juvenile Justice (Care and Protection of Children) Act, 2000
18) Juvenile Justice (Care and Protection of Children) Amendment Act, 2006
19) Juvenile Justice (Care and Protection of Children) Model Rules, 2007
20) Juvenile Justice (Care and Protection of Children) Amendment Act, 2011
21) Juvenile Justice (Care and Protection of Children) Act, 2015
22) Juvenile Justice (Care and Protection of Children) Model Rules, 2016
23) Mental Health Act, 1987
24) Section 2 (13) of the Juvenile Justice Act, 2015

Policies

1) Integrated Child Development Scheme, Ministry of Women and Child Development

2) Integrated Child Protection Scheme, Ministry of Women and Child Development

International Treaties

1) United Nations Declaration on Rights of the Child, 1959
2) Minimum Age Convention, 1973
3) United Nations Convention on the Right of the Child, 1989
4) United Nations Standard Minimum Rules for Administration of Juvenile Justice, 1985
5) United Nations Rules for the Protection of Juveniles Deprived of their Liberty, 1990
6) Hague Convention on Protection of Children and Cooperation in Respect of Inter Country Adoption, 1993
7) Universal Declaration of Human Rights, 1948
8) International Covenant on Civil and Political Rights, 1966
9) International Covenant on Economic, Social and Cultural Rights, 1966

Reports

1) Report of Indian Jail committee 1919–20
2) Coalition for Juvenile Justice (2000), 16th Annual Report on Serving the Mental Health Needs of Young Offenders, Washington DC
3) Justice J.S. Verma (2013), "Report of the Committee on Amendments to Criminal Law"
4) Sinha Committee Report, 1968
5) Ministry of Women and Child Development, "Annual Report 2015–16"
6) Parliamentary Standing Committee on Human Resource Development, *264th Report on Juvenile Justice (Care and Protection of Children) Bill, 2014*

Court Judgements

1) *Abuzar Hussain* v. *State of West Bengal* (2012) 10 SCC 489
2) *Air India Cabin Crew Assn.* v. *Yashaswinee Merchant*, (2003) 6 SCC 277
3) *Akbar Shaikh* v. *State of West Bengal* (2009) 7 SCC 419

4) *Amit Singh* v. *State of Maharashtra and Anr.* (2011) 13 SCC 744
5) *Amit Das* v. *State of Bihar* (2000) 5 SCC 488
6) *Ashwani Kumar Saxena* v. *State of Madhya Pradesh (*2012)
7) *Bai Tahira* v. *A.H.F. Chothia* (1979) 2 SCC 316
8) *Bharat Bhushan* v. *State of Himachal Pradesh* (2013) 11 SCC 274
9) *Bhola Bhagat* v. *State of Bihar* (1997) 8 SCC 720
10) *Bhoop Ram* v. *State of U.P.* (1989) 3 SCC 1
11) *Chandrajeet Kumar* v. *State* Crl. A. 371/2015
12) *Chiranjit Lal Sahu* v. *Union of India*, 1950 SCR 869
13) *Court on its own motion* v. *Department of Women and Child Development, Govt. of N.C.T. of Delhi* (2013) 2 RCR (Criminal) 362
14) *Court on its own motion* v. *Department of Women and Child Development, Govt. of N.C.T. of Delhi* (2013) 3 RCR (Criminal) 362
15) *Court on its own motion* v. *Department of Women and Child Development, Govt. of N.C.T. of Delhi* (2013) 2 RCR (Criminal) 362
16) *D.T.C.* v. *D.T.C. Mazdoor Congress and Ors.*, 1991 SCC Suppl. (1) 600
17) *Dayanand* v. *State of Haryana* (2011) 2 SCC 224
18) *Dayanand* v. *State of U.P* (2011) 2 SCC 224
19) *Dhanna* v. *State of Madhya Pradesh* (2009) 14 SCC 187
20) *Dharambir* v. *State of N.C.T. of Delhi* (2010) 5 SCC 344
21) *Exploitation of Children in Orphanages in the State of Tamil Nadu* (2007), W.P. N. 102 of 2007
22) *Gopinath Ghosh* v. *State of West Bengal* (1984) SUPP SCC 228
23) *Gopinath Ghosh* v. *State of West Bengal* 1984 (Supp.) SCC 228
24) *Gurpreet Singh* v. *State of Punjab* (2005) 12 SCC 615
25) *Hari Ram* v. *State of Rajasthan and Anr.* (2009) 13 SCC 211
26) *Hari Ram* v. *State of Rajasthan and Anr.* (2009) 13 SCC 211
27) *Hari Ram* v. *State of Rajasthan and Anr.* (2009) 13 SCC 211
28) *Jameel* v. *State of Maharashtra* (2007) 11 SCC 420
29) *Jayendra and anr.* v. *State of U.P.* (1981) 4 SCC 149
30) *Jitendra Singh* v. *State of U.P.* (2013) 11 SCC 193
31) *Jitendra Singh* v. *State of U.P.* (2013) 11 SCC 193
32) *Kalu* v. *State of Haryana* (2012) 8 SCC 34
33) *Lakhan Lal* v. *State of Bihar* (2011) 2 SCC 251
34) *Maneka Gandhi* v. *Union of India*, 1978 SCR (2) 621

35) *Mumtaz* v. *State of Uttar Pradesh* 2016 SCC OnLine SC 653
36) *Olga Tellis* v. *Bombay Municipal Corporation*, 1985 SCC (3) 545
37) *People's Union for Democratic Rights* v. *Union of India*, 1983 SCR (1) 456
38) *Pradeep Kumar* v. *State of U.P.* 1995 Supp (4) SCC 499
39) *Pratap Singh* v. *State of Jharkhand and Anr.* (2005) 3 SCC 251
40) *R. K. Tarun* v. *Union of India* (2015) SCC Online Del 13461
41) *Raghbir* v. *State of Haryana* 1982 SCR (1) 686
42) *Raghbir* v. *State of Haryana* 1982 SCR (1) 686
43) *Rajendra Prasad* v. *State of U.P.* (1979) 3 SCC 646
44) *Ranjeet Singh* v. *State of Haryana* (2008) 9 SCC 453
45) *Rohtas* v. *State of Haryana* 1980 SCR (1) 151
46) *Rudal Shah* v. *State of Bihar* (1983) 4 SCC 141
47) *Salil Bali* v. *Union of India and Anr.* (2013) 7 SCC 705
48) *Sampurna Behura Case* W.P. (Civil) No. 473 of 2005
49) *Sampurna Behura* v. *Union of India* (2011) 9 SCC 801
50) *Shah Nawaz* v. *State of U.P. and Anr.* (2011) 13 SCC 751
51) *Sheela Barse* v. *Union of India* 1986 SCALE (2) 230
52) *State of West Bengal* v. *Anwar Ali Sarkar*, 1952 SCR 284
53) *Subramanium Swamy & Ors.* v. *Raju* (2014) 8 SCC 390
54) *Swati Maliwal Jaihind, Chairperson, Delhi Commission of Women* v. *Raju through Juvenile Justice Board & Ors.* CRLMP No. 22044-22045 of 2015
55) *Tehseen Poonawala* v. *Union of India* W.P. 94 of 2016
56) *Tehseen Poonawala* v. *Union of India* W.P. No. 94 of 2016
57) *Umesh Chandra* v. *State of Rajasthan* (1982) 2 SCC 802
58) *Upendra Kumar* v. *State of Bihar* (2005) 3 SCC 592
59) *Vijay Singh* v. *State of Delhi* (2012) 9 SCC 768
60) *Vimal Chadha* v. *Vikas Choudhary and Anr.* (2008) 8 SCALE 608

Websites

1) http://www.manupatra.co.in/
2) https://www.jstor.org/
3) home.heinonline.org
4) https://www.kluwerlawonline.com
5) http://www.legalservicesindia.com
6) http://lawcommissionofindia.nic.in
7) http://censusindia.gov.in
8) http://www.undp.org/
9) http://ncrb.nic.in/
10) http://www.scconline.com/
11) http://judis.nic.in/
12) https://scholar.google.co.in/
13) http://www.wcd.nic.in/
14) http://mha.nic.in/
15) http://indiabudget.gov.in/
16) http://www.wcddel.in/
17) http://ncpcr.gov.in/
18) http://www.hrln.org/
19) http://www.crin.org/
20) http://www.childlineindia.org.in/
21) http://mospi.nic.in/
22) http://finmin.nic.in/
23) http://indiabudget.gov.in/
24) http://haqcrc.org/
25) http://pib.nic.in/
26) http://www.nls.ac.in/
27) http://altlawforum.org
28) http://legalsutra.com
29) http://www.livelaw.in/

Index

A

addiction 23, 101, 111–116, 124–125, 154, 160–164, 209–211
Adenwalla, Maharukh 25
adolescent 17, 113, 116, 189
adult 7, 14, 20–22, 26, 32, 63, 72, 103, 117–118, 121, 157, 182
Agnew, Robert 14
Ameen, E.J. 29, 181
Ashok, K.M. 90

B

Barton, W.H. 128, 131
Beijing Rules 3, 25, 41
Bharucha, R.N. 31
Bishop, Donna M. 26
Blakemore, S.J. 202
Bouffard, Jeffrey A. 182
Brown, R.A. 7, 169, 171
Brownell, P. 8

C

Chilton, R.J. 16, 127
child abuse 7, 9, 15, 17, 19, 43, 49, 59, 61, 69, 120, 188, 221–223
children 2–10, 15–16, 18–19, 30–31, 41–44, 59, 72, 76
children's committee 138–139, 142, 175–176
children's court 51, 55–56, 63, 69, 189, 193–194, 197–198, 211, 213
children in conflict with the law 1, 4–6, 10, 24, 31, 33–40, 41–56, 58–59, 71–101, 187–205
children in need of care and protection 4–6, 24, 40–44, 56–59, 82
Chung, H.L. 118
Clarke, Stevens H. 24–25
Code of Criminal Procedure 2, 40, 55, 63, 71, 194
Cottle, C.C. 119, 124, 166
counselling 8, 37, 59, 65, 79, 126, 148, 183–186, 197, 201, 224–225
counsellor 8, 48, 64, 69, 147–148, 150, 153, 183–186, 197, 202, 225–226
custody 22, 24, 37, 43, 125, 127–130, 133, 166–167, 192, 213–214, 216

D

de-addiction 59, 68

delinquents 3, 6, 9, 15–23, 28, 32, 71–72, 83, 87, 98, 104, 109, 117, 157, 160–161, 168
delinquent behaviour 15–23, 104, 109, 117–122, 161
DeRosier, M.E. 16, 18
Dietrich, K.N. 161
Dirikx, Astrid 7
drug abuse 16, 18, 23, 48, 112–116, 120, 125, 161, 210

E

education 3–6, 9–10, 19–20, 29, 31, 33, 41, 46, 48–49, 58, 63, 67, 69, 101–107, 114–115, 123–124, 130–132, 138, 145–150, 152, 155, 157–158, 162, 165–168, 171, 178, 181–182, 224
Elrod, P. 20

F

Farrington, D.P. 15, 17, 105, 119, 122
first aid 45, 48, 68, 136, 138, 176, 221

G

Grisso, T. 22–23

H

Hansaria, Vijay 28
Hansen, Mark 21
Heishman, S.J. 116
Hirschi, Travis 15
Hoeve, M. 15

I

Individual Care Plan 41, 43, 52, 55, 57, 59, 148, 151, 178, 186, 193, 222–223
Izzo, Rhena L. 183

J

Jagota, Rupam 9, 30
Jeenger, K. 25
Johnson, R.E. 108
juvenile delinquency 1, 9, 14–24, 27–28, 30, 33, 103–104, 108–110, 112, 125–126, 159, 164, 183, 210–211
juvenile justice 1, 3, 8, 24
juvenile justice boards 8, 36, 52, 65, 76, 78–81, 99, 148, 194
Juvenile Justice (Care and Protection of Children) Act 2000 4, 8, 34–41, 73, 85–93, 192–196
Juvenile Justice (Care and Protection of Children) Act 2015 50–61, 74, 82, 100, 163, 187–205
Juvenile Justice (Care and Protection of Children) Rules, 2007 41–50
Juvenile Justice (Care and Protection of Children) Model Rules, 2016 61–70

K

Katsiyannis, Antonis 19
Kerig, P.K. 22

Khan T.H. 28
Kolivoski, Karen M. 27
Kotov, R. 115
Kumari, Ved 1–2, 8, 29
Kupersmidt, J.B. 16

L

Levitt, Steven D. 21–22
Lipsey, M.W. 29
Loeber, R. 109, 112, 125, 166
Lundman, Richard 25

M

Maguin, Eugene 19, 126
Mahoney, A.R. 30
Masten, A. 109
McCord, J. 108
medical care 39, 48, 59, 64 (suggested staffing patterns), 64
medical check-up 48, 136, 138, 143–144, 176, 221
Monahan, K.C. 118, 121
Mulder, E. 120
Murray, J. 17

N

Narrain, A. 23
NCRB 103–104, 106, 109, 122, 156, 191, 196

O

observation homes 28, 36, 44, 53, 56, 62, 134, 136, 139, 154–155, 172, 180, 185, 192–193
Ollendick, T.H. 29
Osgood, D.W. 16

P

Pande, B.B. 24, 32
Parker, J.G. 18, 20
parole 136, 138, 143, 177
Paus, Tomas 202
Peters, C.M. 183
Petrosino, Anthony 126
Piliavin, Irving 6–7, 168, 171
Pillai, G. 33
Pitts, John 1–2
POCSO Act 51
police abuse 6–7, 10, 168–169, 215
Porter, S.R. 116
Post Release Plan 13, 145, 201
post release prospects 13, 23, 145–155, 178–185, 201, 222–227
Prakash, A. 32
principle of reformation 1–3, 24–33, 71–74, 195–196
punishment 17, 25–26, 51, 59–60, 98–100, 187

R

Rakshit, Shiladitya 26
recreation 46, 48, 49, 59, 67, 69, 136, 138, 143, 217
reformation 1–3, 24–33, 71–74, 195–196, 223–224
rehabilitation 3–4, 24–33, 35, 42–43, 50, 55, 58–59, 68, 71–75, 126, 148, 188, 196, 207, 212, 222–224

Reiss, Albert J. Jr. 119, 122
Rickard, E. 10, 30
Rodriguez, N. 27

S

Sampson, R.J. 17
Santesso, D.L. 115
Sawyer, S.M. 21
segregation 44, 64, 134, 137, 144, 172, 217
Sen, Satadru 2
Scott, E.S. 118–119
Shaw, Clifford R. 15
Sher, K.J. 115, 161
Sinha, R. 112
special home 28–29, 36–38, 44, 56, 64, 134, 139, 154, 172, 180, 185, 189, 200
staff 64, 136, 139, 142–144, 148, 150, 222
Sterling, R.W. 31
Stolzenberg, L. 103–104, 119, 122, 156, 165
stigmatising semantics 43, 51, 125, 133, 171, 195, 212, 216
Sullivan, Mercer L. 157

T

teacher 64, 104, 146, 149, 152
therapy 48, 54, 59, 69, 145, 147, 149–155, 183–186, 197, 201, 224
Thornberry, T.P. 16
Tittle, Charles R. 159
Tiwari, M. 19
Tremblay, R.E. 18
trainers 69, 146, 149, 152, 180–181, 183, 224, 226

U

Umbreit, M.S. 26
UNCRC 195

V

Vacca, J.S. 157, 161, 181–182
Van Dam, C. 124
vocational training 28–30, 33, 46, 48, 63, 82, 146, 148, 151–152, 154–155, 179–183, 223
victim 26–27, 32–33, 59

W

Warr, Mark 17
Wasserman, G.A. 23
Widom, C.S. 9, 15
Witte, A.D. 104

Z

Zabel, Robert 27

About the Author

G.S. Bajpai is an internationally renowned scholar, currently serving the dual role of Professor of Criminology and Criminal Justice as well as Registrar at National Law University, Delhi. He is the President of the Indian Society of Victimology, an elected Executive Member of the World Society of Victimology and Vice President of Victim Support Asia.

Dr Bajpai has contributed significantly to the digitalisation of legal education through E-PG *pathshala* projects in law and criminology as well as guided the launch of massive open online courses in law for the first time in India. He has authored 15 books and more than 80 papers along with leading several research projects. He is the editor of three acclaimed journals—*Journal of Victimology and Victim Justice, Journal of National Law University Delhi and Indian Journal of Criminology*, published by the Indian Society of Criminology.

www.ingramcontent.com/pod-product-compliance
Ingram Content Group UK Ltd.
Pitfield, Milton Keynes, MK11 3LW, UK
UKHW041307110926
15112UKWH00010B/18/J

9 789388 414647